IMAGES
of America

Point Pleasant
Volume II

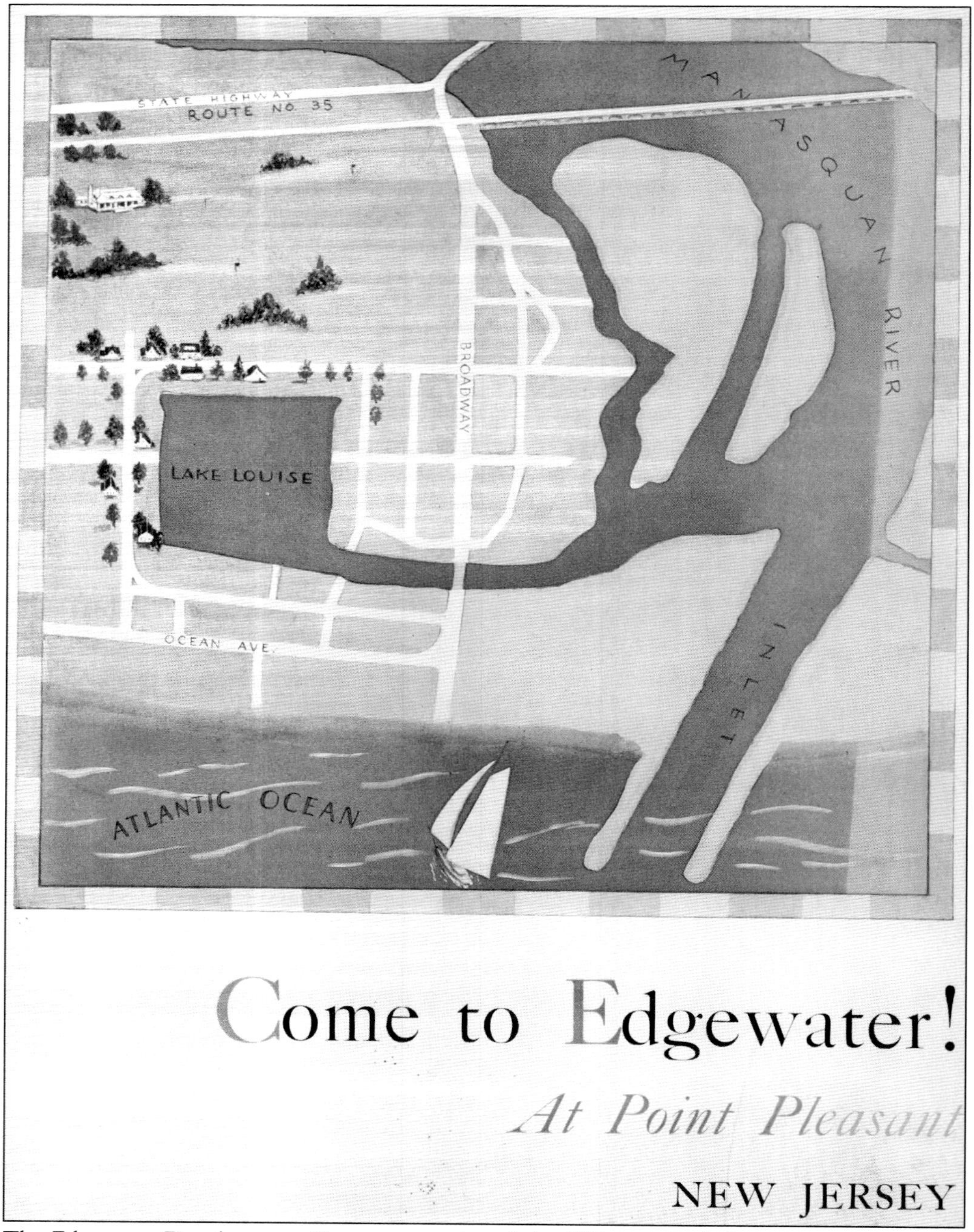

The Edgewater Development Company purchased the 275-acre Cook farm tract in 1927 from the River and Oceanfront Land Company, and proceeded to aggressively develop the property. Improvements were made to Cook's Pond, which was renamed Lake Louise, and streets and lots were carefully laid out.

IMAGES
of America

POINT PLEASANT VOLUME II

Jerry Woolley

ARCADIA
PUBLISHING

ISBN 978-0-7385-6379-4

Published by Arcadia Publishing
Charleston, South Carolina

Printed in the United States of America

For all general information contact Arcadia Publishing at:
Telephone 843-853-2070
Fax 843-853-0044
E-mail sales@arcadiapublishing.com
For customer service and orders:
Toll-Free 1-888-313-2665

Visit us on the Internet at www.arcadiapublishing.com

*This book is dedicated to my loving wife Lee,
whose patience and support helped make this book a reality;
and to our daughter Katie, whose genuine curiosity over the
"very old" pictures and maps is a real source of inspiration.*

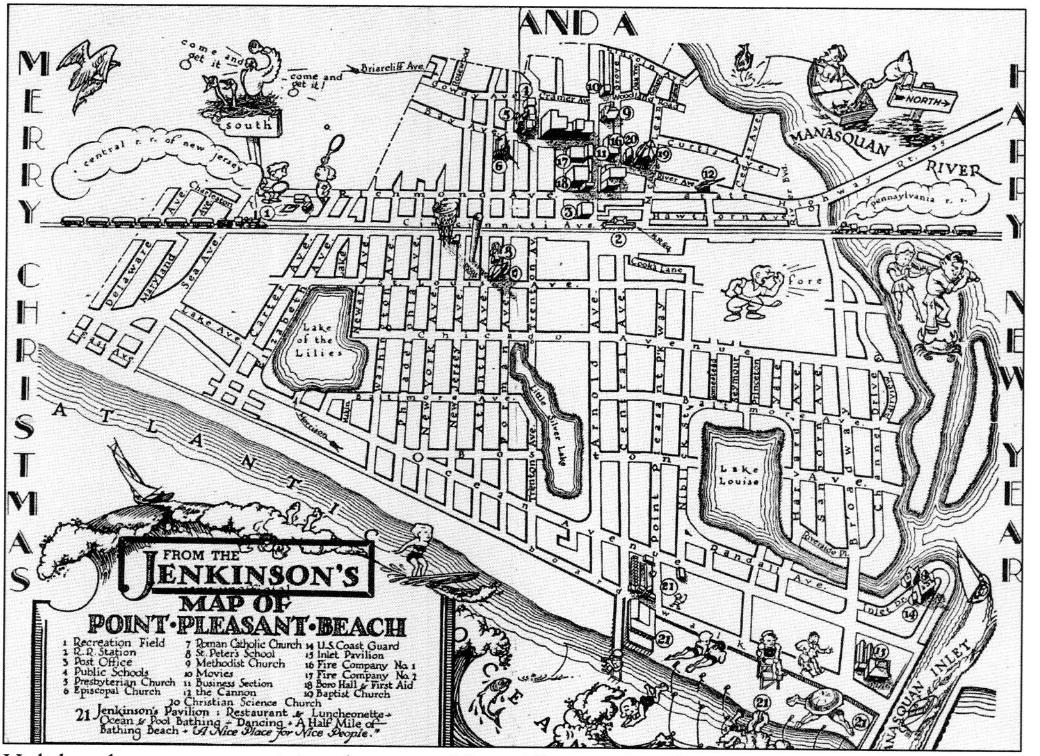

Holiday place mats containing this map of Point Pleasant Beach and its attractions adorned the restaurant tables in Jenkinson's Pavilion *c.* 1940.

Contents

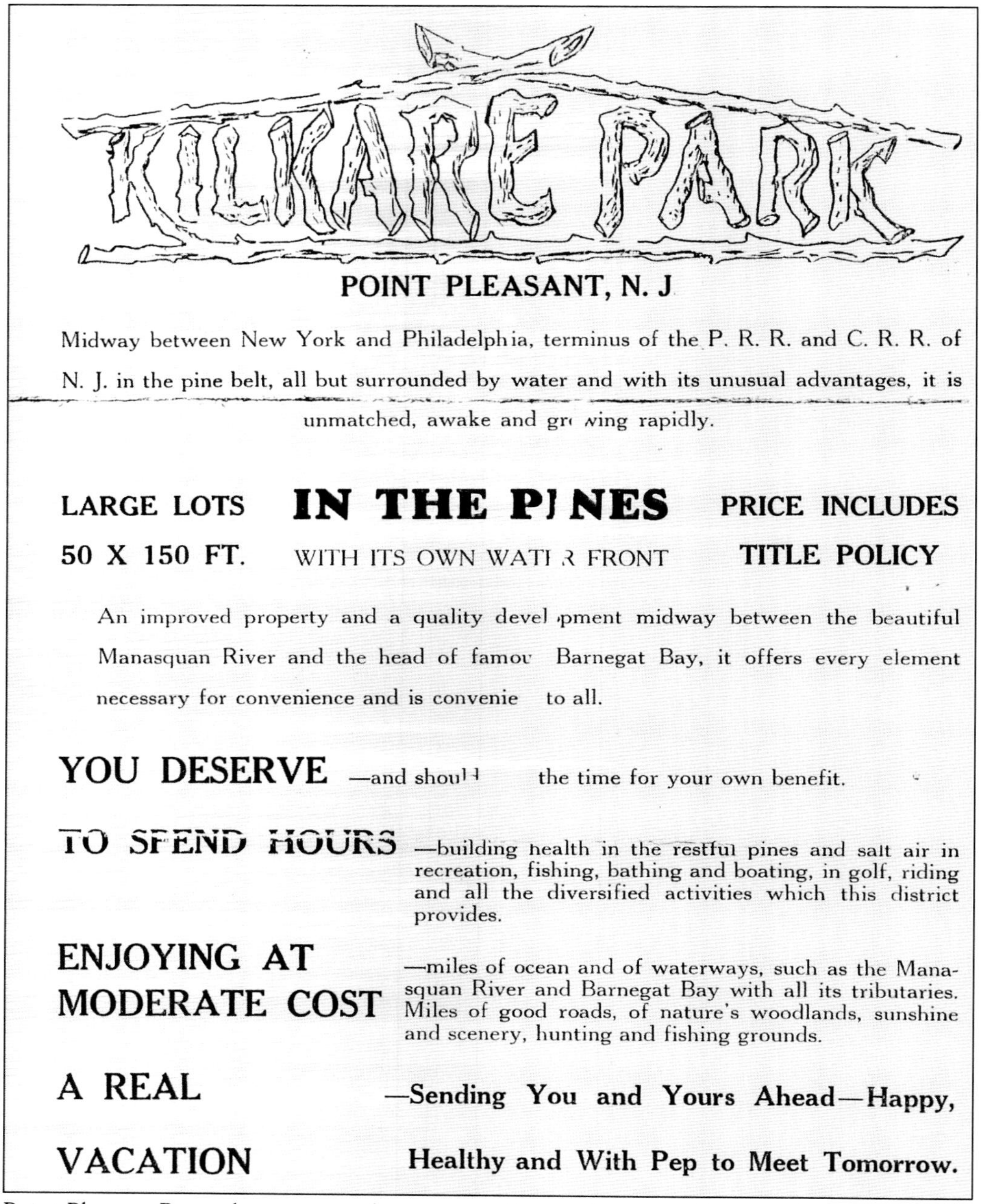

KILKARE PARK

POINT PLEASANT, N. J

Midway between New York and Philadelphia, terminus of the P. R. R. and C. R. R. of N. J. in the pine belt, all but surrounded by water and with its unusual advantages, it is unmatched, awake and gr wing rapidly.

LARGE LOTS 50 X 150 FT. **IN THE PI NES** WITH ITS OWN WATI R FRONT PRICE INCLUDES TITLE POLICY

An improved property and a quality devel pment midway between the beautiful Manasquan River and the head of famou Barnegat Bay, it offers every element necessary for convenience and is convenie to all.

YOU DESERVE —and shou the time for your own benefit.

TO SPEND HOURS —building health in the restful pines and salt air in recreation, fishing, bathing and boating, in golf, riding and all the diversified activities which this district provides.

ENJOYING AT MODERATE COST —miles of ocean and of waterways, such as the Manasquan River and Barnegat Bay with all its tributaries. Miles of good roads, of nature's woodlands, sunshine and scenery, hunting and fishing grounds.

A REAL VACATION —Sending You and Yours Ahead—Happy, Healthy and With Pep to Meet Tomorrow.

Point Pleasant Borough experienced its own land boom during the Roaring Twenties. Most of the land speculation was occurring along the new Manasquan River-Bay Head Canal. Small neighborhoods, or developments, sprang up with such names as Waterway Park, Riviera Park, and Kilkare Park.

Introduction

This second picture history of Point Pleasant and Point Pleasant Beach continues where volume one ended. The format is nearly identical to that of the first book (why tinker with a good thing?), but I have attempted to include more recent photographs of places and events while not duplicating what has already been presented in volume one of *Point Pleasant*.

The publication of the first book met with such enthusiasm that it seem inevitable a second book would follow. Every criticism and suggestion, positive and negative, was considered while compiling this material. My sincere appreciation goes out to all of you who shared your thoughts, photographs, and memorabilia.

"The neck of land that holds the towns of Point Pleasant, Point Pleasant Beach and Bay Head is unique. It is surrounded by water on three sides . . . the Manasquan River on the north, Atlantic Ocean on the east, and Barnegat Bay and Beaver Dam Creek to the south. Such a diversity of aquatic environs is one of the chief reasons for this area's popularity back through time to its earliest inhabitants and visitors."

The above paragraph is from the first chapter of a detailed history of the Point Pleasant area which has been my ongoing project for the past ten years. It will be completed eventually and the research toward that undertaking was used heavily in these works. Until that time comes, I hope these fascinating picture histories will serve as a reminder of our rich past and the people and events that made it.

Jerry A. Woolley
December 1996

Acknowledgments

Of course, everyone who contributed toward *Point Pleasant Volume One* also played an important role toward the completion of this book. Additional thanks go to the following: Francis Tomaino; Emidio Caruso Jr.; Greg Hoffman; Tom Vogel; Frank Bryant; Skeeter O'Dell; George Morris; Ben Goble; Jan Newman; Jill Lockwood Bennett; Barbara Scharmann; Peter Brookes of Fables of Bay Head; Barry Lubin of Borden's; Jerry Colagiovanni of Jenkinson's; Saint Peter's Church; The Squan Village Historical Society, especially George Williams and Wesley Banse; The Point Pleasant Beach Library Board of Trustees; and the Friends of the Point Pleasant Library.

Special thanks to the Point Pleasant Historical Society and the society museum in the Point Pleasant Beach Municipal Building for their generosity in sharing their ever-expanding collection of local artifacts and information. For more details about the society, or to become a member, write PO Box 1273, Point Pleasant Beach, NJ 08742.

One

Down by the Water

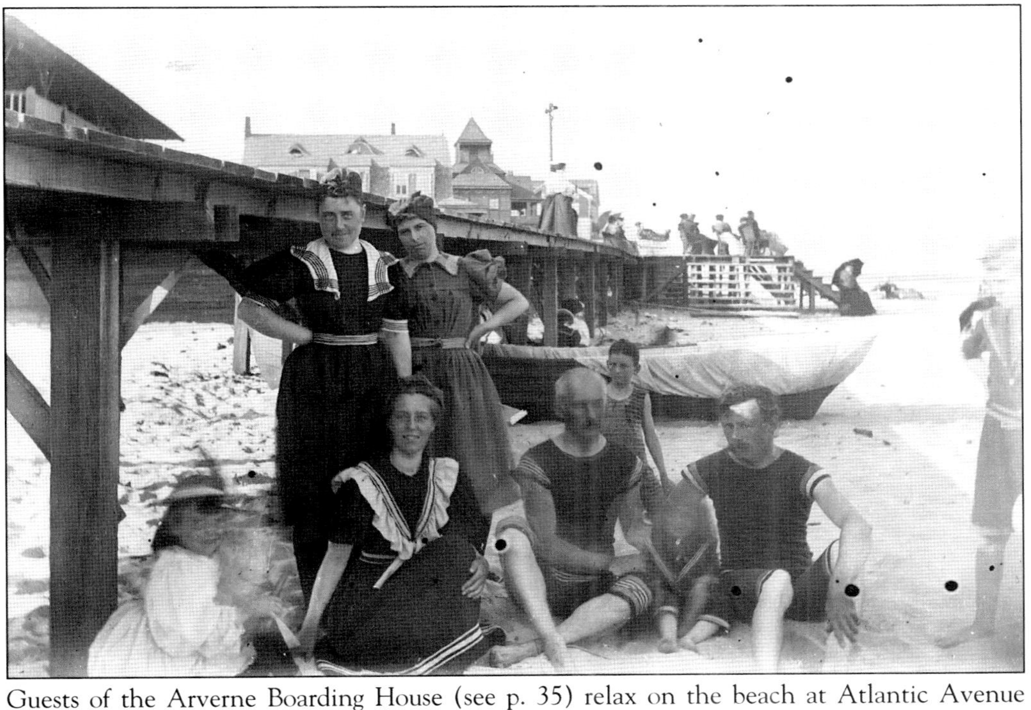

Guests of the Arverne Boarding House (see p. 35) relax on the beach at Atlantic Avenue in 1899. The boardwalk seen here was portable, meaning it was removed and stored during the winter months. At the time this photograph was taken, the boardwalk extended from the Leighton Hotel at Trenton Avenue south to the Stratford Hotel at Philadelphia Avenue.

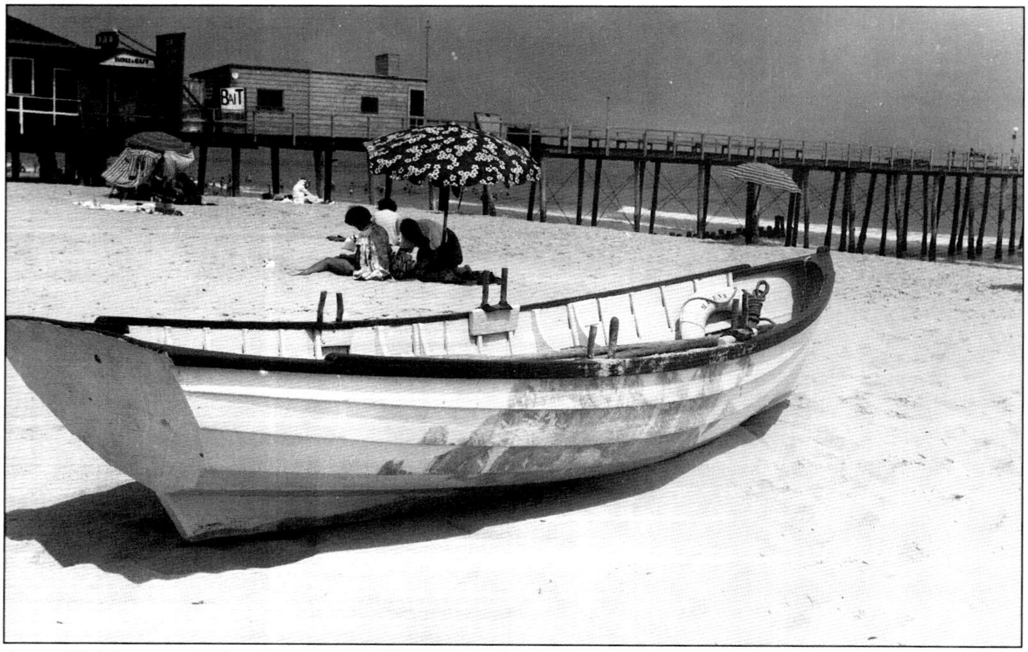

A surf lifeboat, or "Sea Bright Skiff," awaits the next rescue on Havens Beach in 1939. Most of these cedar boats were built locally and were often used for rescues when rip currents carried unsuspecting bathers out to sea. The Point Pleasant Fishing Club pier is in the background.

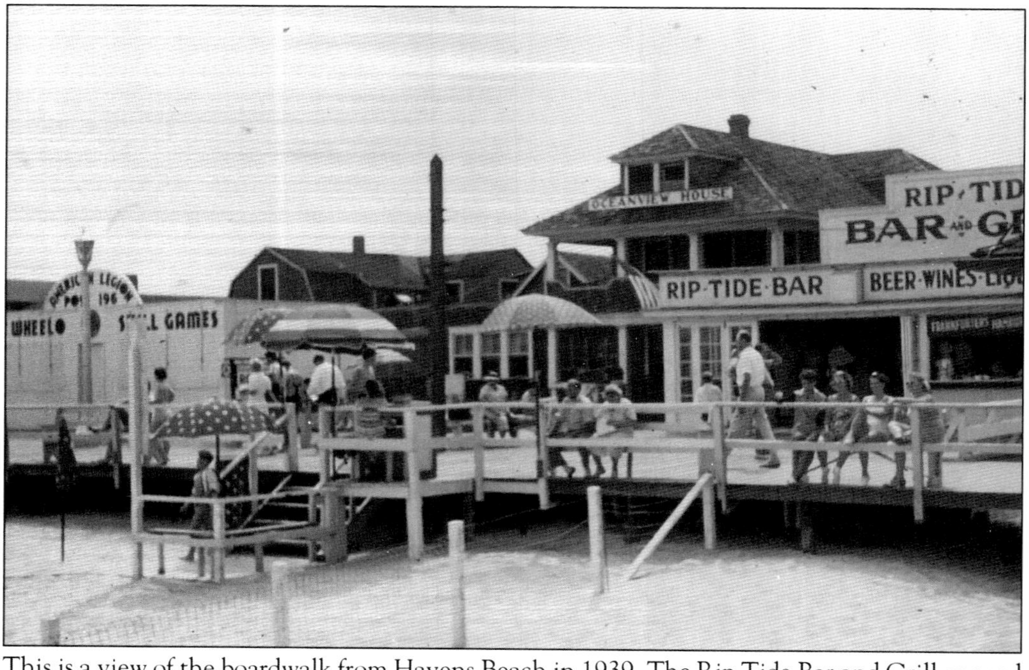

This is a view of the boardwalk from Havens Beach in 1939. The Rip Tide Bar and Grill opened the previous year and remained a boardwalk landmark for four decades. The Oceanview House was an early beachfront boarding home owned by Ethel Hutchinson and is still visible today above the Char-broil Grill. Compare this photograph with the one in Vol. I on p. 118.

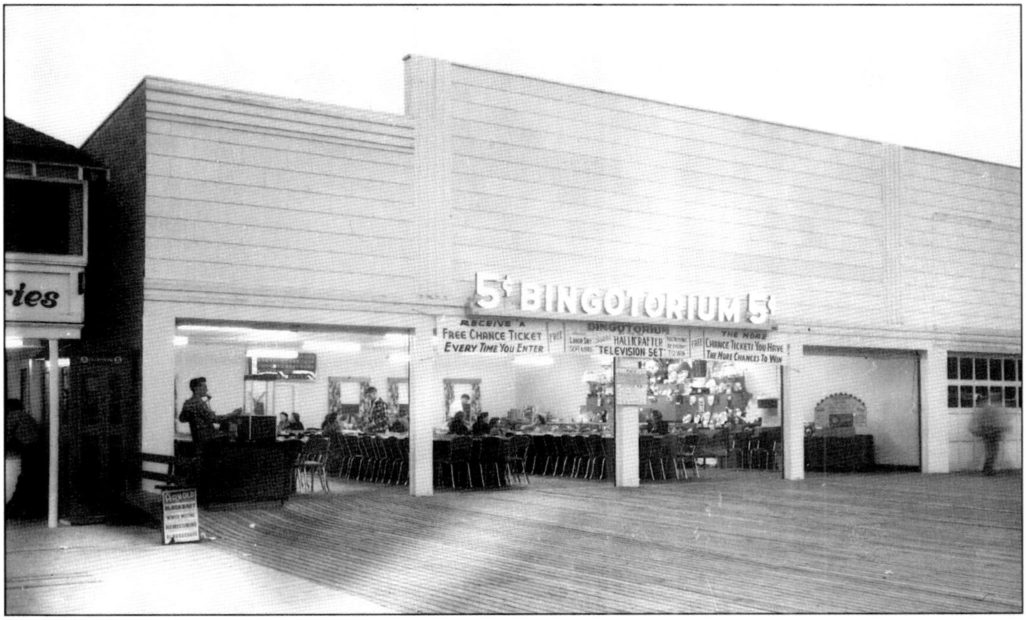

By the mid-1940s, boardwalk bungalows between the Oceanview House and Havens Pavilion were replaced by an arcade building, later to become Frank's Arcade. Before Frank's, part of this building housed a then-popular Bingotorium (a boardwalk bingo game house), shown here in 1948.

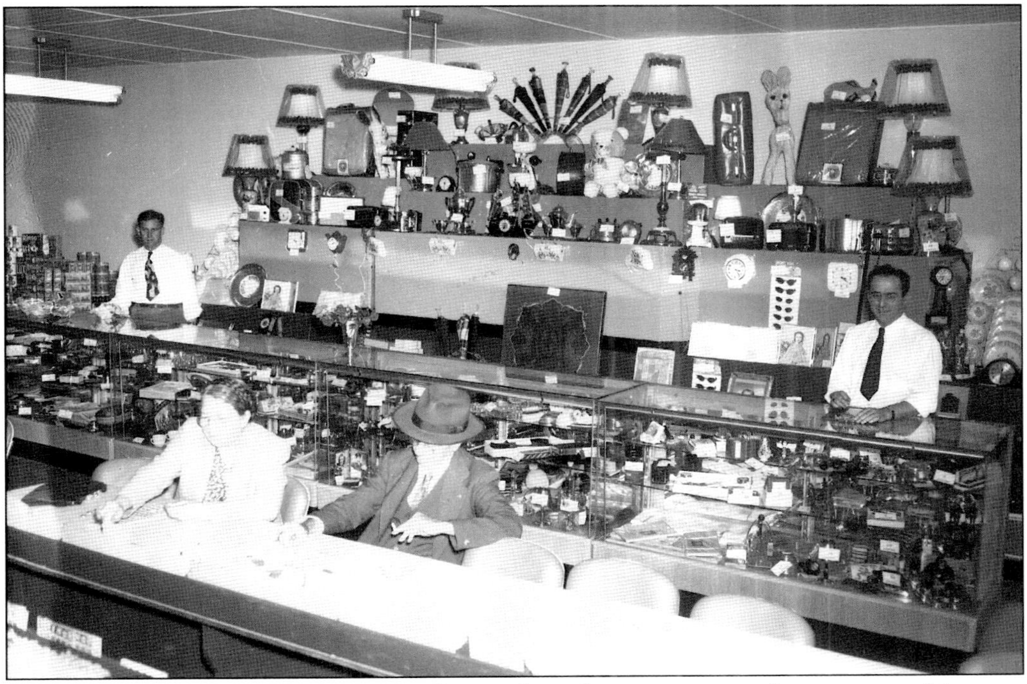

The Bingotorium prize cases contained everything from cameras and toasters to china sets and televisions. By the 1950s, boardwalk games geared toward a younger crowd replaced the bingo houses.

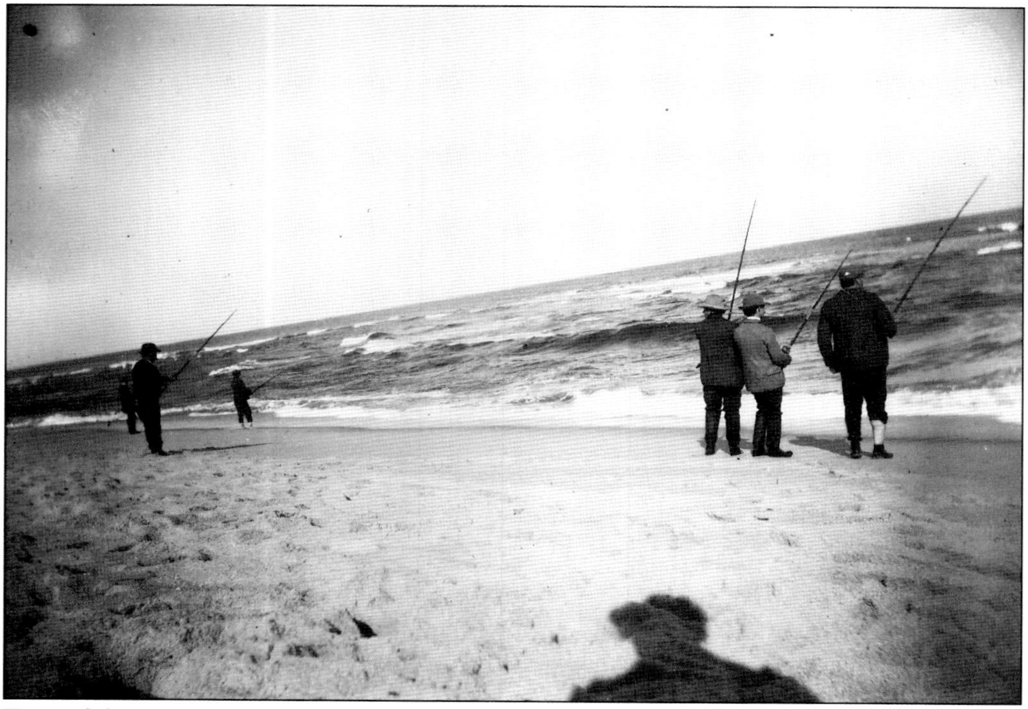

Turn-of-the-century rod and reel surf fishing is shown here at Point Pleasant Beach. Extensive sand bars were common along the beaches until the 1940s when the Manasquan Inlet jetties caused the bars to "fill in" from north to south and gradually disappear. Today the only bars that remain are at the southern end of town.

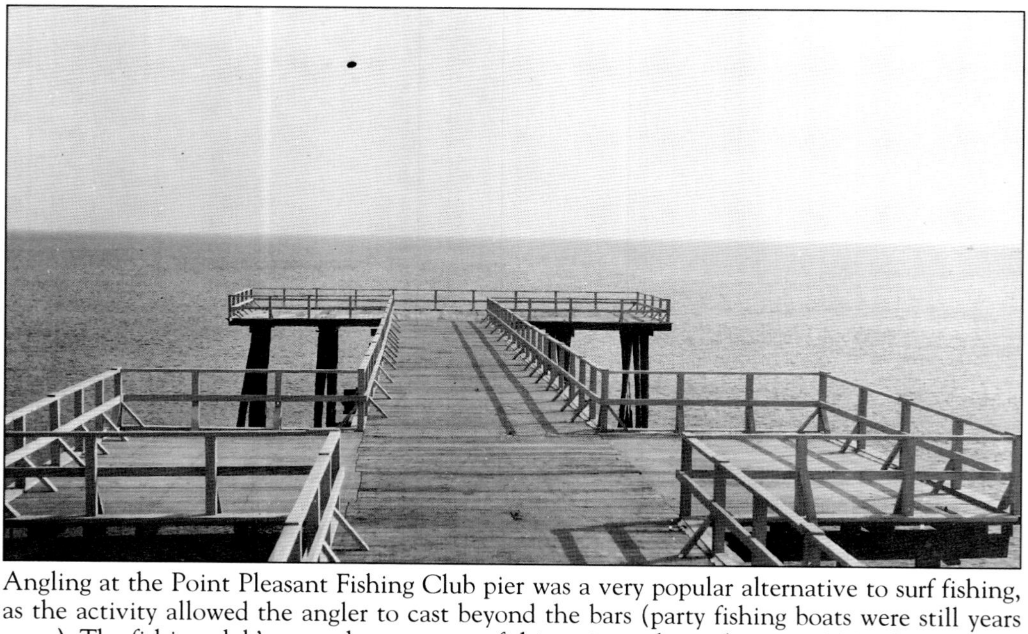

Angling at the Point Pleasant Fishing Club pier was a very popular alternative to surf fishing, as the activity allowed the angler to cast beyond the bars (party fishing boats were still years away). The fishing club's second attempt at a fishing pier is shown here in 1920. The common T-shape design provided additional railing space for the growing club membership.

Hugo G. Wagner organized the fishing club in 1918 and immediately had a 12-foot-wide, 300-foot-long pier built at the foot of Central Avenue. Another 400 feet was added in the spring of 1919 before the entire thing was washed away in August. Not to be discouraged, the club built an even longer second pier by the following summer. The main gate to this second pier is shown here about 1922.

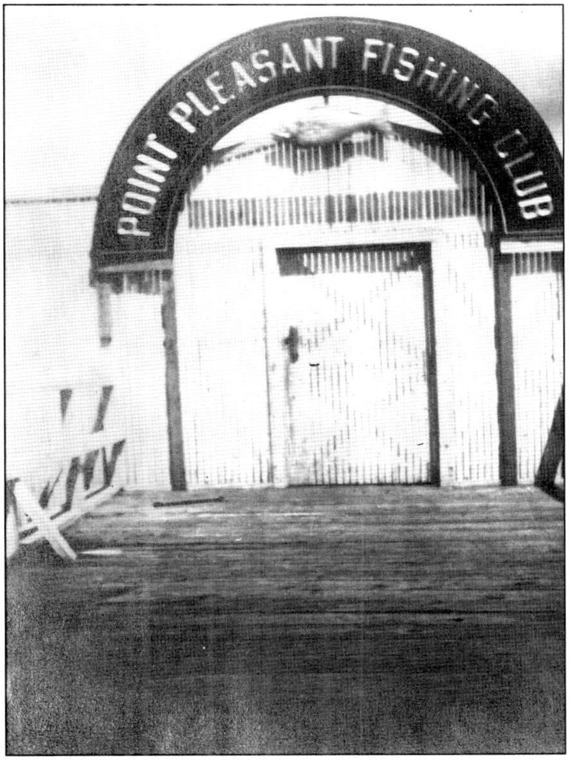

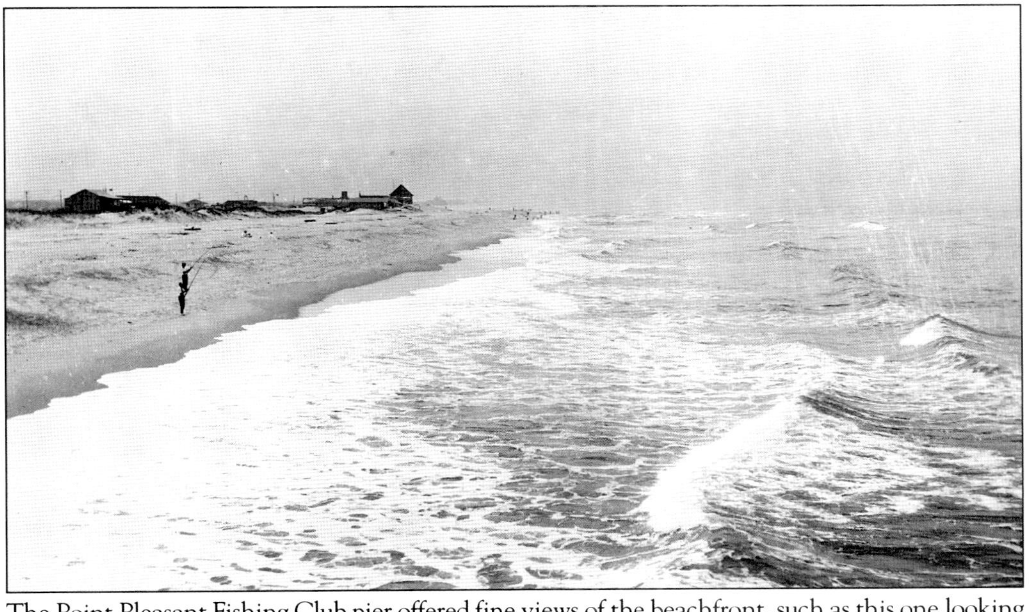

The Point Pleasant Fishing Club pier offered fine views of the beachfront, such as this one looking north about 1922. The bungalow colony had just been started the previous year by such enterprising residents as Edward Griggs, Earl Limroth, Augustus Hayes, and Dr. Frank Denniston.

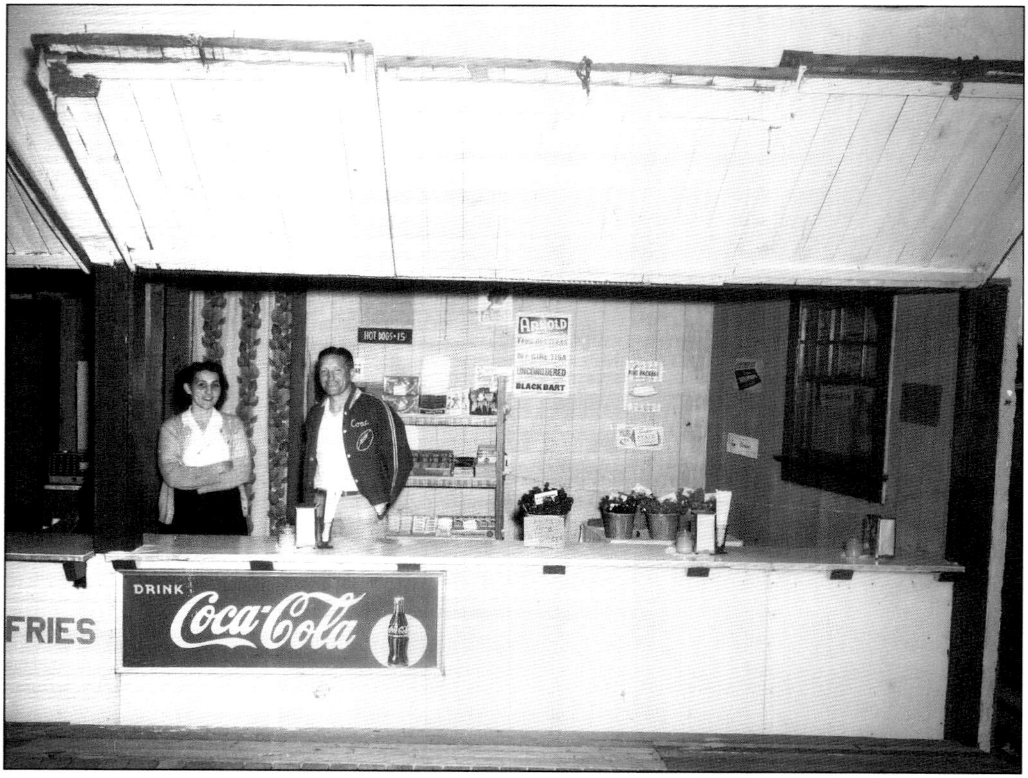

Point Pleasant Beach High School football coach and teacher William "Rock" Strattan appears with his boardwalk stand in 1948. The building containing this concession was one of the first on the boardwalk south of Arnold Avenue. Jenkinson's Midway stand occupies the site today.

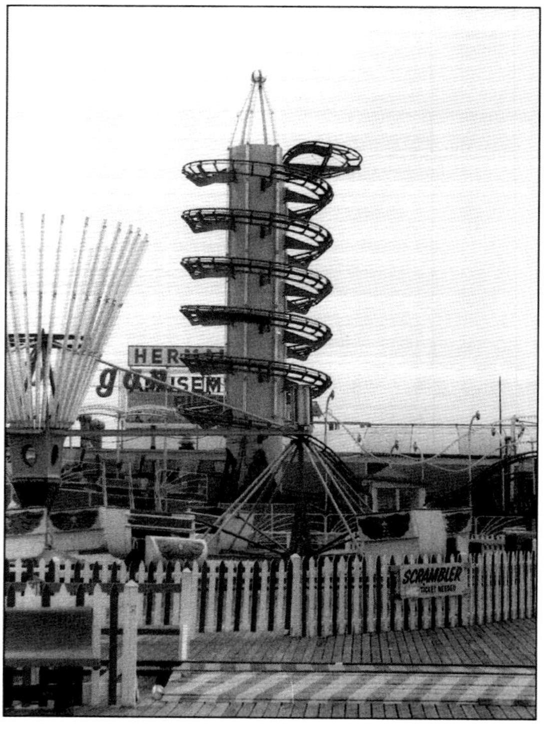

The Toboggan Rocket Ride was a familiar landmark at the beachfront during the 1970s, which was a transitional period for the boardwalk. Many longtime businesses changed ownership or were ravaged by fire during this period. The Toboggan had a 55-foot circular drop that ended with a head-banging dip for those novice riders who didn't hold tight.

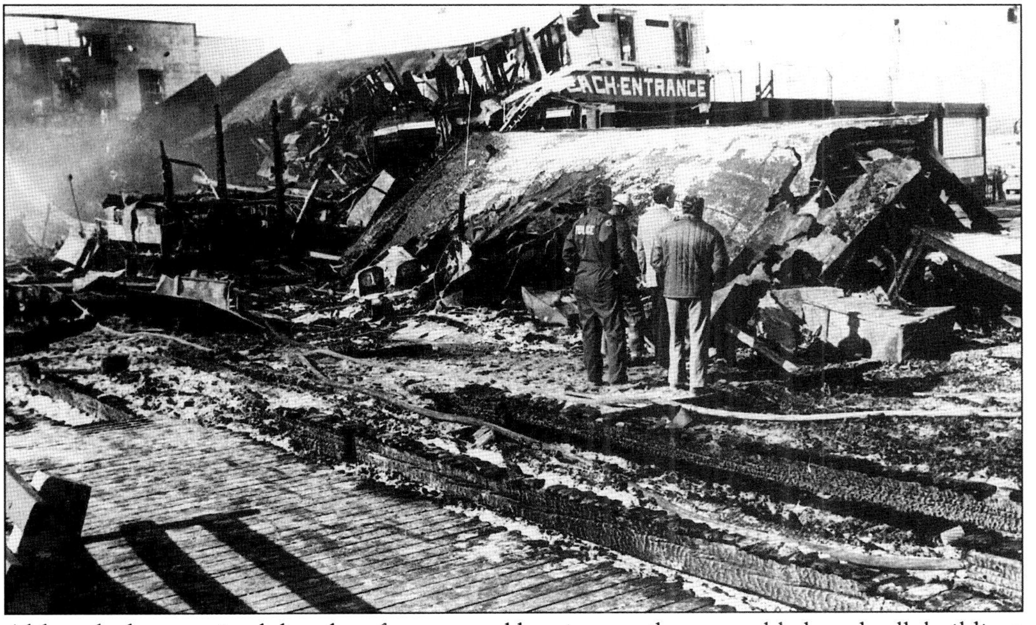

Although they survived decades of storms and hurricanes, the venerable boardwalk buildings at the foot of Arnold Avenue fell in a matter of hours when they were swept by fire in April 1975. Nine buildings were destroyed along with hundreds of feet of boardwalk. After the destruction of Martell's by fire the following September, the boardwalk had lost most of its early pioneer buildings.

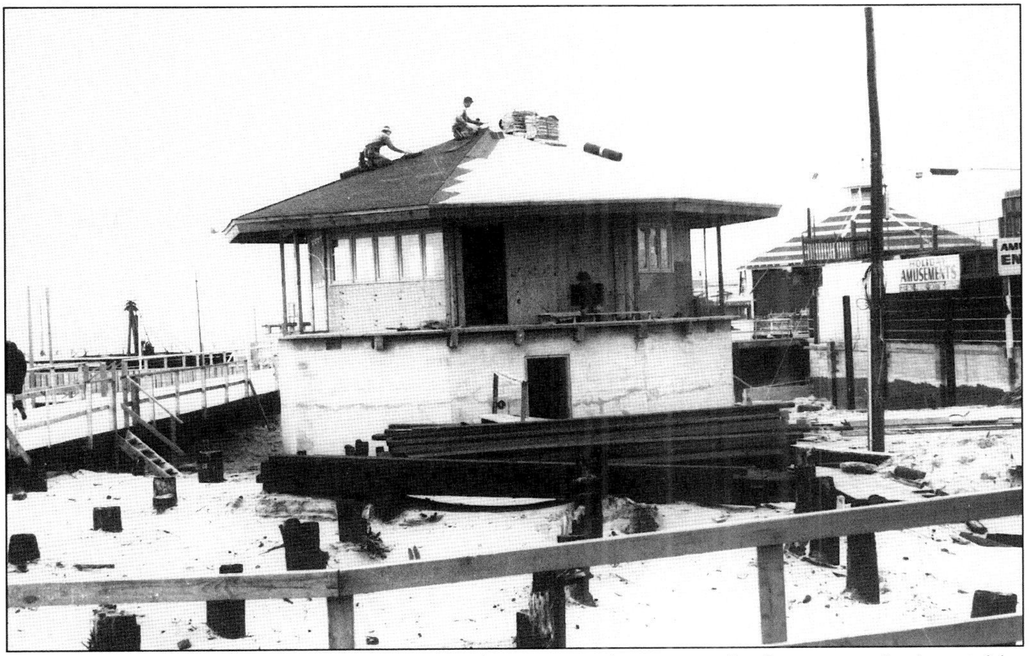

Following the April 1975 blaze, the police substation and rest room facility were rebuilt quickly; the police were housed inside a new circular building. Most of the lost buildings were eventually rebuilt with modern, fireproof construction.

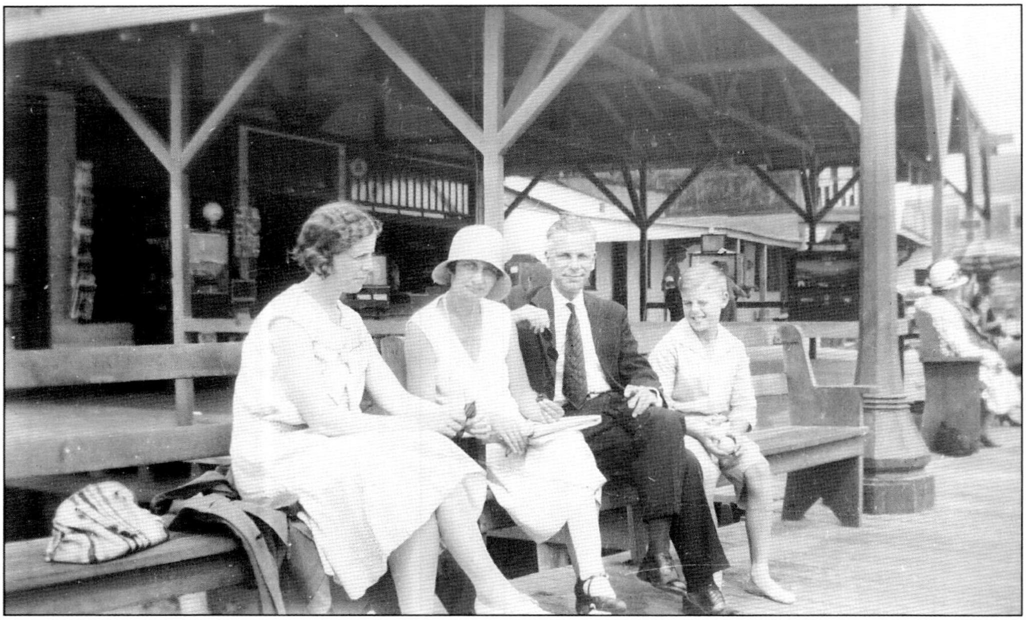

Summer visitors relax on the boardwalk outside of Risden's Casino near New Jersey Avenue in 1930. Joseph Risden purchased the casino from E.E. Johnson in 1916 and the Risden family ran the restaurant and dance hall until it was sold in 1954 to August Hoffman, who continued the business as the Hoffman House. The building was gutted by fire and torn down in 1969.

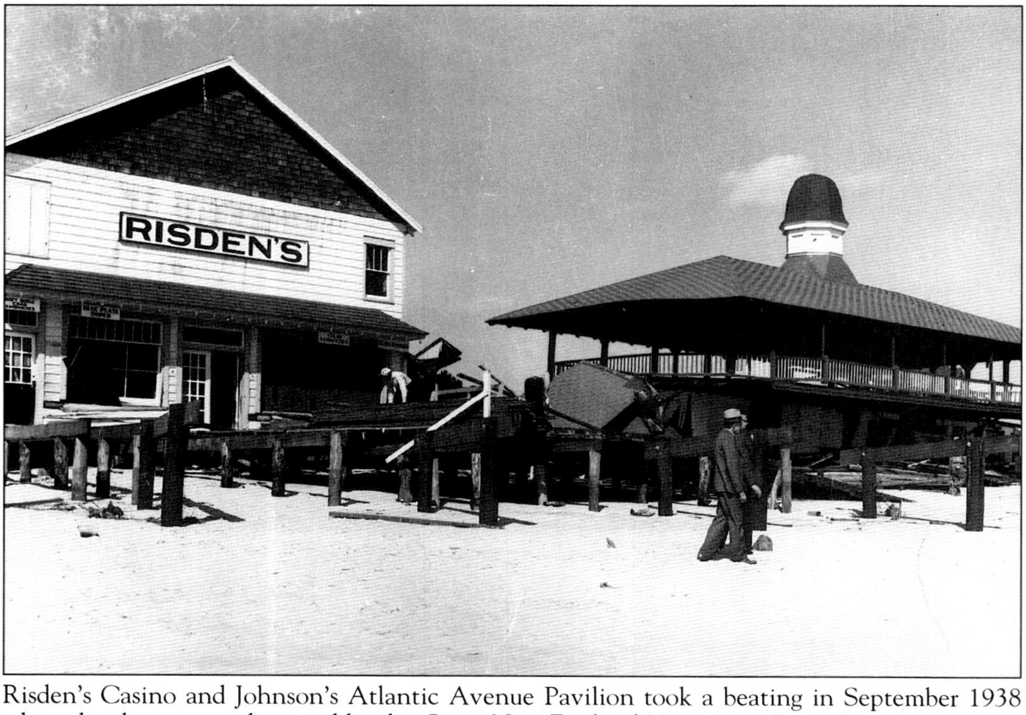

Risden's Casino and Johnson's Atlantic Avenue Pavilion took a beating in September 1938 when the shore was sideswiped by the Great New England Hurricane. Even though the storm center was 150 miles offshore, the high tides and gale winds took their toll on the beachfront.

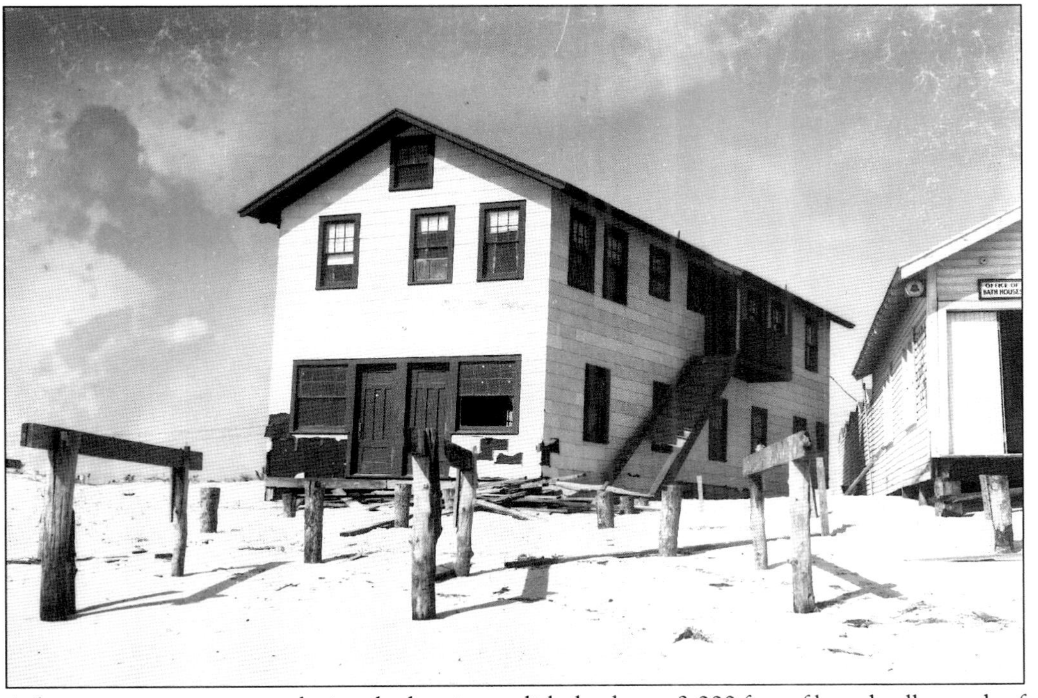

A fast-moving storm surge during the hurricane dislodged over 3,000 feet of boardwalk, much of which was never rebuilt. Above, David Abromowitz's new concession and apartment at Beacon Beach was tossed off its piling. The fishing pier, completely rebuilt four years earlier, lost more than 75 feet to the towering surf.

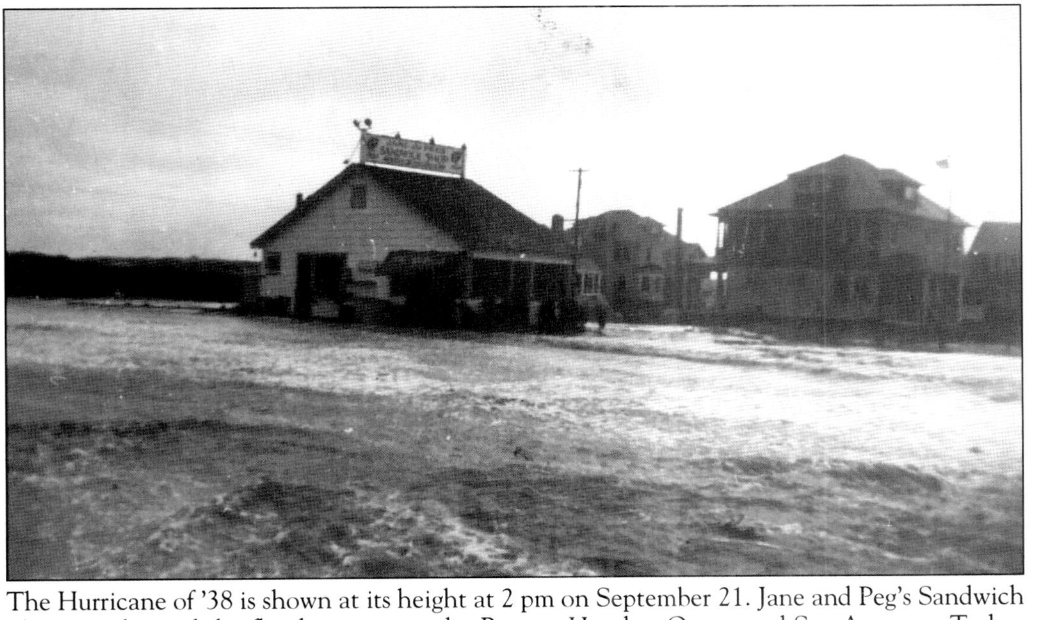

The Hurricane of '38 is shown at its height at 2 pm on September 21. Jane and Peg's Sandwich Shop stands amid the floodwaters near the Beacon Hotel at Ocean and Sea Avenues. Today, this is the site of the Bay Head Pointe housing development. Sandwich shop owners Jane Green and Peg Dunne soon afterward moved their shop west to where McDonald's is today.

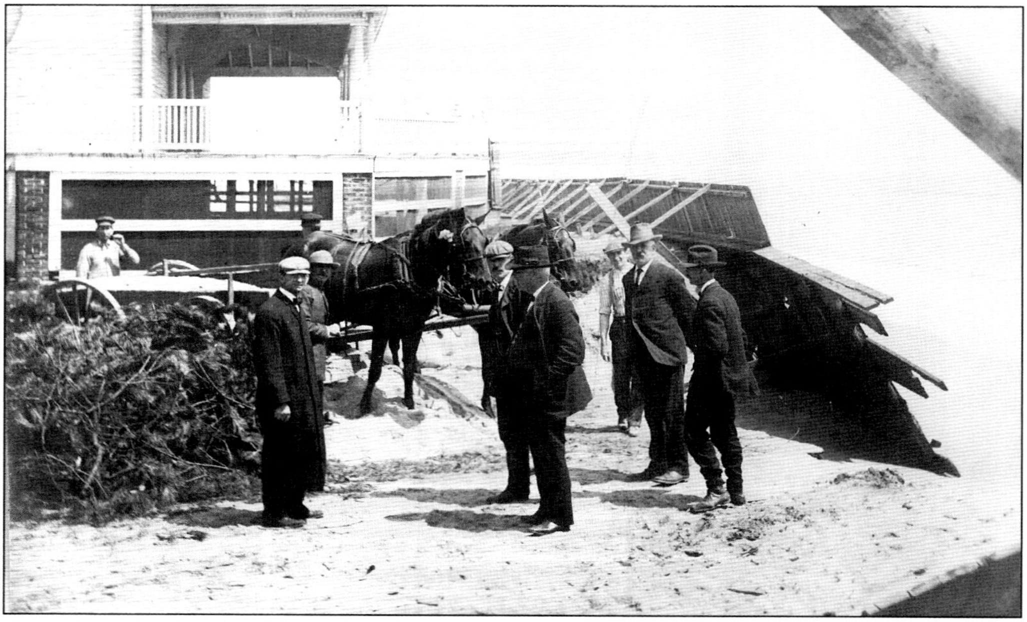

Ever since the first beachfront buildings were put up in the early 1880s, erosion of the bluffs has been an ongoing threat and concern. The seaward end of the massive Leighton Hotel on Forman Avenue was constantly being challenged by the Atlantic. Here, trees and other fill are carted in to help shore a disintegrating bulkhead in 1910.

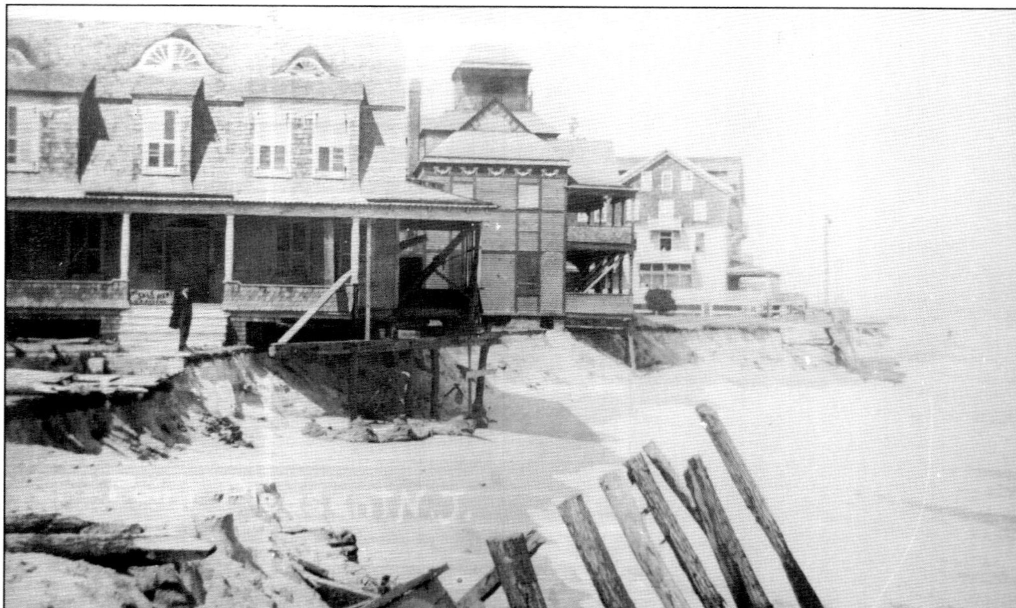

A badly eroded beachfront is shown in this view looking north from Atlantic Avenue in 1910. The Atlantic Apartments (in the foreground) had numerous close encounters with Mother Nature over the years, only to be wrecked by a bulldozer in 1994. The Murphy Cottage to the rear was moved inland 150 feet and still exists today as the Ocean Point Hotel.

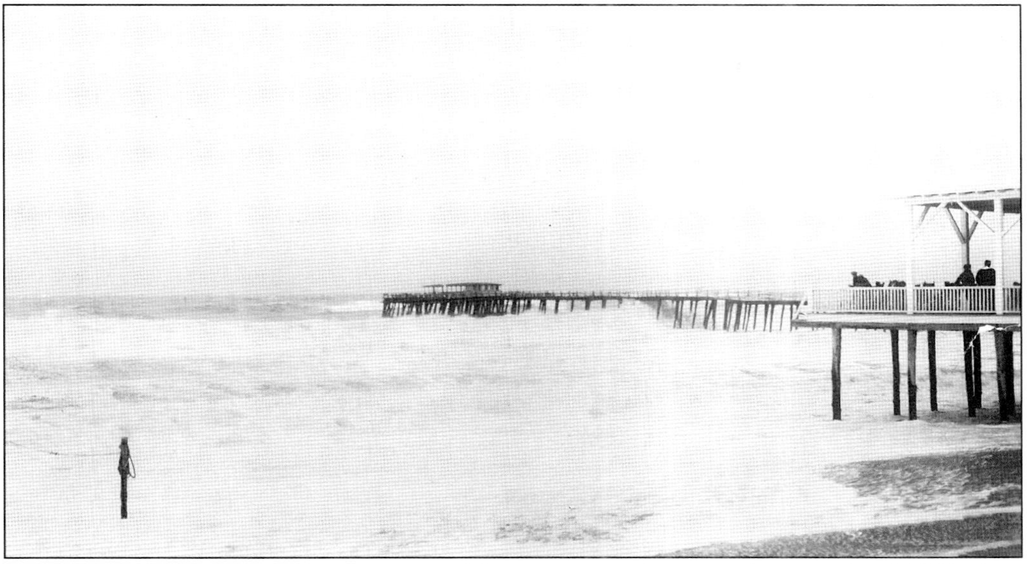

Point Pleasant Beach's ongoing erosion problem came to a dramatic climax in April 1929 when two intense coastal storms bore down on the shore and devoured what little beach was left. During the first storm, huge waves crest at the decking of the fishing pier while the one-year-old Jenkinson's Pavilion is awash in the undertow.

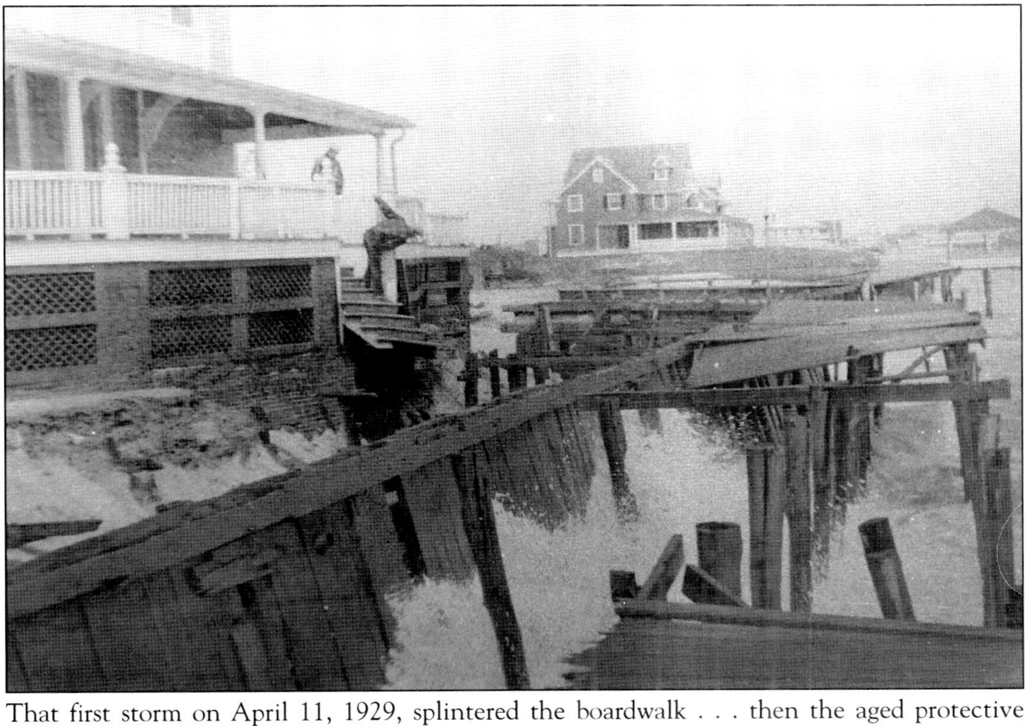

That first storm on April 11, 1929, splintered the boardwalk . . . then the aged protective bulkhead in front of the Leighton Hotel. Once again the Leighton is attacked, while a hotel caretaker balances on a dangling stairway and checks for damage. The Leighton Hotel survives yet another onslaught.

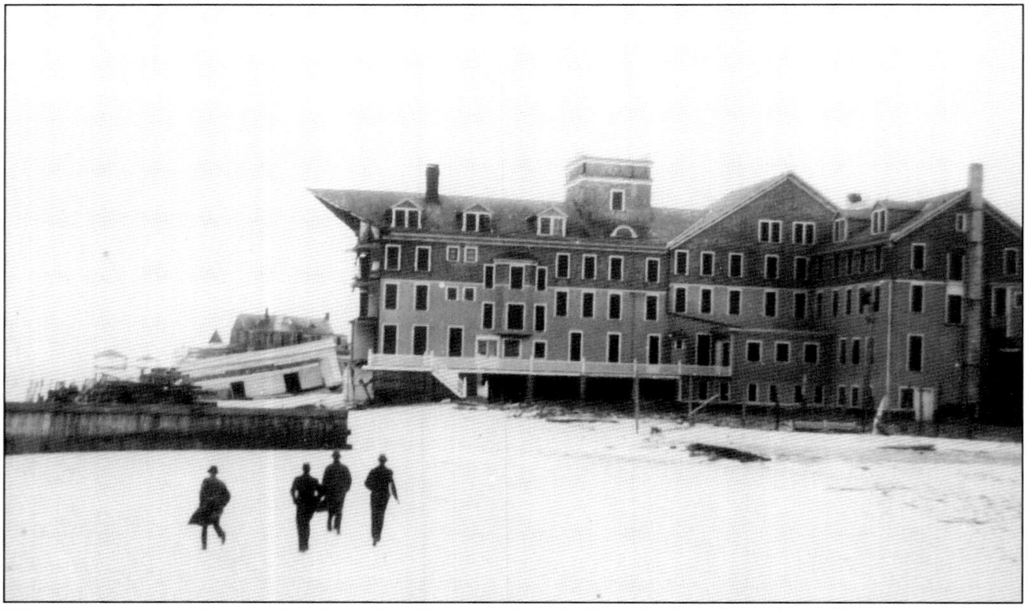

The second coastal storm hit four days later on April 15 and 16, and, with its defenses gone, the entire east wing of the Leighton Hotel collapsed into the raging surf on the morning of the 16th in front of a large crowd of spectators.

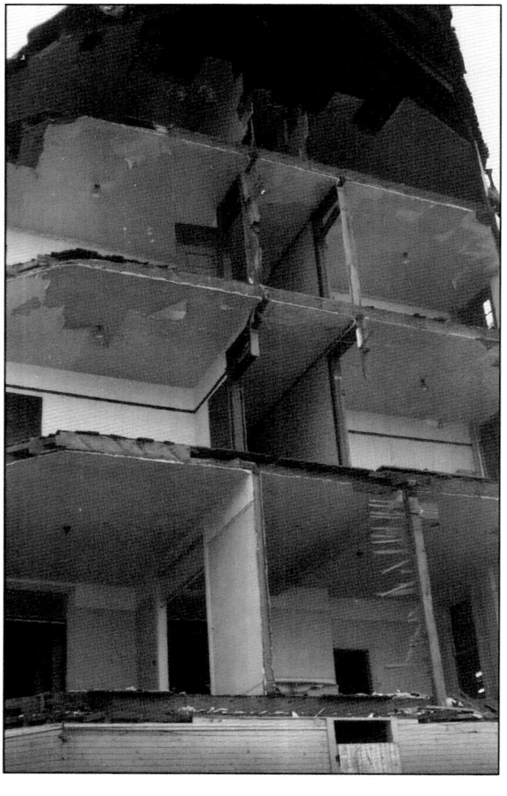

The Leighton's main ballroom was lost along with twenty-five oceanfront rooms and accompanying furniture. The hotel's weak spot is evident here, where the main building and east wing connected. Repairs were quickly made in the following months and the Leighton opened for business as usual in time for the summer crowds.

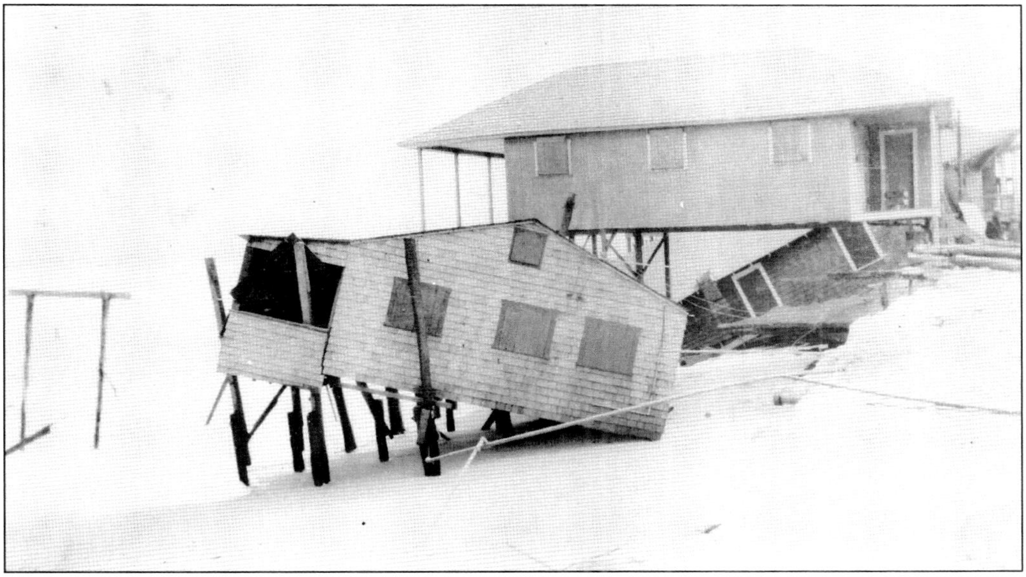

The main focus of the news media during the twin storms of April 1929 was the bungalow section of the beachfront, and rightly so. Thirteen houses were lost, with another dozen moved out of harm's way. At one point, it was feared a new inlet would form along Costa Row and connect the Atlantic Ocean with Lake Louise.

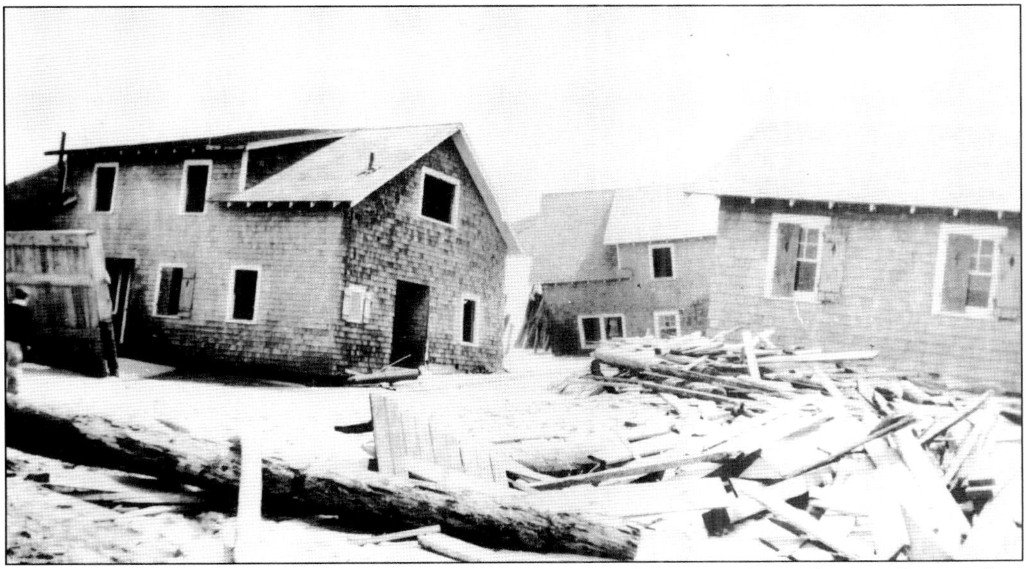

Hundreds of spectators kept vigil on the beach day and night to watch one house after another wash away. Workmen were kept busy removing furniture while every available plumber was called by the frantic homeowners to remove valuable plumbing and bathroom fixtures. The total damage from these storms in Point Pleasant Beach alone amounted to three-quarters of a million dollars (see Vol. I, p. 117).

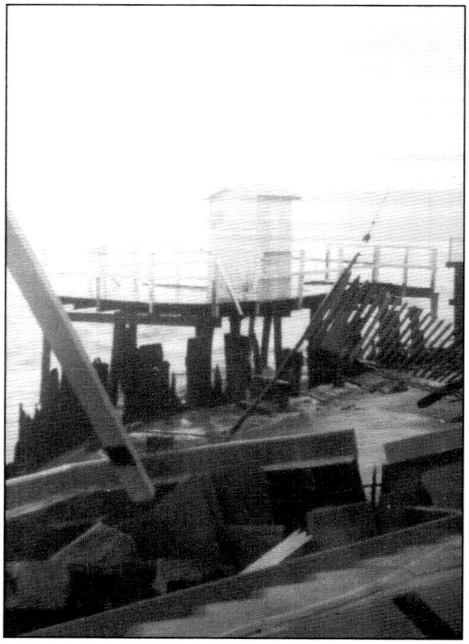

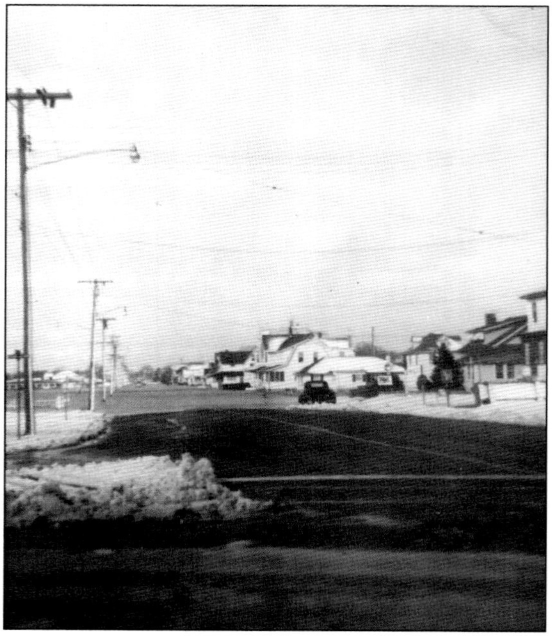

Thirty-three years after the 1929 storms, the Great March Storm of 1962 struck Point Pleasant Beach, causing extensive erosion but only minor beachfront damage. The reduced amount of damage may be attributed to the three decades of beach replenishment provided by the Manasquan Inlet jetties. On the left, the foot of New York Avenue is awash, while on the right tidal flooding inundates Arnold Avenue. Perhaps the most crippling effect the March 1962 storm had in the Point Pleasant area was the collapse of the original Lovelandtown Bridge over the Point Pleasant Canal. Temporary repairs were quickly made and lasted until the entire bridge was replaced with the present vertical-lift bridge in 1972.

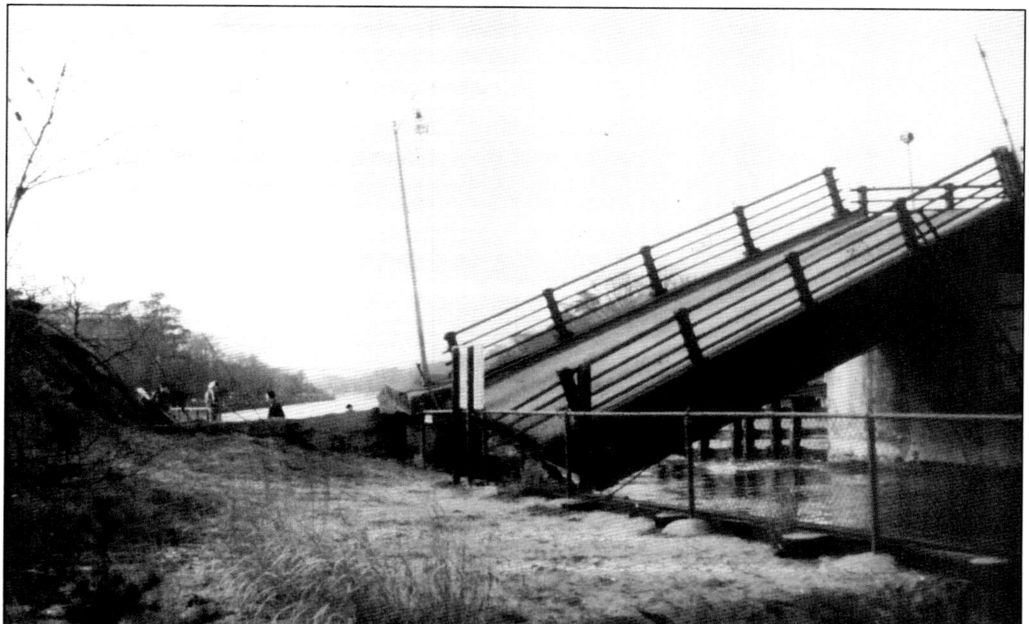

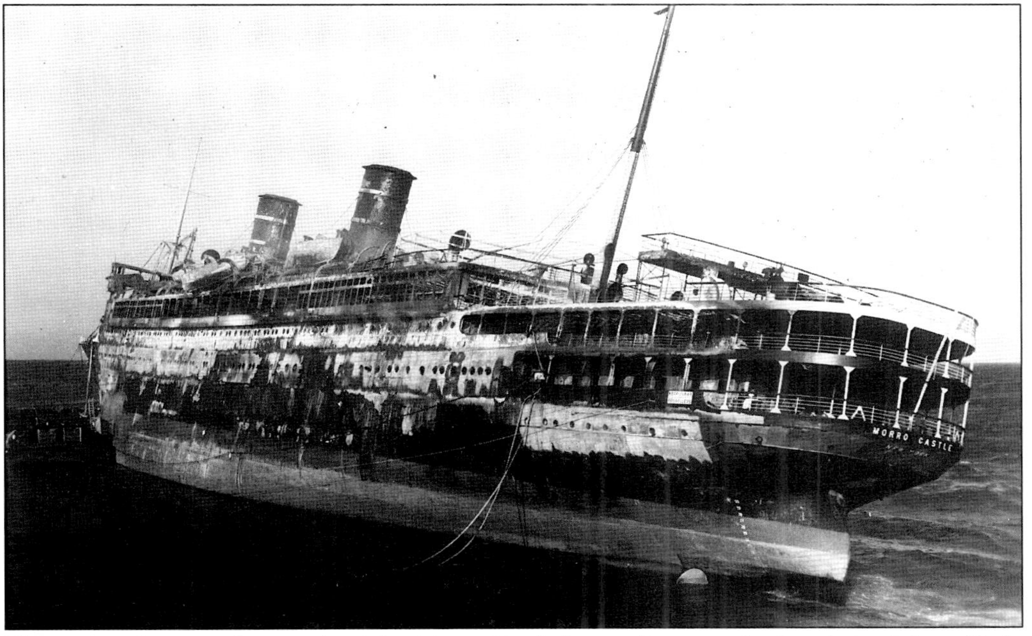

This image features the wreck of the *Morro Castle* luxury liner on the beach in Asbury Park. The *Morro Castle* was bound from Havana to New York City when it caught fire in heavy weather off Ocean County on September 8, 1934. The disaster claimed 134 lives.

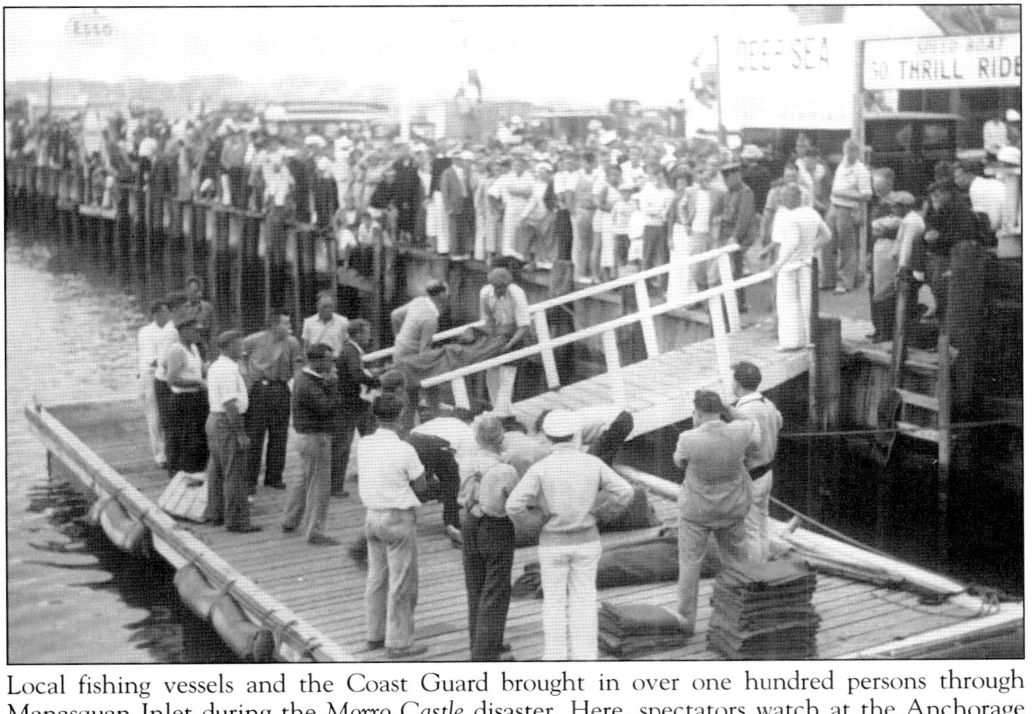

Local fishing vessels and the Coast Guard brought in over one hundred persons through Manasquan Inlet during the *Morro Castle* disaster. Here, spectators watch at the Anchorage Landing in Cook's Creek as bodies are taken to the morgues of David DeRoche and H. Allen Van Hise.

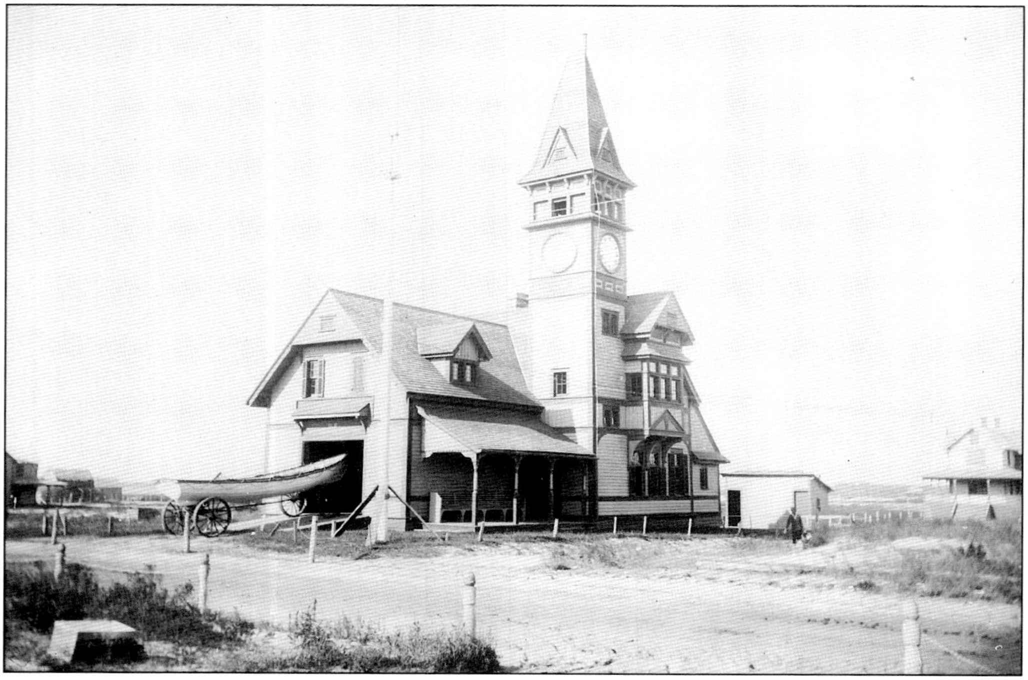

Life Saving Service Station #10 on East Avenue in Bay Head featured an impressive clock/watch tower. Built in 1889, this building housed the U.S. Government Life Saving crew, and later Coast Guard crews that kept watch along the shoreline in Bay Head and Point Pleasant Beach into the 1940s.

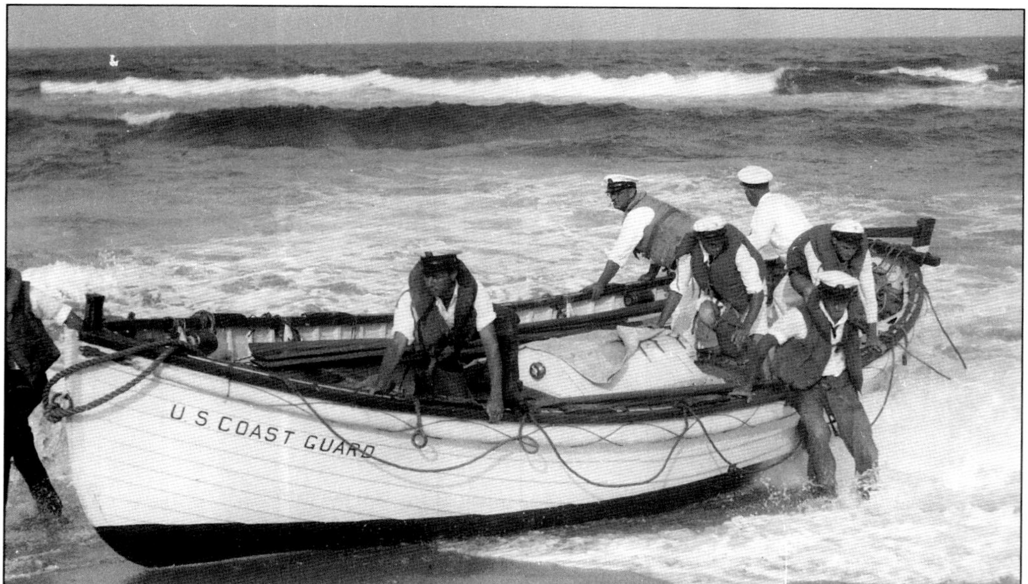

A Manasquan Beach Coast Guard skiff comes ashore in the summer of 1931. At this time, the Manasquan Inlet Station was located on Ocean Avenue in Manasquan. The Manasquan and Bay Head Life Saving crews often shared their areas of responsibility when the need arose.

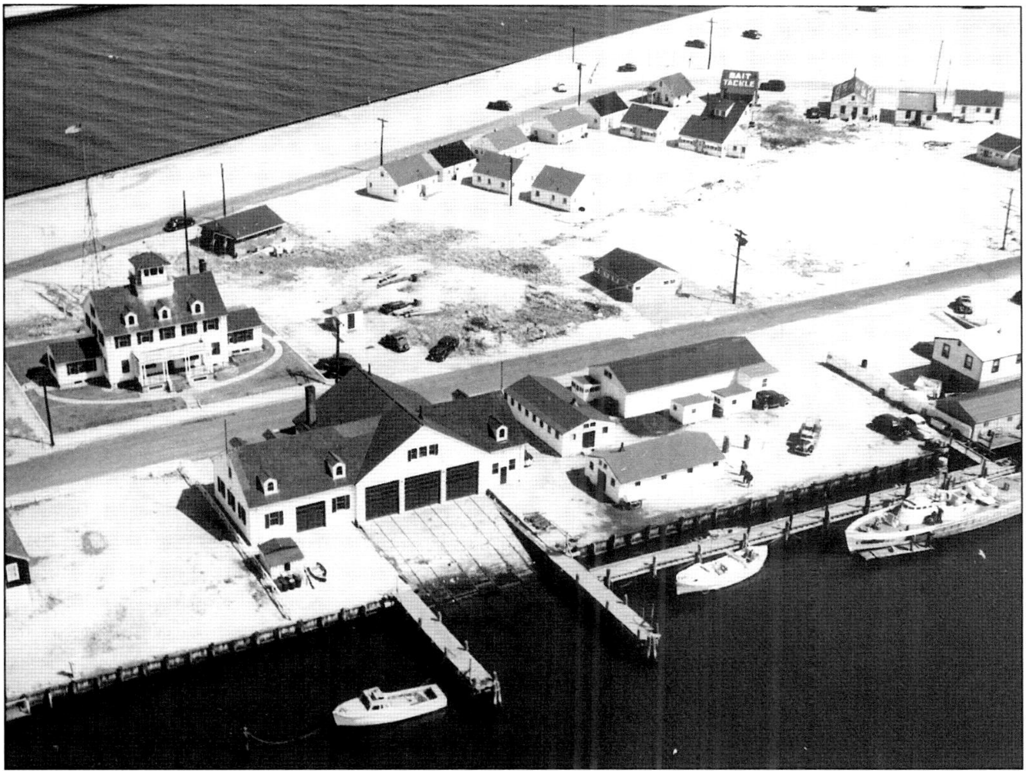

The Manasquan Inlet Coast Guard Station and boathouse on Inlet Drive are shown here about 1950. Construction of surrounding summer homes and businesses on Inlet Drive began after World War II and continued through the 1950s.

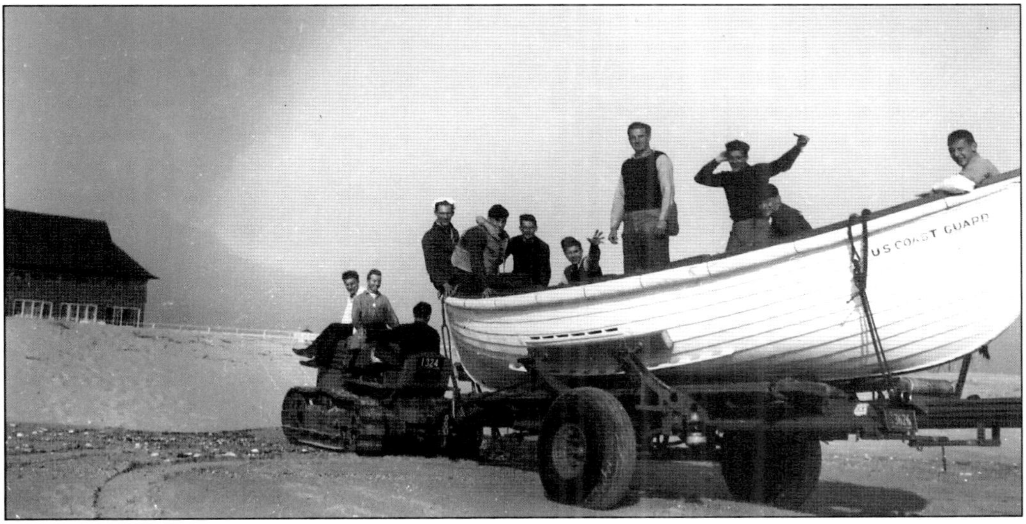

It's September 1947 and the Coast Guard drills are now held at the Inlet Pavilion beach at the foot of Broadway. Tractor and trailer have replaced horses, rollers, and human muscle to haul the boats onto the beach. The old Inlet Pavilion (in the background), built in 1903, was torn down just weeks after this photograph was taken.

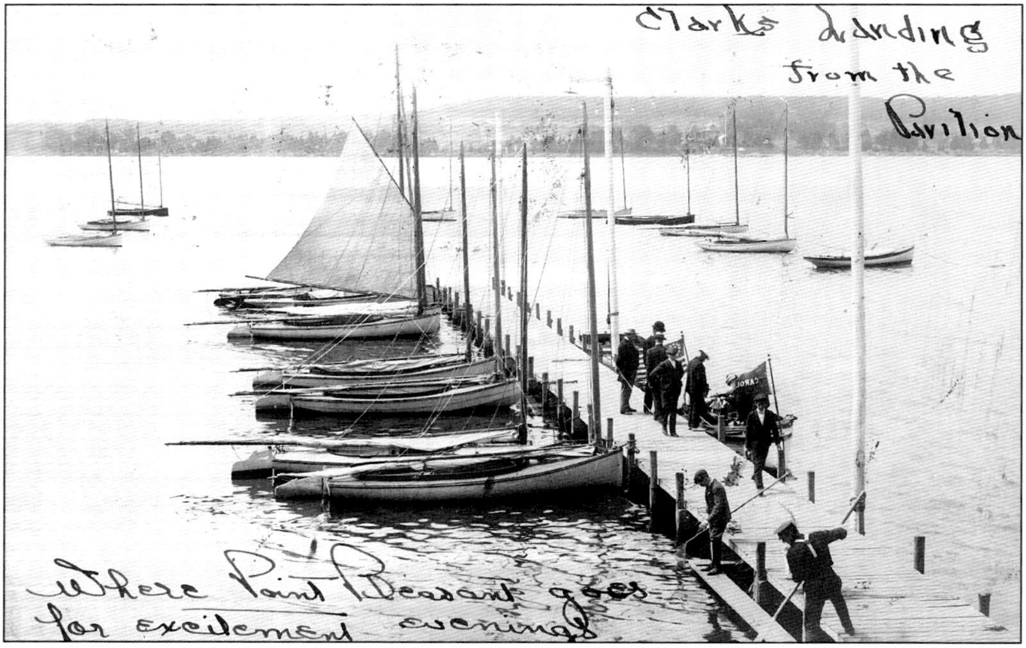

The message on this 1905 postcard identifies Clark's Landing on the Manasquan River distinctly and precisely: "Where Point Pleasant goes for excitement evenings." Indeed, Clark's Landing was the one place to go for such a wide variety of exciting activities day and night. Many longtime residents have such fond memories of Clark's Landing in its heyday.

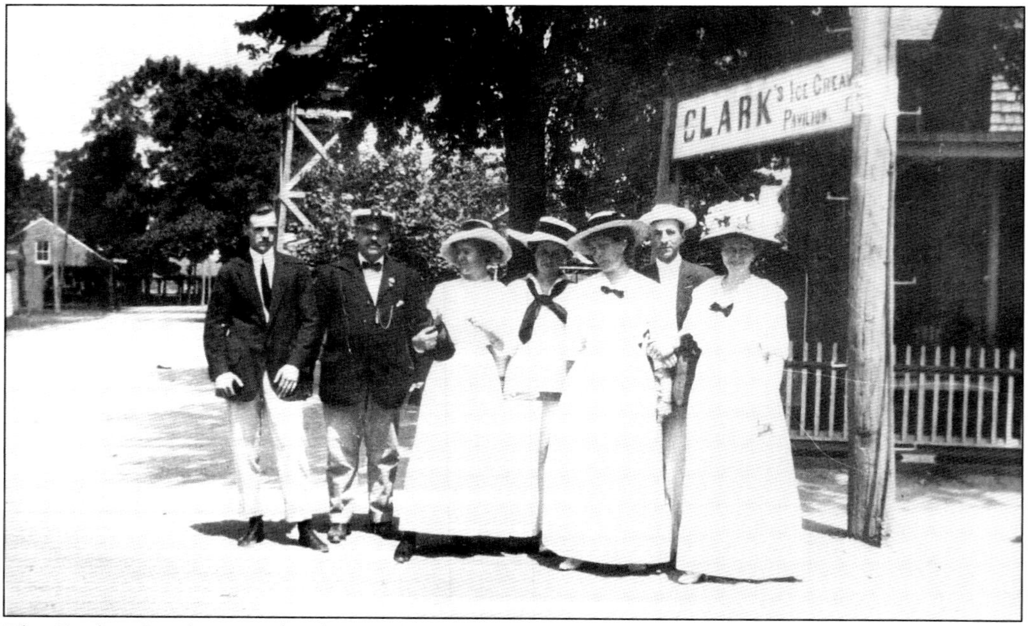

The Fischer family waits for the trolley at the entrance to Clark's Landing on Arnold Avenue in 1910. The Fischers summered across the river in Brielle and T.T. Fischer (second from the left) was the commodore of the Manasquan River Yacht Club during the teens.

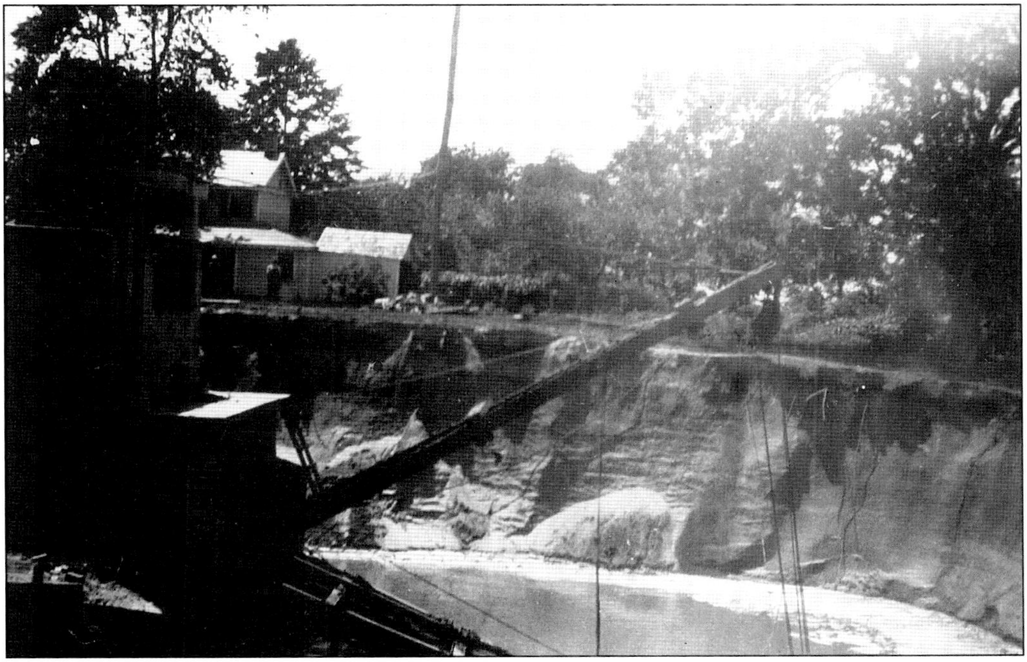

A suction dredge is hard at work digging the Manasquan River-Bay Head Canal in 1922. Already four years behind schedule, the canal didn't officially open until 1926. This dredge pumped sand onto the nearby banks; a good portion of this earth was trucked to Point Pleasant Beach and used in the construction of the new (third) Manasquan River highway bridge causeway.

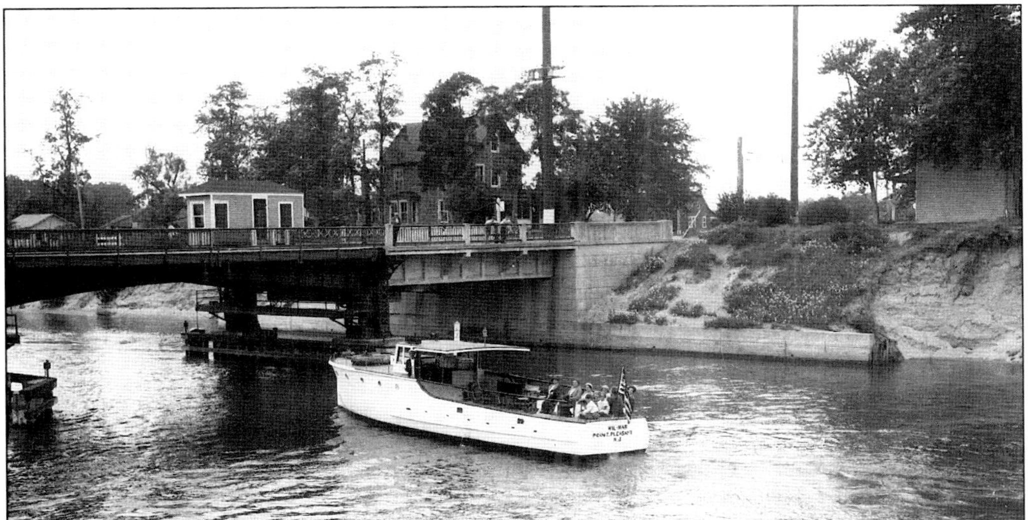

Captain Charles Gifford pilots his vessel, the *Wil-Mar*, under the old Route 4 (now Route 88) drawbridge in 1933. The view is toward the southwest. The house behind the trees in the background was the Tylee Allen store and dwelling. Allen was an early Point Pleasant dry goods merchant during the mid- and late 1800s. He also served as postmaster in the 1860s and '70s.

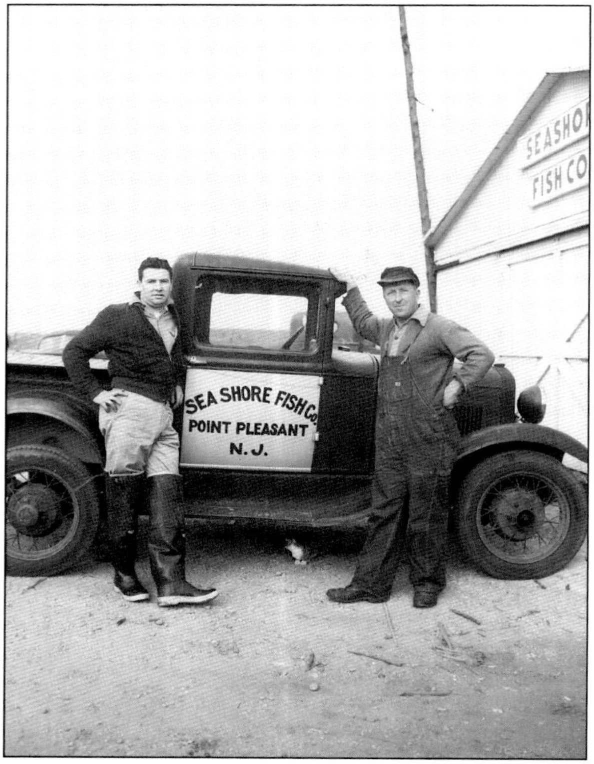

Wilbur Gifford, Hans Nelson, and their feline friend are at the Seashore Fish Company on Channel Drive in 1942. Cats were plentiful and well-fed around the fishery docks along Will's Hole Thorofare.

The humble but profitable Seashore Fish Company dock appears here in 1943. The Seashore Fish Company was one of the early centers of commercial fishing along Will's Hole Thorofare. Notice the net drying reel on the dock, which was used in connection with the offshore pound fishing operations (see Vol. I, p. 109).

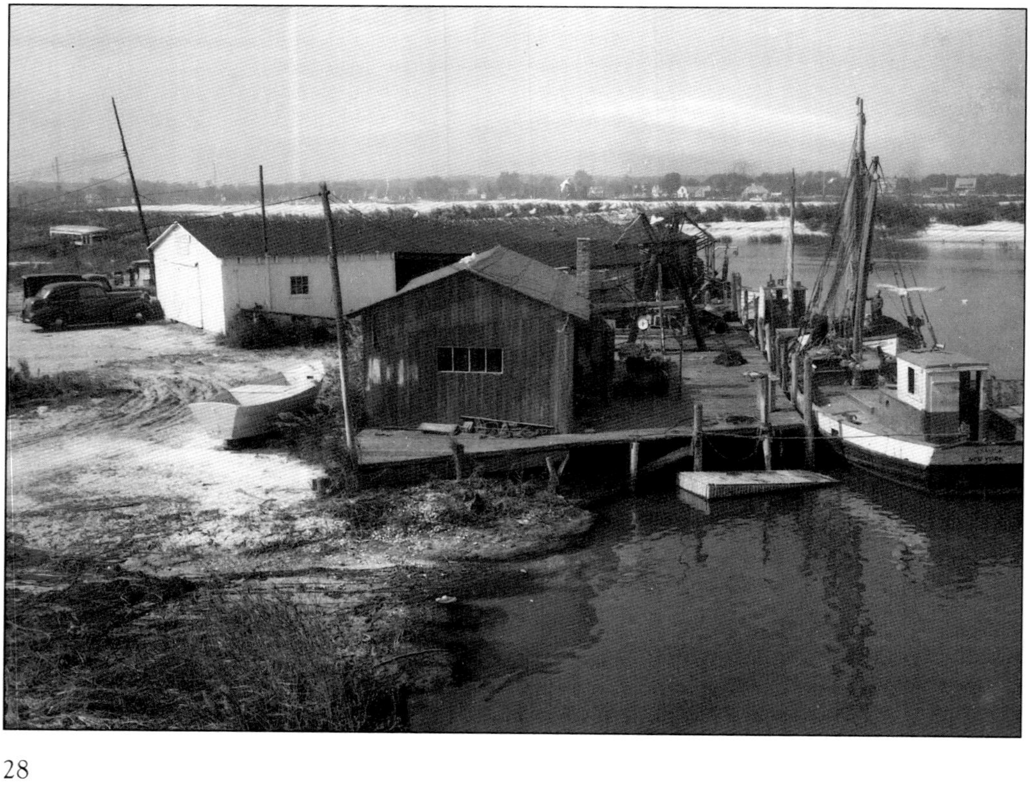

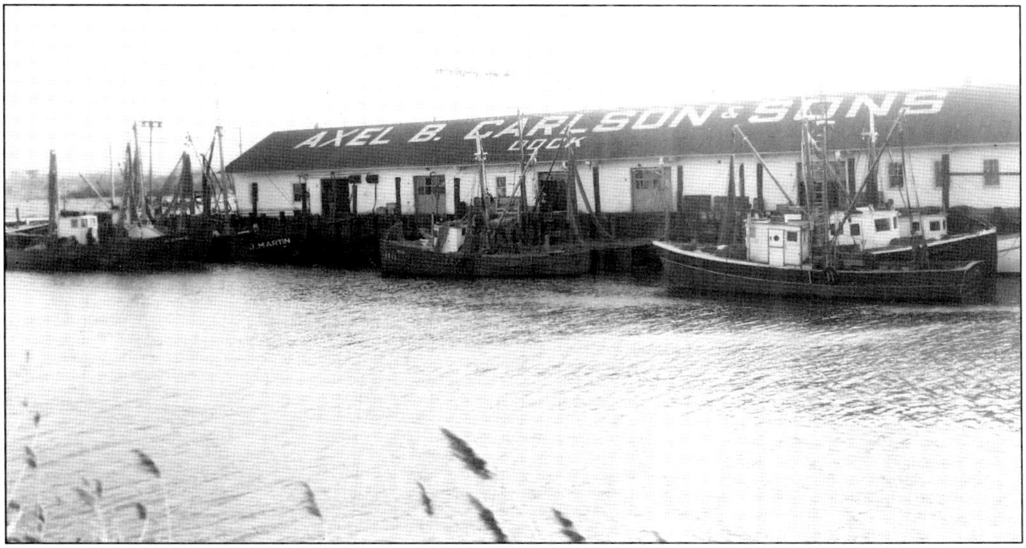

Axel B. Carlson's Point Pleasant Fishery at the foot of Baltimore Avenue appears here in 1946. This fishery expanded over the ensuing years to include a retail store and restaurant. The original wood and concrete packing and freezer building (above) was destroyed by fire in 1982.

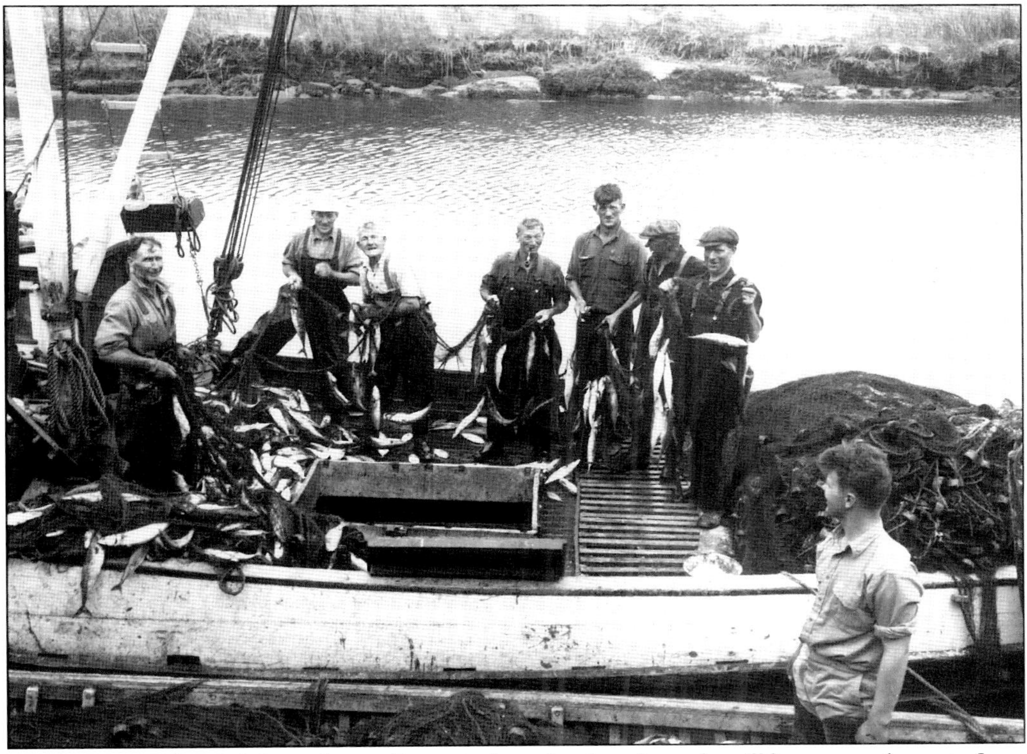

Workers at Carlson's fishery show off a typical catch taken from the offshore pound nets in June 1943. Standing in the foreground is Axel "Junie" Carlson. This catch would be kept on ice. By the 1960s, special refrigerated holding pens were in operation and could hold up to 10,000 pounds of deep water lobsters, each weighing 25 pounds or more.

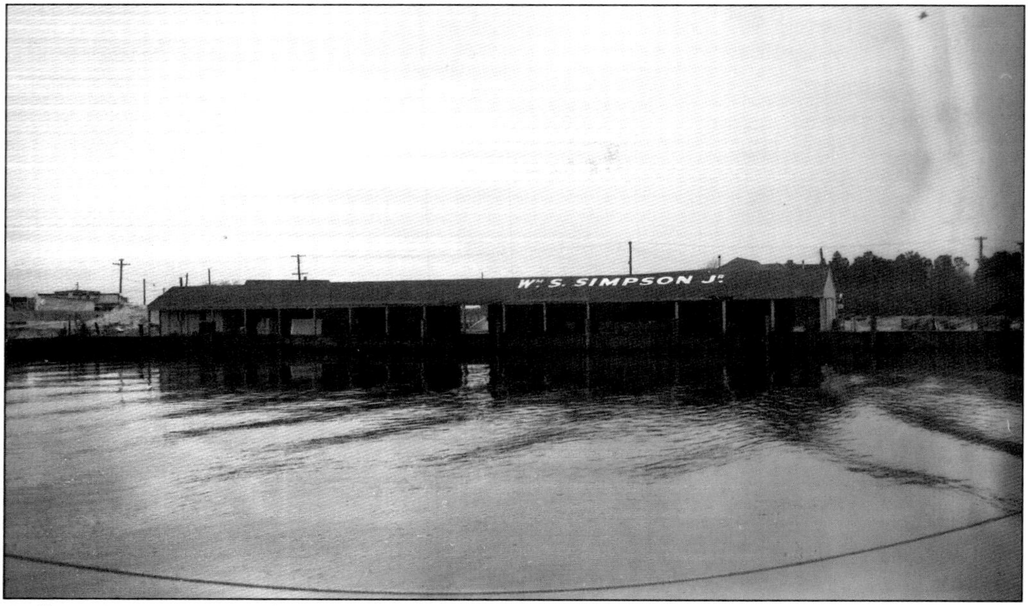

William S. Simpson Jr. of Mantoloking operated this fishery for several years on the west side of Cook's Creek on Channel Drive, shown here in 1946. Today the Fisherman Co-Op dock and seafood market occupies the site.

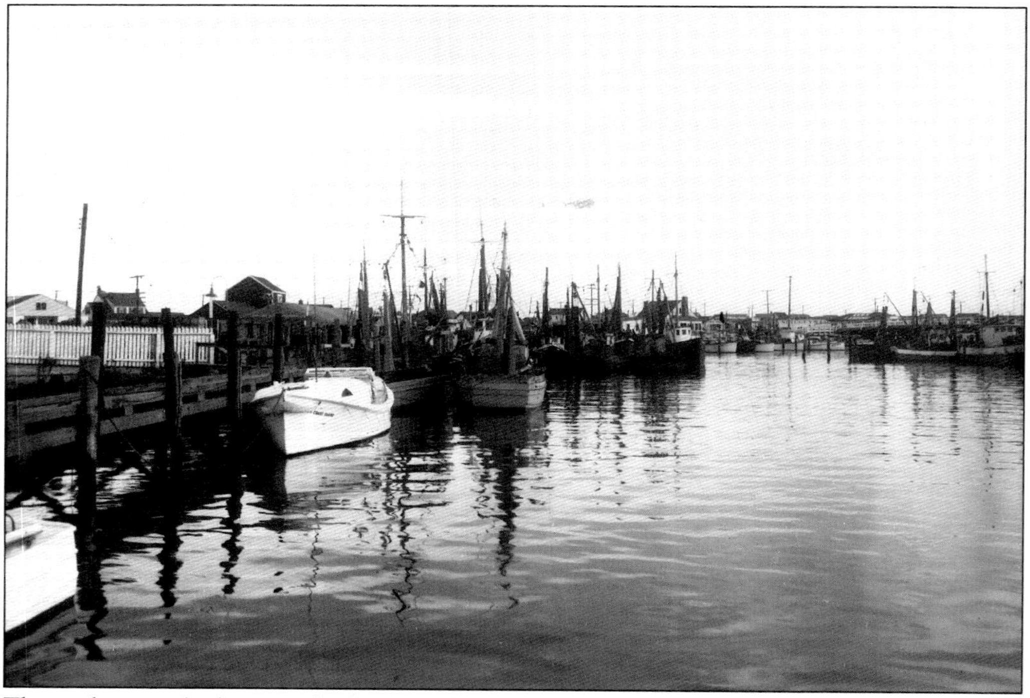

This is the view looking south along Cook's Creek toward Broadway and Lake Louise in 1946. On the left is Frank Barmore's dock, now the site of the Shrimp Box Restaurant. Barmore's wife Edith started the restaurant in 1953 as a small take-out stand with four counter stools and fresh seafood taken right off the boats.

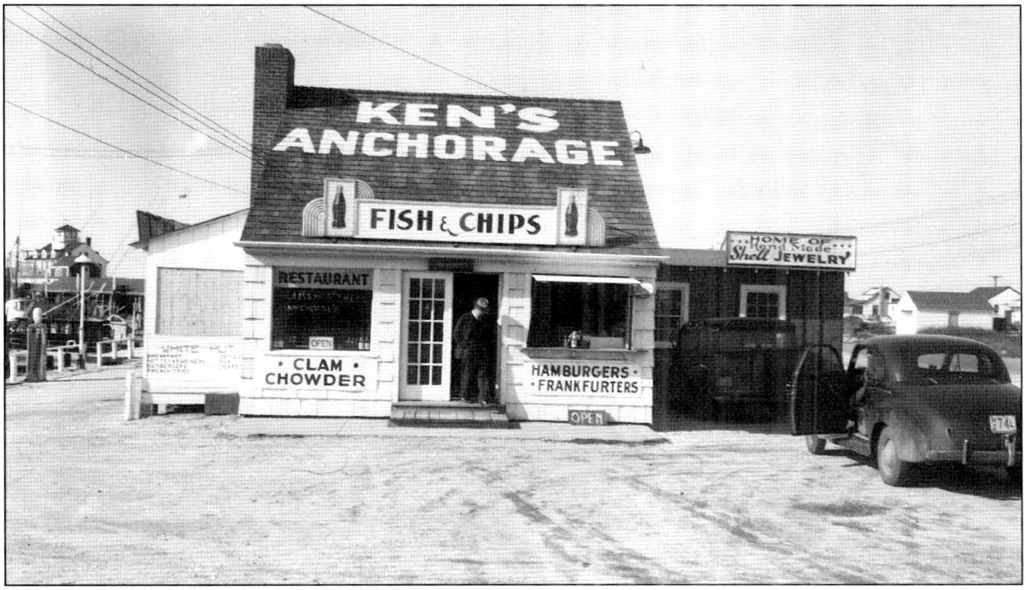

The "Anchorage" on the north side of the Broadway bridge is shown in 1948. The property, confiscated from Hubert Johnson by the Coast Guard during World War II, was sold to Jack Kennel in 1945. The small building on the property (above) was built around 1930 and is one of the oldest buildings in the Inlet area. Today it is the Cottage Restaurant.

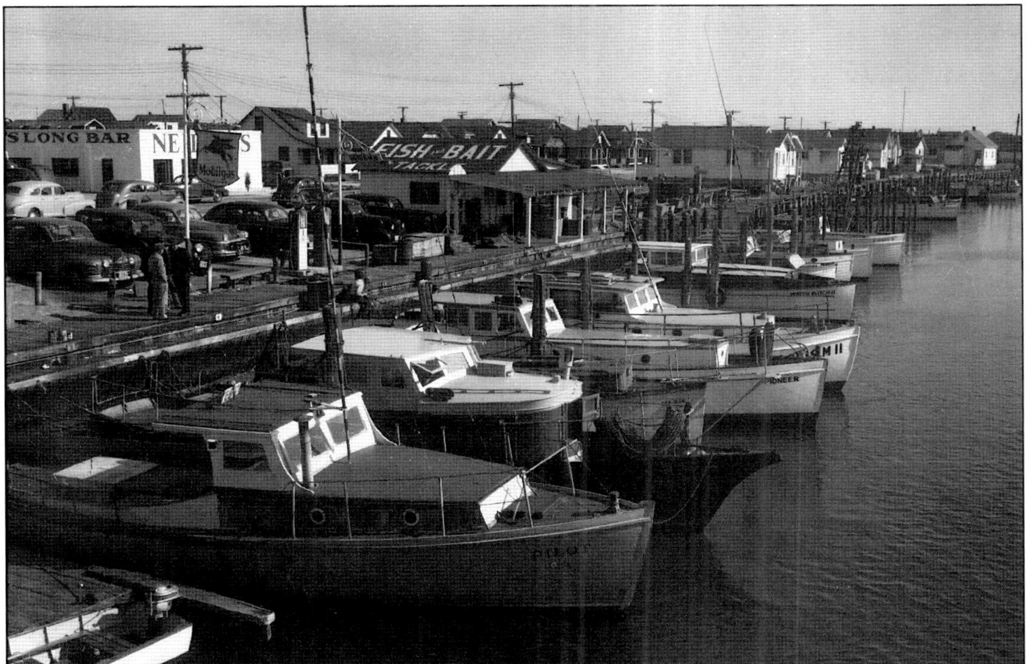

John P. Kennel founded Ken's Landing on the south side of the Broadway bridge in 1934. With nearly 400 feet of waterfront, Ken's Landing flourished. The south dock is shown here in 1948. The former Neilly's Long Bar, now the Broadway Grill, is on the left.

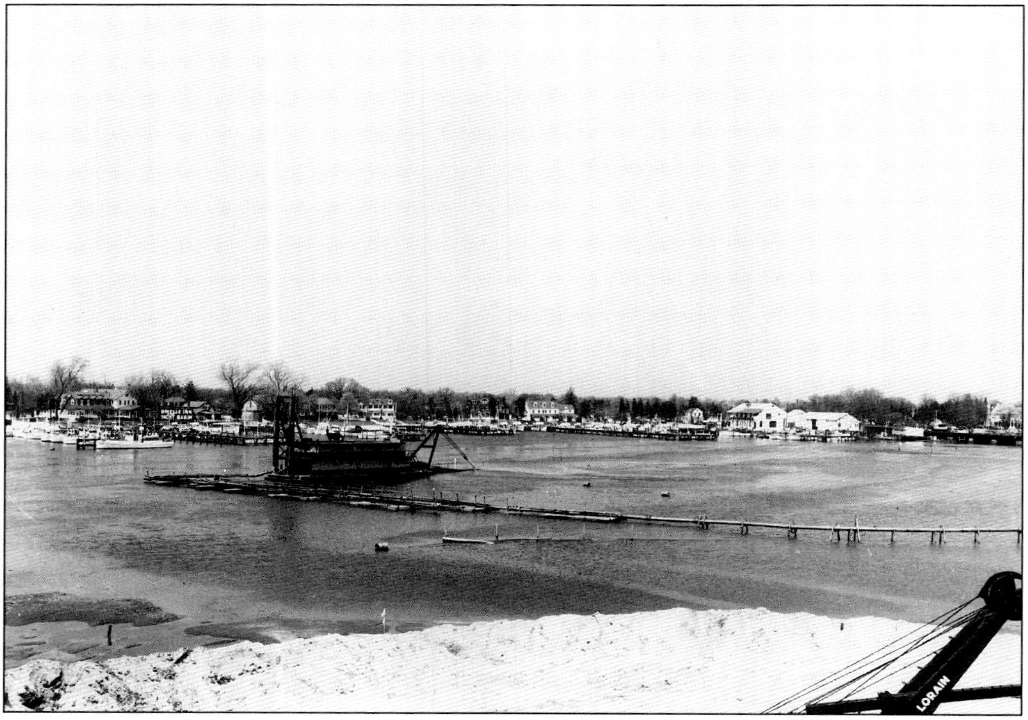

With the construction of the present Route 35 bridge in 1950 and the relocation of the main river channel, the Manasquan River became the site of the most extensive dredging to be undertaken in many years. This dredge is cutting the new river channel in May 1950 as the sand is pumped through pipes onto Gull Island.

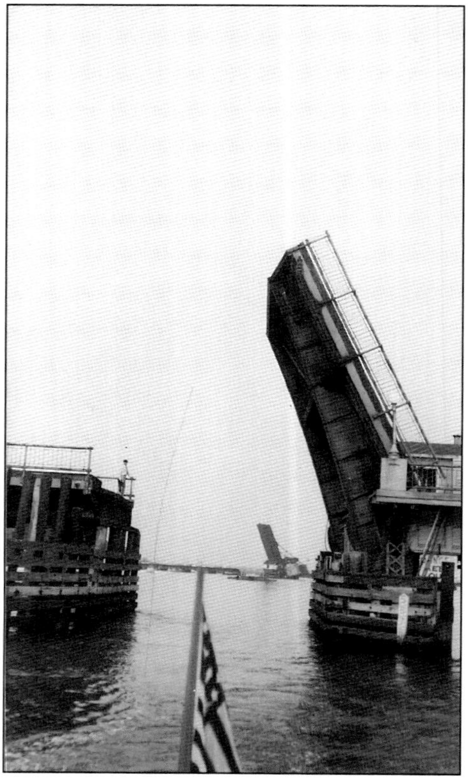

This interesting view shows the Inland Waterway on the Manasquan River *c.* 1935 as it passes under the Route 35 highway bridge and the railroad bridge. This is the third highway bridge—a nightmare for motorists and boaters alike with an average clearance of 10 feet.

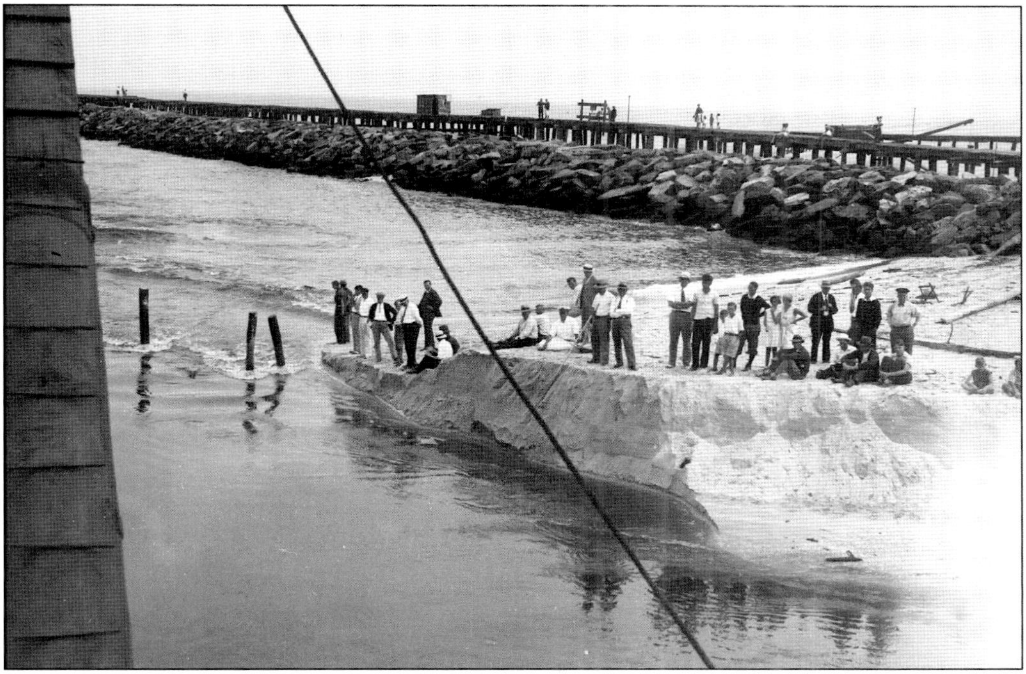

Spectators keep tabs on the progress of the Manasquan Inlet in July 1931. Rocks for the south jetty (in the background) were trucked out over the sand on heavy wooden piers and dropped in place by a crane. The piers were later removed with the support piling cut off at the water line.

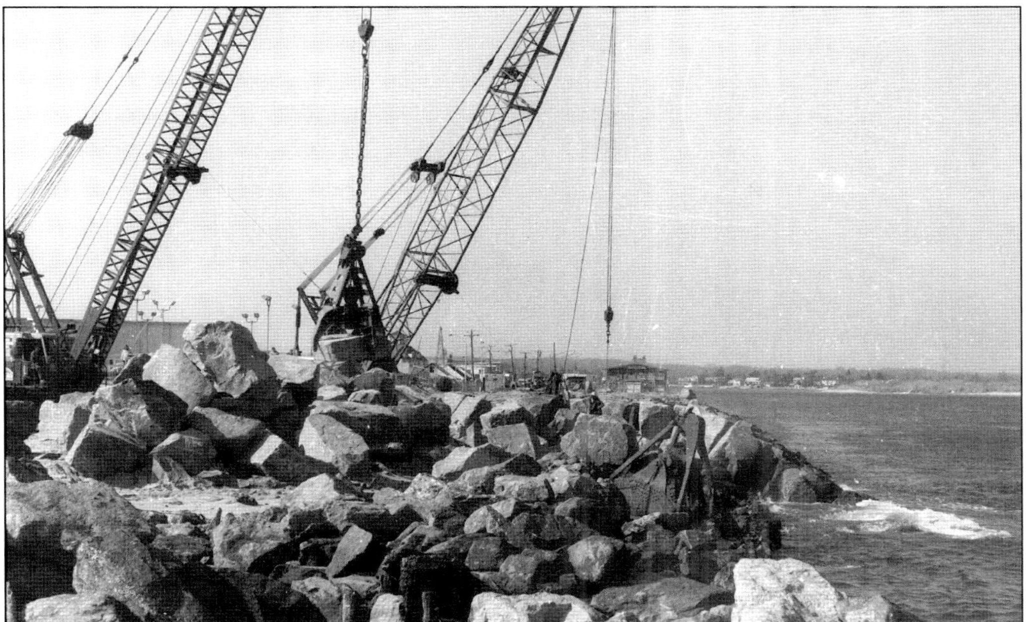

The Manasquan Inlet jetties got a complete makeover in 1980–81. A new type of interlocking "jacks" called "dolos" were placed at the seaward end of both jetties and have held up well. Notice the old 1930 construction pier piling at the bottom of the photograph.

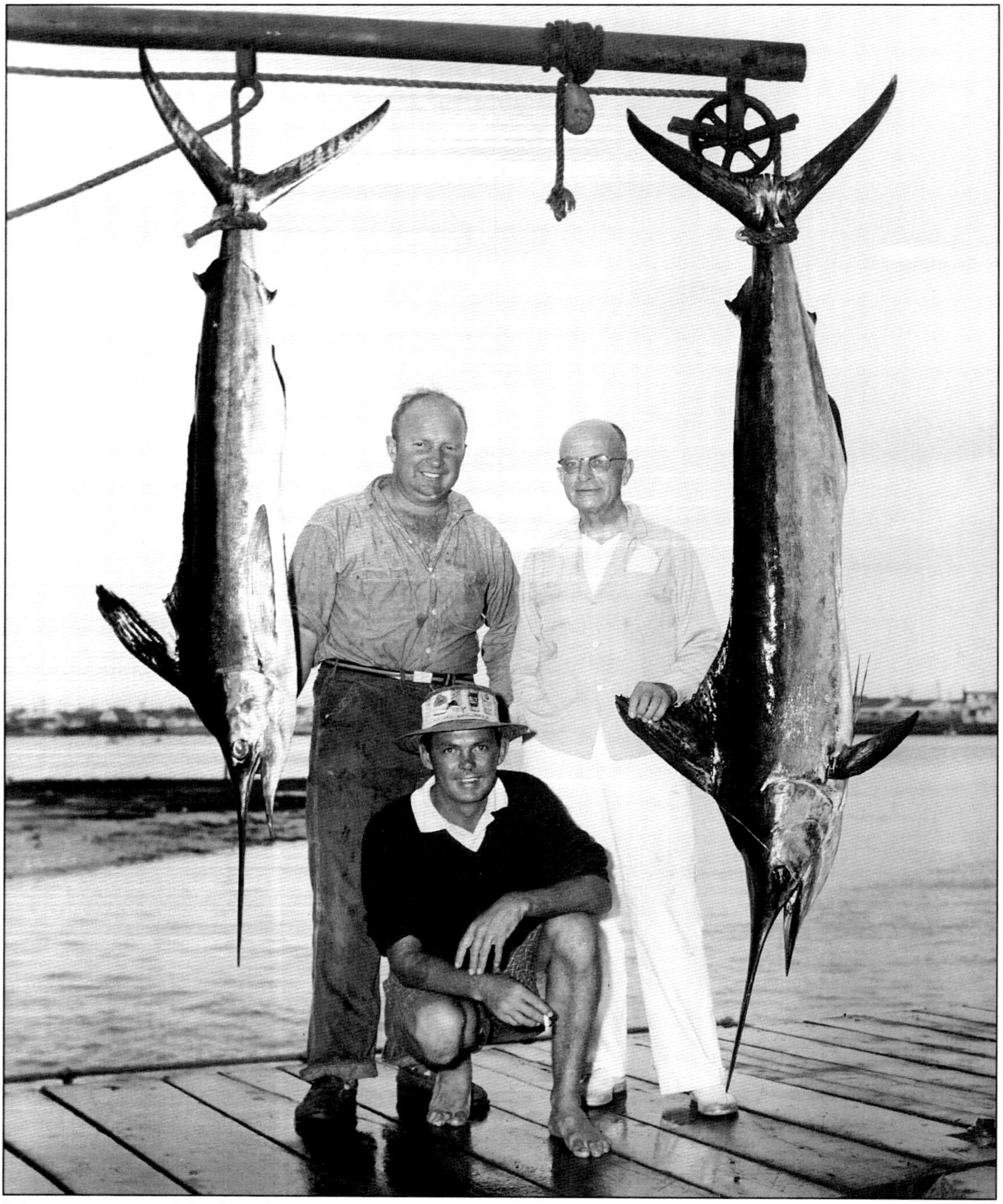

This is just one of the hundreds of prize catches brought in at Carlson's dock over the years. Kneeling on the dock is Captain Lyman "Sonny" Barr; behind him on the left is Walter "Buddy" Carlson.

Two

Cottages and Inns

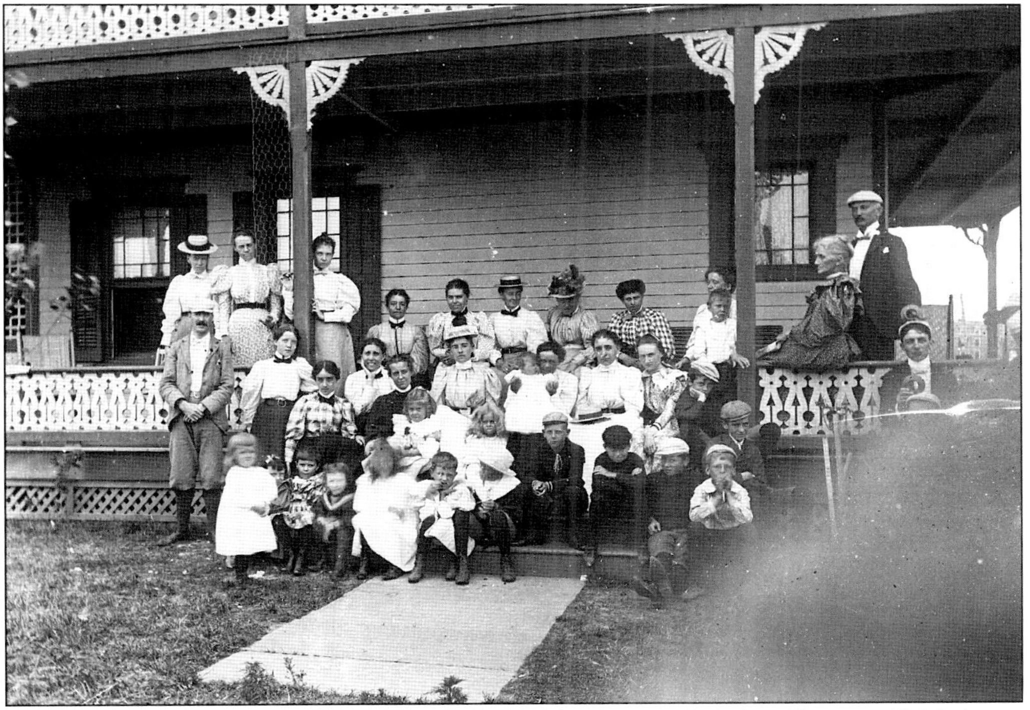

Family and friends gather on the east porch steps of the Arverne Boarding House at 406 Atlantic Avenue in 1897. The proprietress of this expansive and popular summer retreat, Miss Joan Pierce, is sitting on the porch railing to the right.

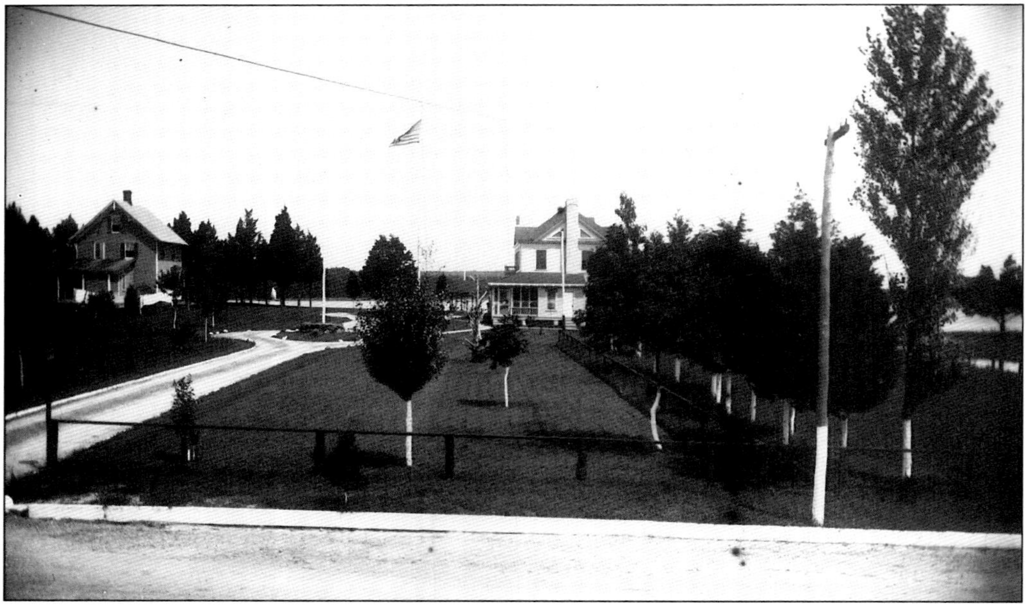

Many fine houses were built along the Manasquan River in Point Pleasant and Point Pleasant Beach during the latter part of the 1800s. This turn-of-the-century scene shows the Cooke mansion on the river with Front Street (now River Road) in the foreground. The Cedar Bluff Cottage is on the left.

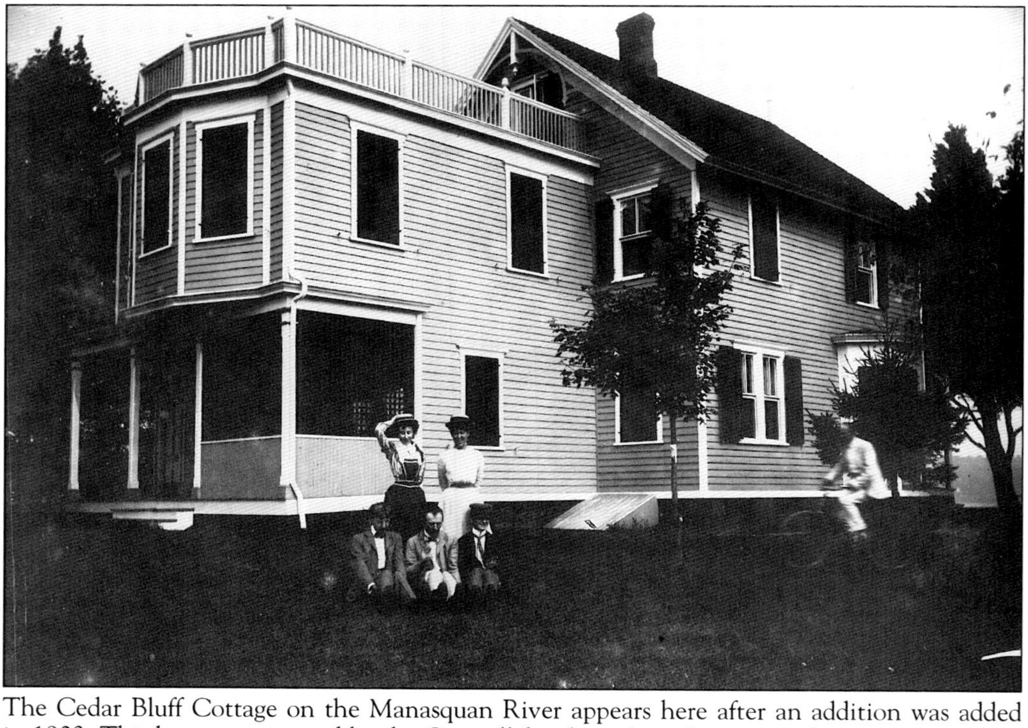

The Cedar Bluff Cottage on the Manasquan River appears here after an addition was added in 1903. This house was owned by the Connell family and was later moved to 1137 Pine Bluff Avenue, where it still stands. The Joseph Moran estate was then built on this site.

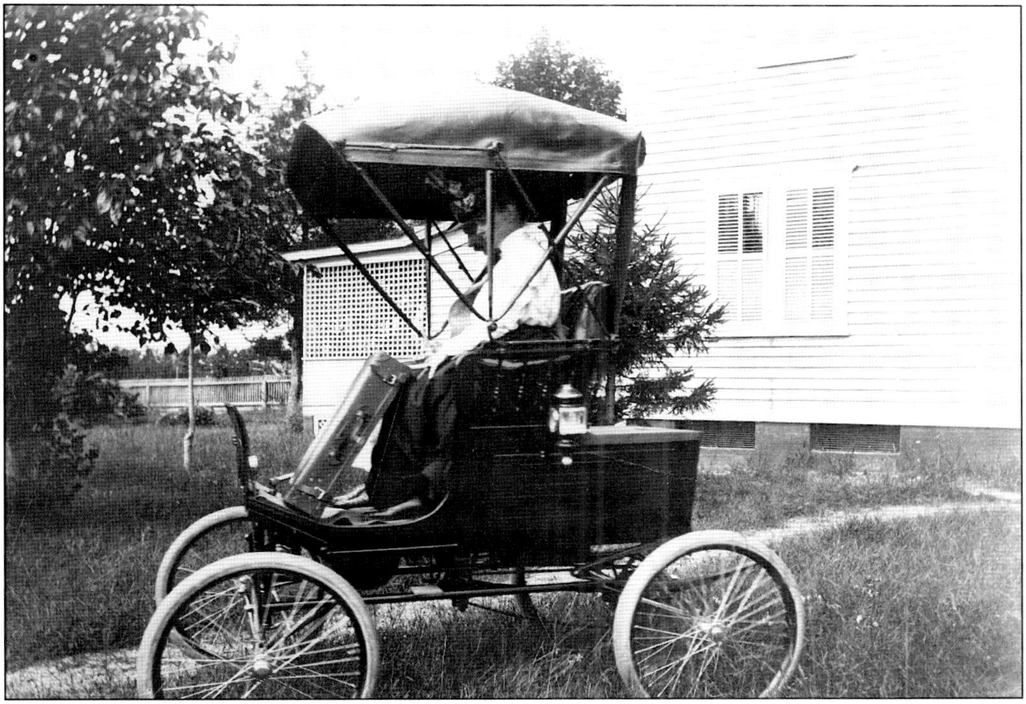

Mildred Connell married Daniel Mason, who worked for the Produce Exchange. The Masons later resided in Point Pleasant Beach. Here, the Masons show off their electric automobile at the Cedar Bluff Cottage in 1901.

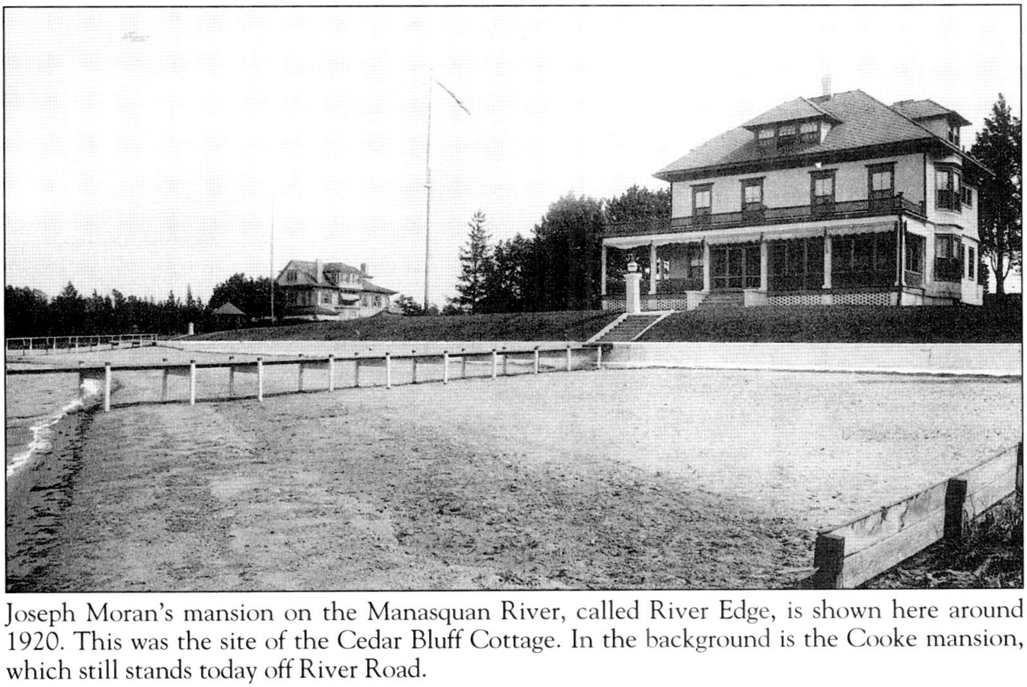

Joseph Moran's mansion on the Manasquan River, called River Edge, is shown here around 1920. This was the site of the Cedar Bluff Cottage. In the background is the Cooke mansion, which still stands today off River Road.

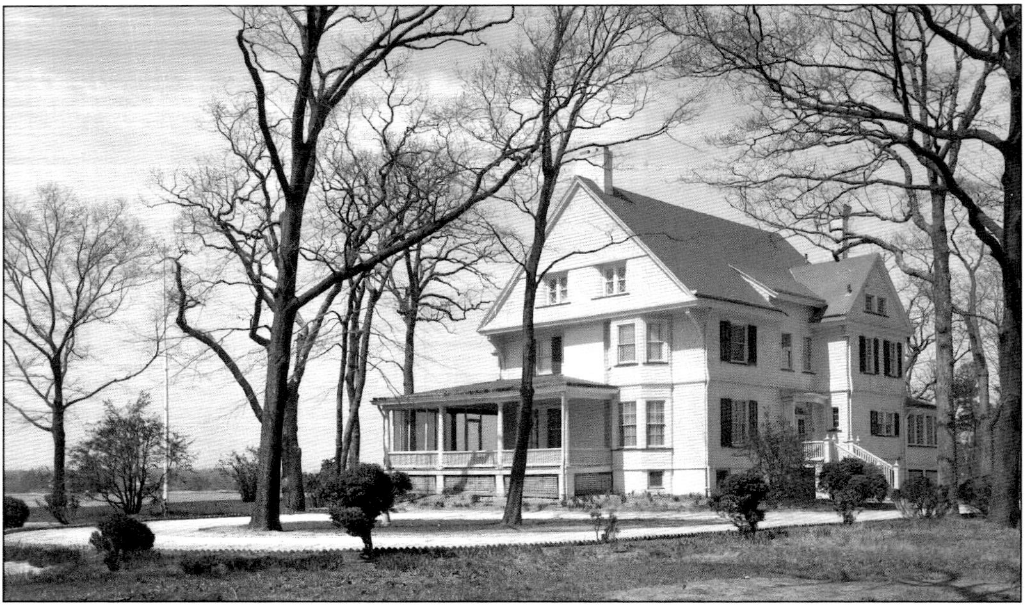

The Severance house on the Manasquan River in Point Pleasant Beach appears here in 1946. This house is typical in size of the late-nineteenth-century mansions built on the banks of the river. Following a 1939 fire, the house was completely remodeled and still exists today at the end of Woodland Road.

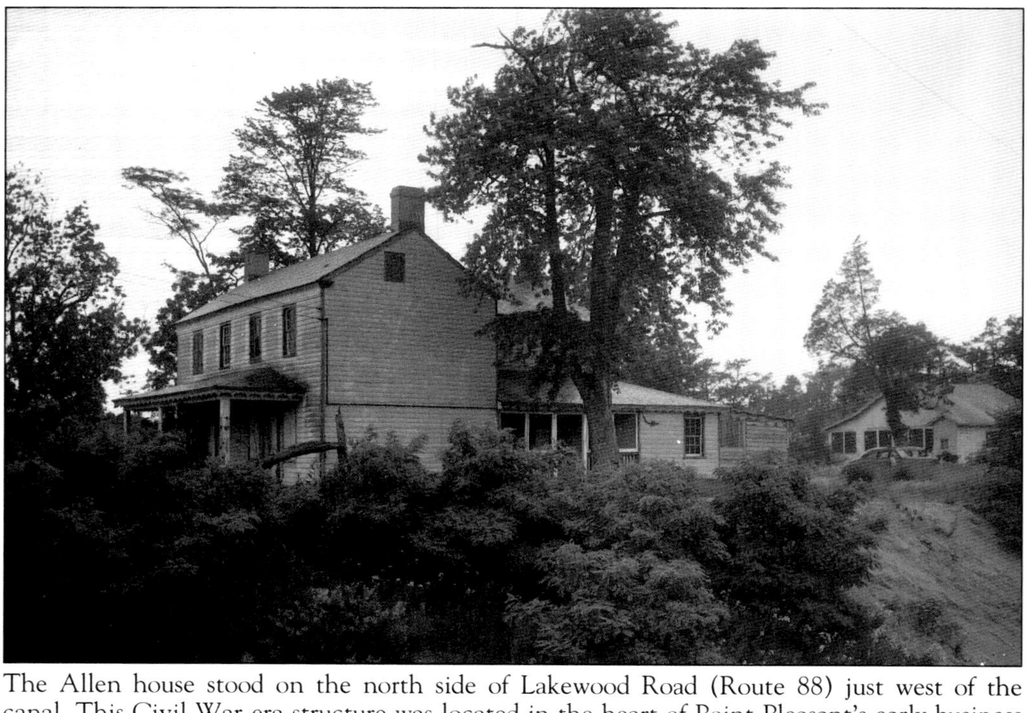

The Allen house stood on the north side of Lakewood Road (Route 88) just west of the canal. This Civil War-era structure was located in the heart of Point Pleasant's early business community and was undoubtedly a place of commerce as well. In disrepair by 1945 (above), this landmark was eventually torn down.

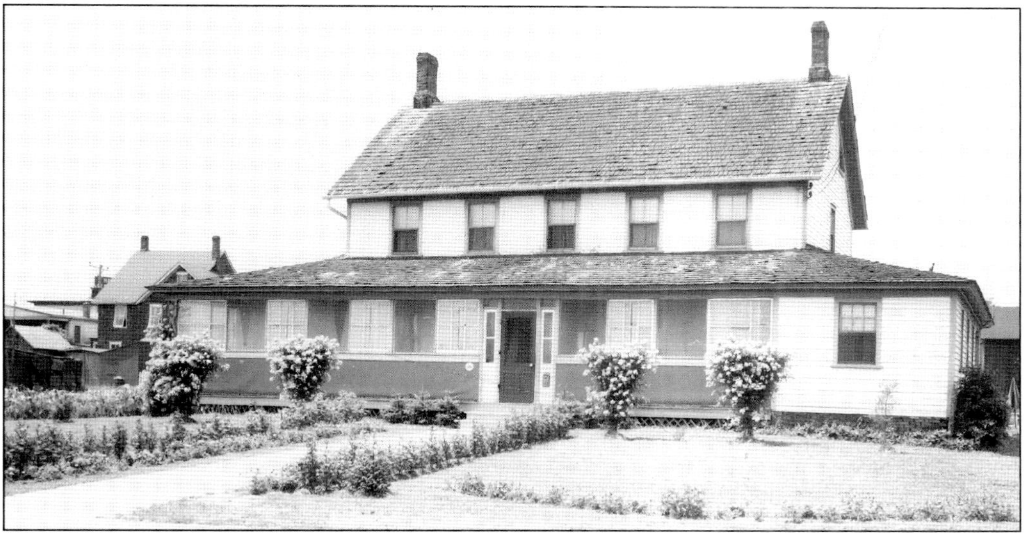

Located at what was once number 133 Railroad Square, the Thomas Williams house, shown here in 1939, was one of the earliest homes built within the present boundaries of Point Pleasant Beach that survived well into the twentieth century (see p. 107). During the 1880s, Williams and Charles Knox owned much of the land along the present Route 35 between McLean and Holly Avenues. This land was originally purchased from John Arnold.

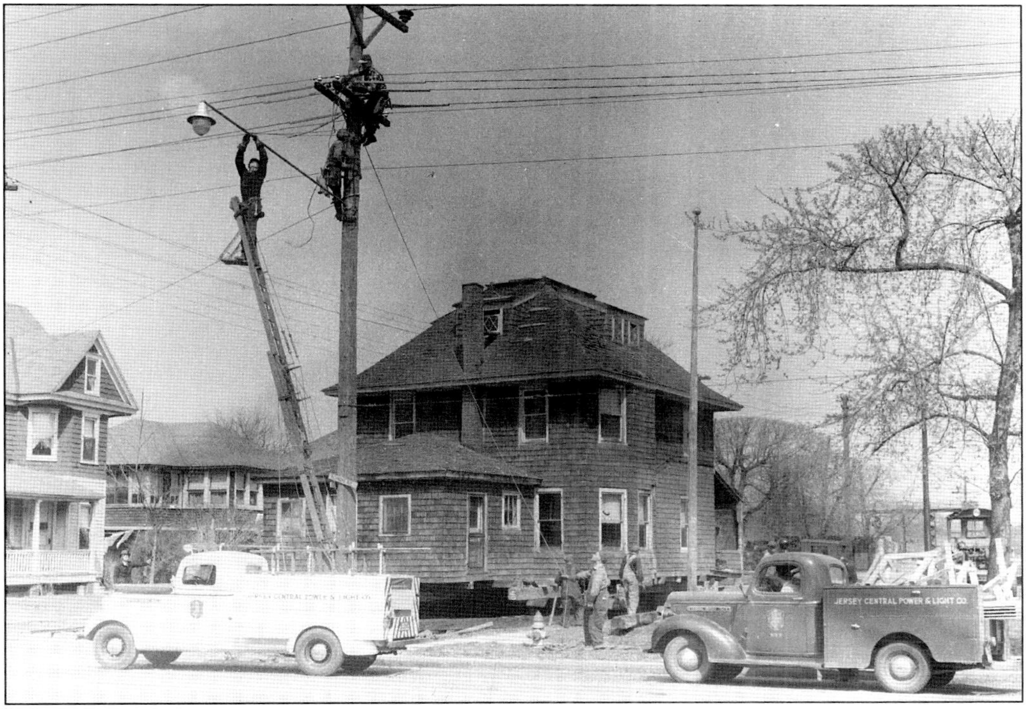

House moving was a common practice during the first half of the 1900s. The building would ride on heavy timber beams and rollers while electric and telephone wires, street lights, and tree limbs were temporarily removed or trimmed to make room for the passage of a house. This dwelling is heading east on McLean Avenue in 1941 to its new home at 131 Railroad Square.

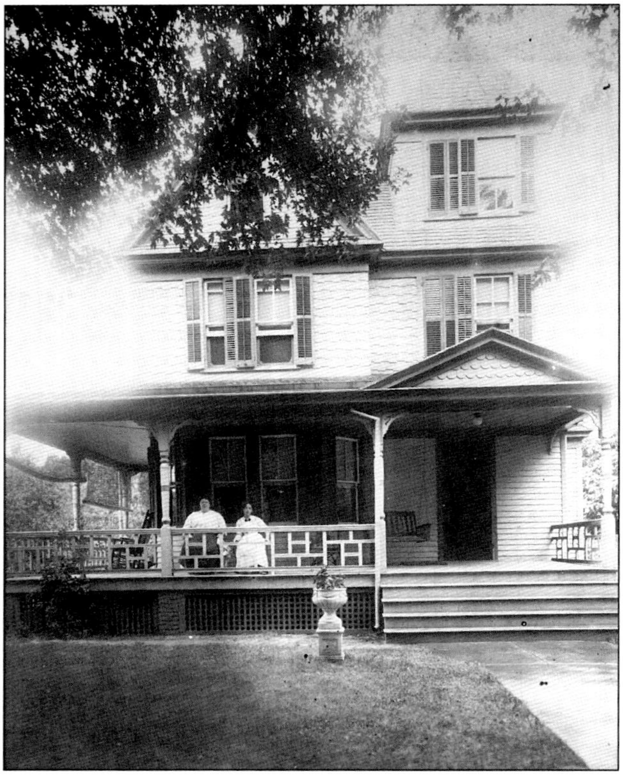

In 1910, Bessie Betts Hollingsworth (left) and Josephine Lynch sit for the camera at the Joseph Lynch house at 417 River Avenue. This house was built about 1892 by Horace Allen and still stands today at River Avenue and Grove Street.

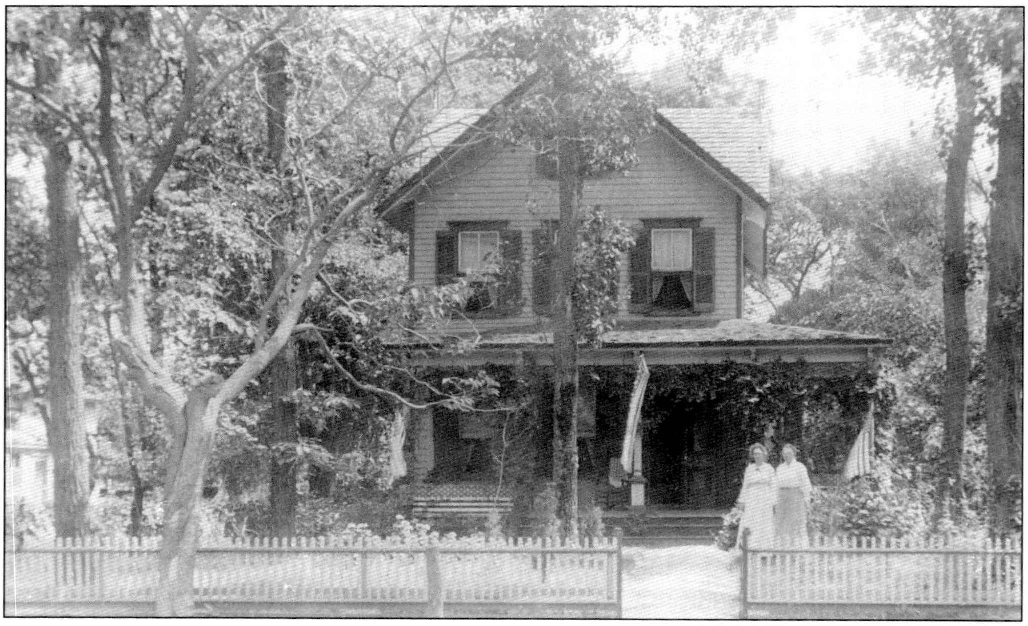

In 1880, Philadelphia lumber merchant George Russell had four cottages built on Arnold Avenue between Cramer Avenue and the Allen house. Three of these houses still exist. The easternmost, shown above *c.* 1910, was torn down in the early 1950s.

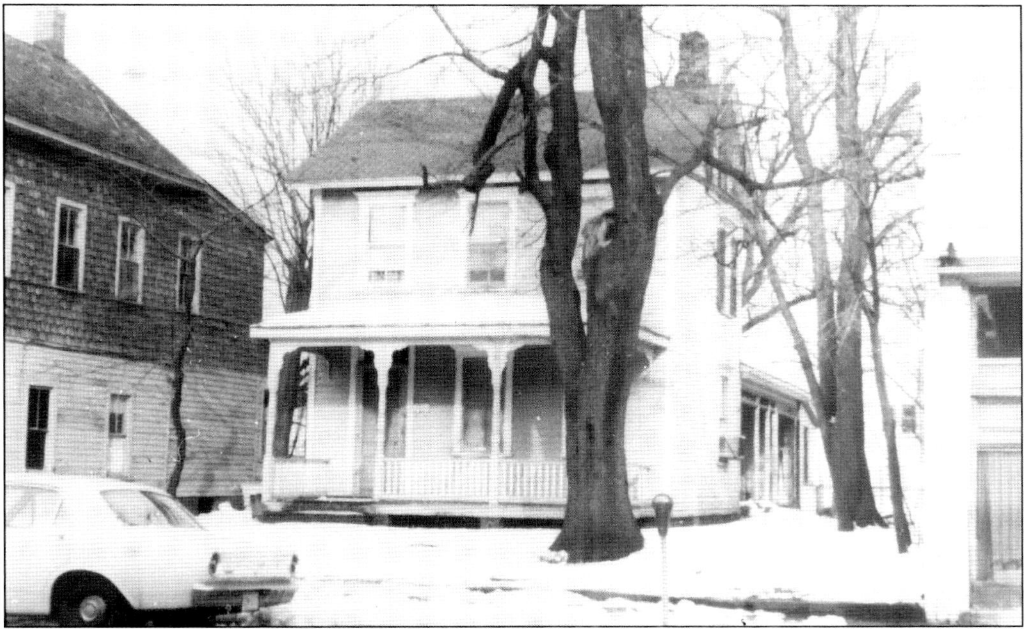

The Charles Johnson house was situated on the east side of Bay Avenue between Laurel and Arnold Avenues. Built around 1890, this dwelling survived two major fires on either side in 1899 and 1906. The Johnson house was demolished in 1969 and the site is now a municipal parking lot next to Bay Point Optical.

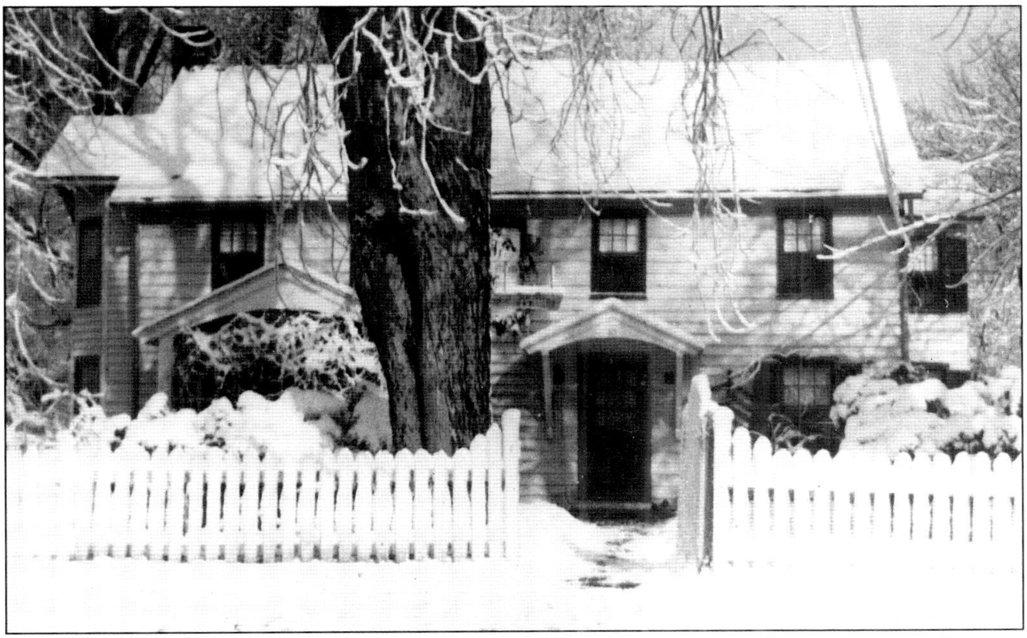

The Morris Homestead at 817 Ocean Road is the oldest known existing house in Point Pleasant. Captain John Morris purchased 250 acres of land from the Board of Proprietors of Eastern New Jersey in 1750 and built the house about 1768. Except for two brief periods, the house has remained in the Morris family for over 225 years.

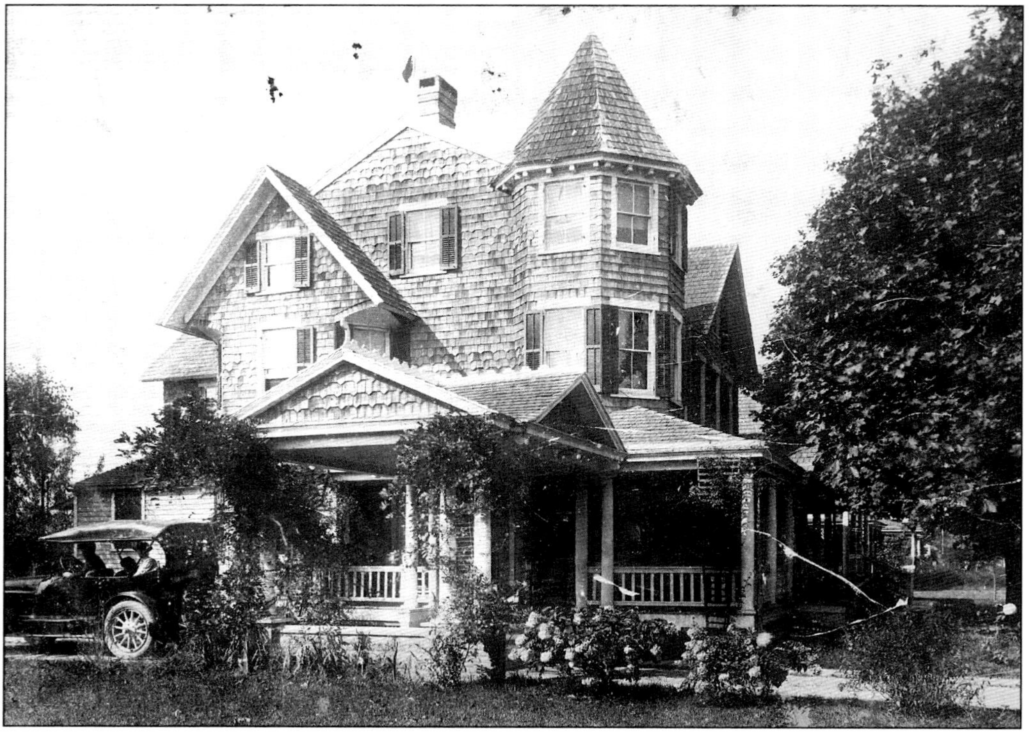

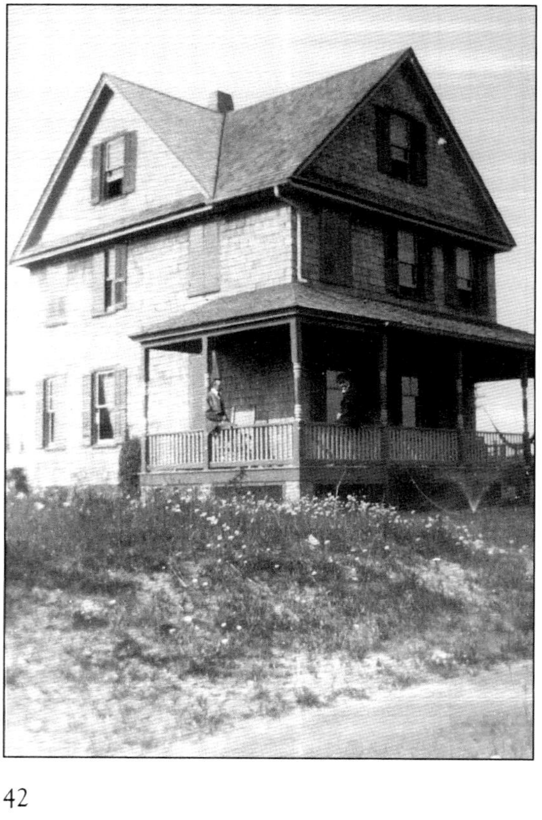

The VanNote house at 704 Forman Avenue is shown here about 1918. Zebulon VanNote built this house in 1882 at a cost of $1,200. It featured a lean-to kitchen in the rear and a cedar water tank in the attic. VanNote had the house enlarged in 1897. This house is now the parsonage for the Point Pleasant Presbyterian Church.

This was the residence of Point Pleasant Hardware Company owner Joseph W. Johnson. In this 1915 photograph the house was located on the present site of the Hoffman Doughnut Shop on American Legion Way. In 1949, the house was moved across the street and still stands next to the American Legion Building.

In 1870, Reverend Charles Knox of Bloomfield purchased property from John Arnold which ran from near Bay Avenue east to the beach and south of Arnold Avenue. The Knox family took up residence during the summer months in the old Harker Homestead on the property, shown here in 1900. This homestead was located on Richmond Avenue where Foodtown stands today. These buildings were torn down in 1916.

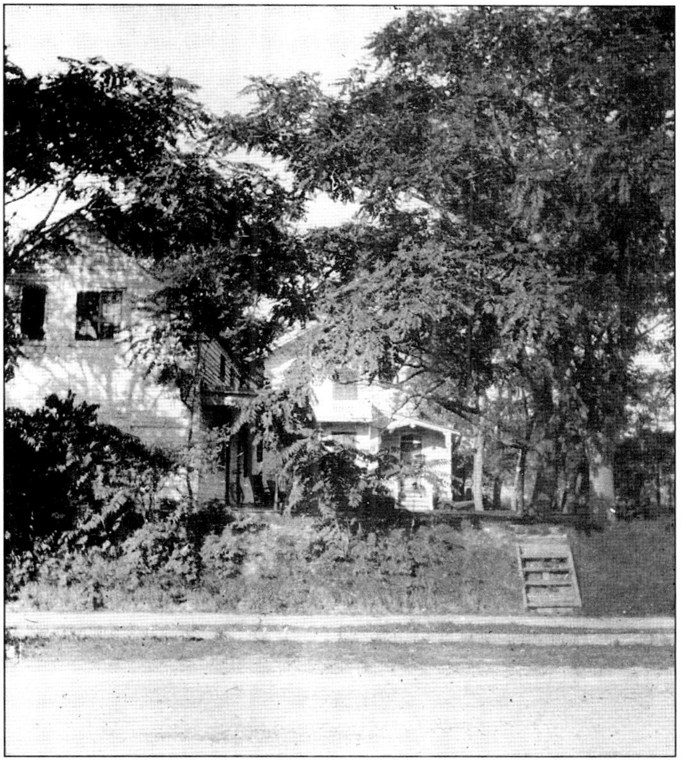

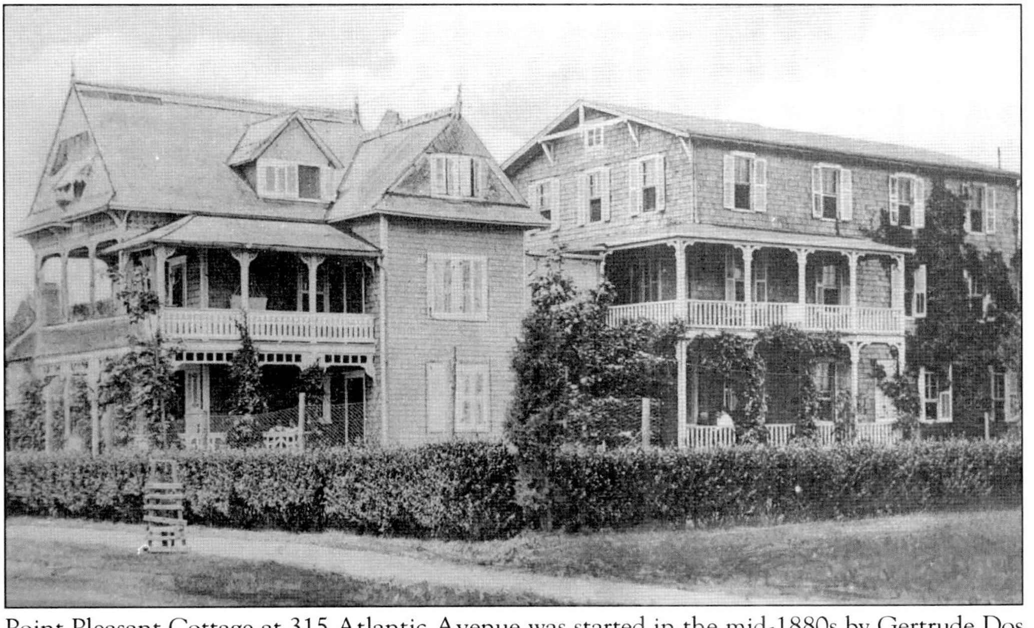

Point Pleasant Cottage at 315 Atlantic Avenue was started in the mid-1880s by Gertrude Dos Santos. The house was later doubled in size when another building owned by Dos Santos was moved from Ocean Road and placed at the rear of the cottage. Practically unchanged from its original appearance, the Point Pleasant Cottage still takes in summer guests today.

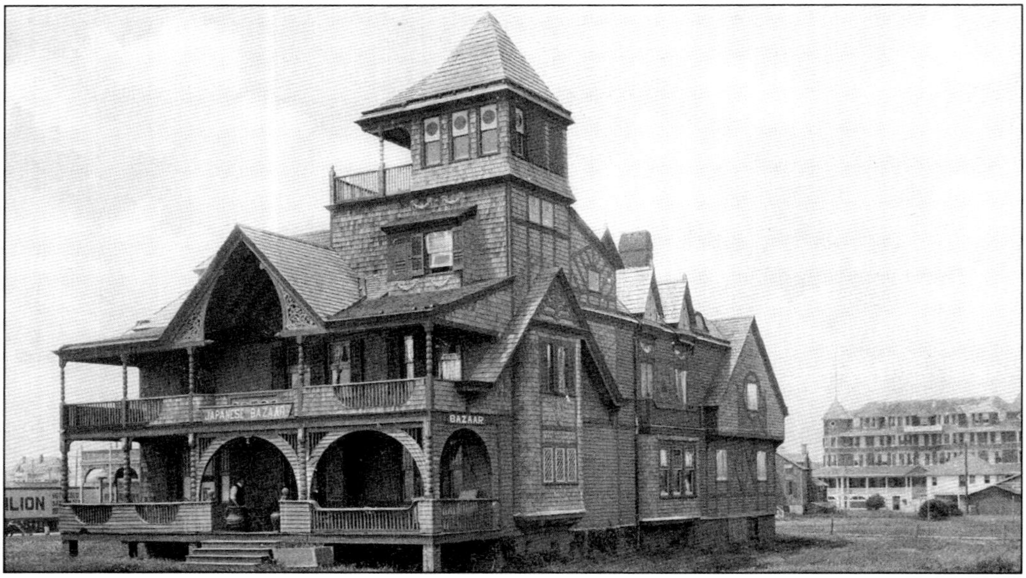

This massive boarding house has been a landmark on the beach for the past 110 years. Originally built as a summer cottage by the Murphy family, it came close to toppling into the Atlantic on several occasions. It was finally moved inland about 150 feet in 1910 (see p. 18). Notice the Carrollton Hotel in the background.

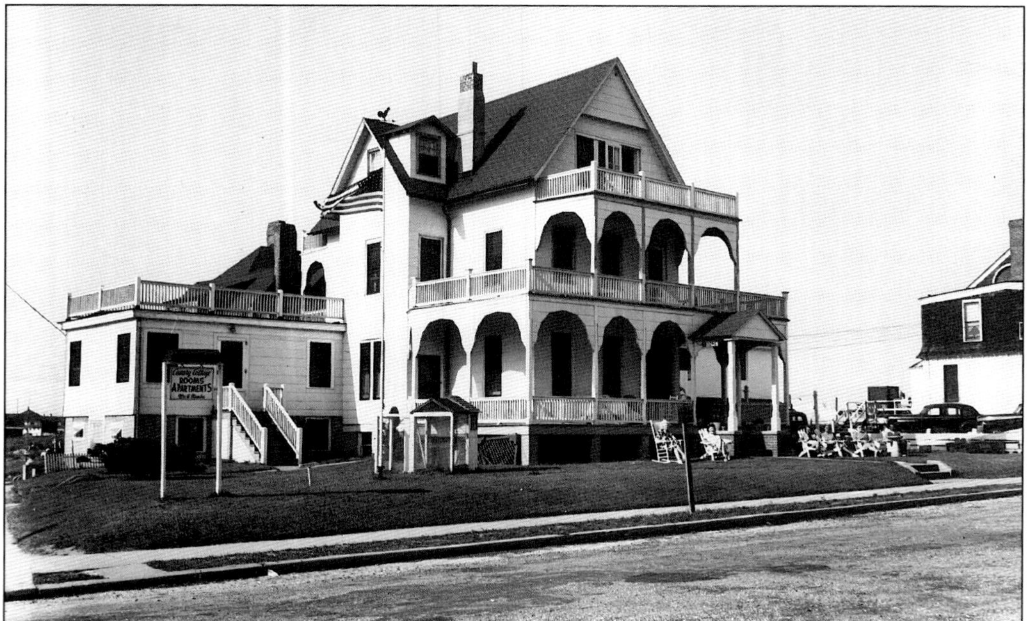

The Canary Cottage at Ocean and Atlantic Avenues appears here in 1946. This house, along with the Atlantic Apartments (on the extreme right) and the Murphy Cottage (top), is part of a cluster of beachfront homes that were built during the first several years of the Point Pleasant Land Company's promotion of Point Pleasant City (see Vol. I, p. 17).

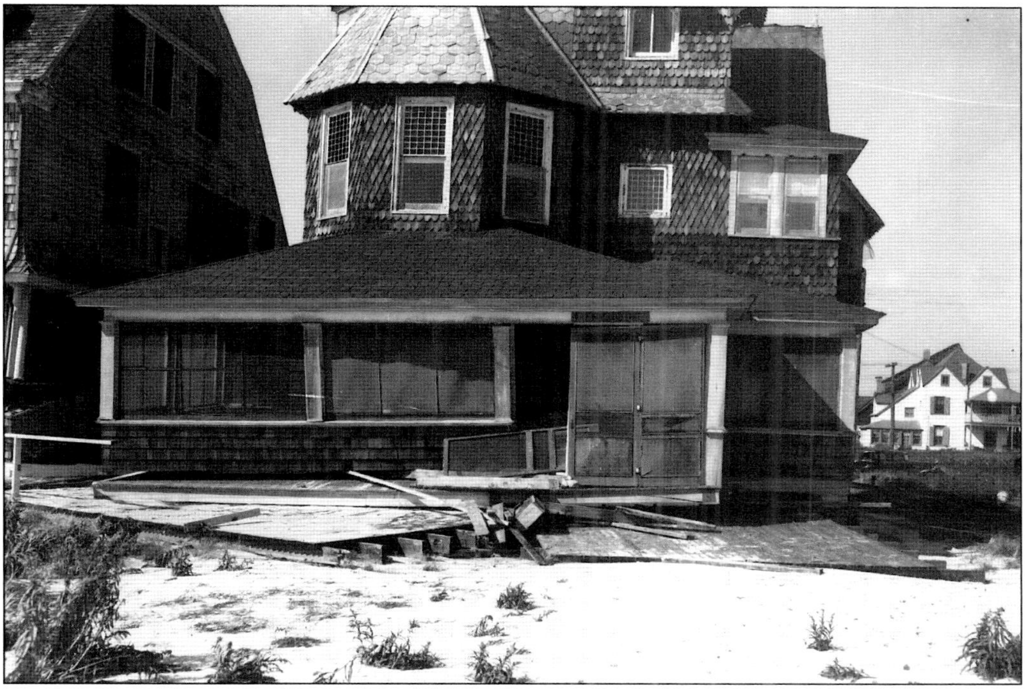

It's the day after the Hurricane of 1938 (see p. 17) and the Wild Waves cottage on the beach south of New Jersey Avenue has again survived the ocean's fury. Sections of boardwalk have sliced through the front porch. Later known as the Uhl cottage and the Ocean House, this building was razed in 1995.

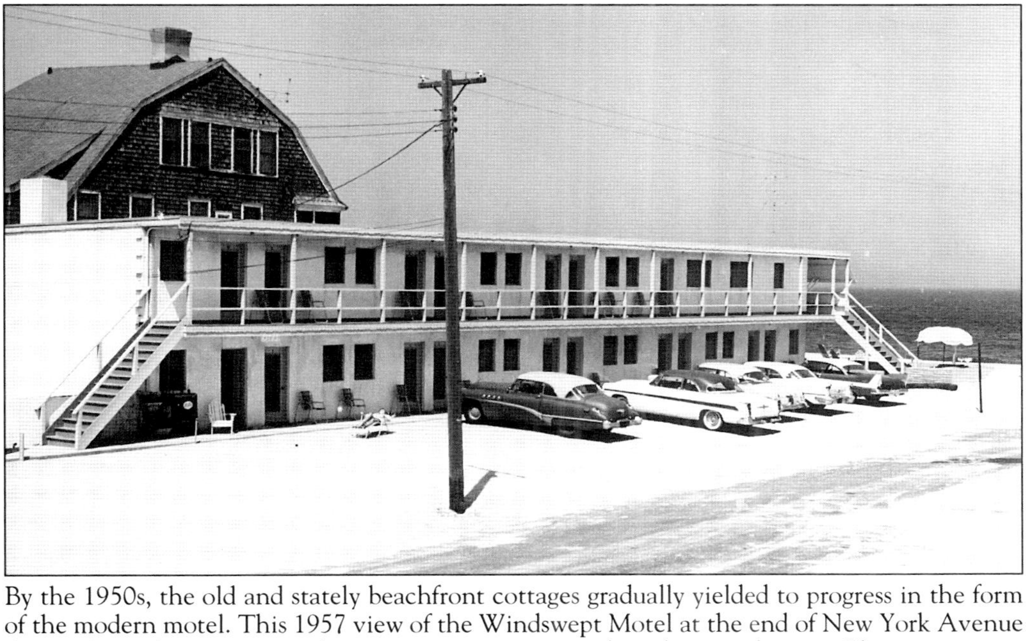

By the 1950s, the old and stately beachfront cottages gradually yielded to progress in the form of the modern motel. This 1957 view of the Windswept Motel at the end of New York Avenue shows this. The cottage to the rear was soon removed as the motel grew. Changing tastes, changing times.

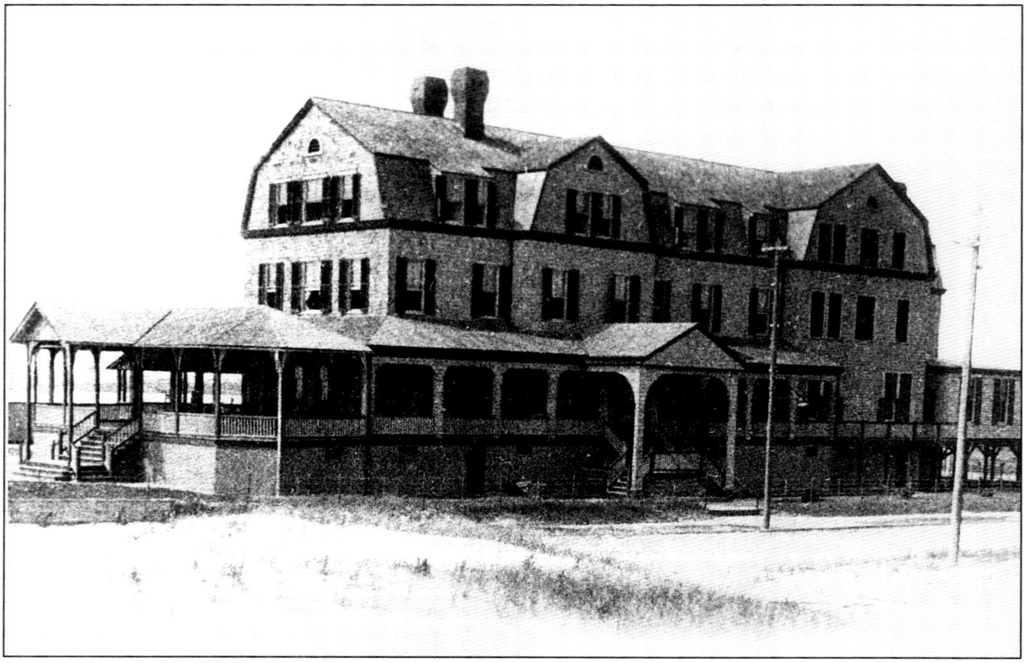

Along with the Leighton, Carrollton, and Beacon Hotels, another popular beachfront resort was the Stratford By-the-Sea. Situated at the foot of Philadelphia Avenue, the Stratford was built for Mrs. William O'Brien in 1892 and featured running water from an 800-foot-deep artesian well on the property. Unfortunately, the fifty-room hotel was destroyed by fire in 1905.

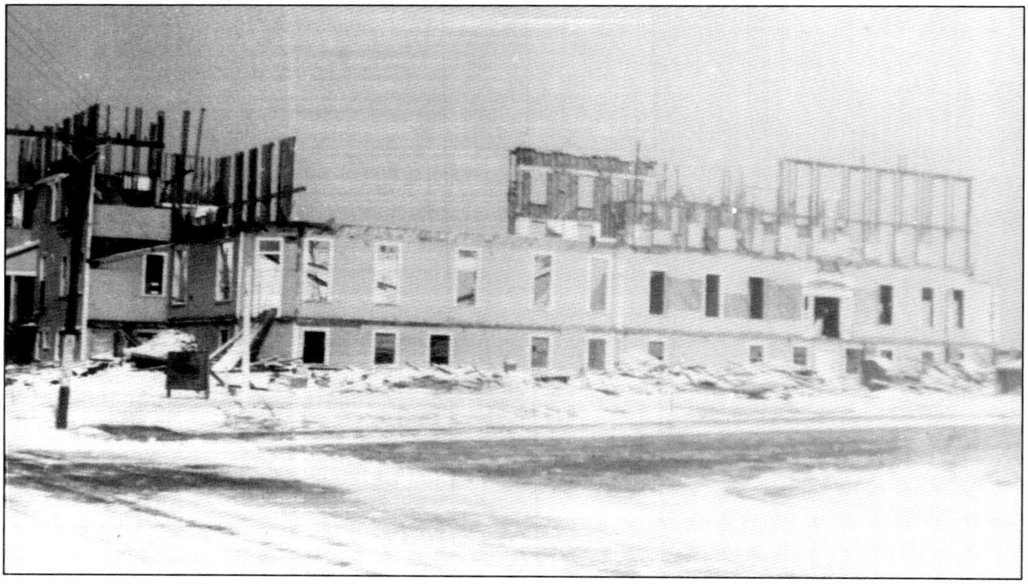

Not all of Point Pleasant Beach's stately hotels went up in flames. The Leighton Hotel comes down in 1943 as it went up in 1893—piece by piece. Built by George Newbury of Manasquan, the hotel contained as many as one hundred rooms before 1929 (see Vol. I, p. 21). The country was now involved in World War II and every usable piece of lumber from the Leighton was being salvaged for the war effort.

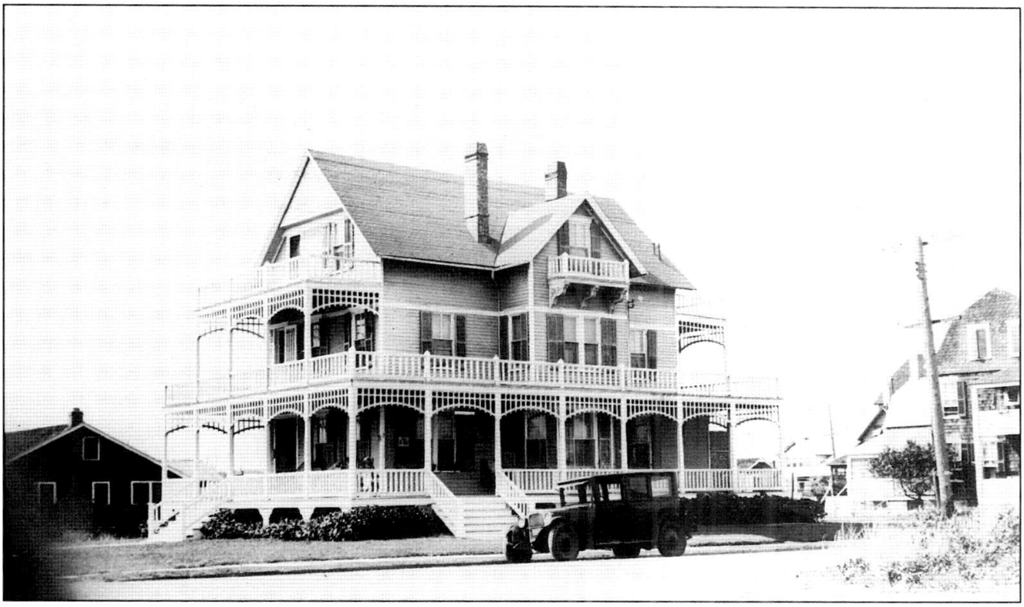

To take advantage of a refreshing summer sea breeze, many of the early cottages featured expansive porches and balconies with ornamental and sometimes exotic woodwork. This house at New York and Boston Avenues in 1931 is a good example of the porch making the house.

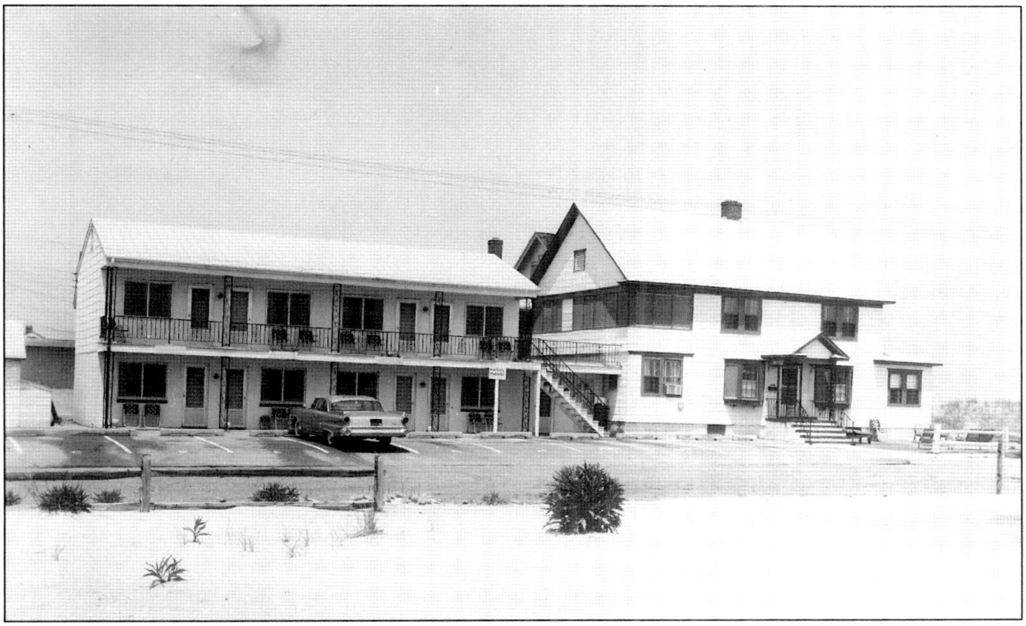

During the motel boom of the 1950s, some of the old beachfront homes became incorporated into newer motels. The Mary Francis Motel, shown here in 1961, was added onto a cottage at the end of Philadelphia Avenue. The Driftwood Motel on Ocean Avenue is another example of this idea.

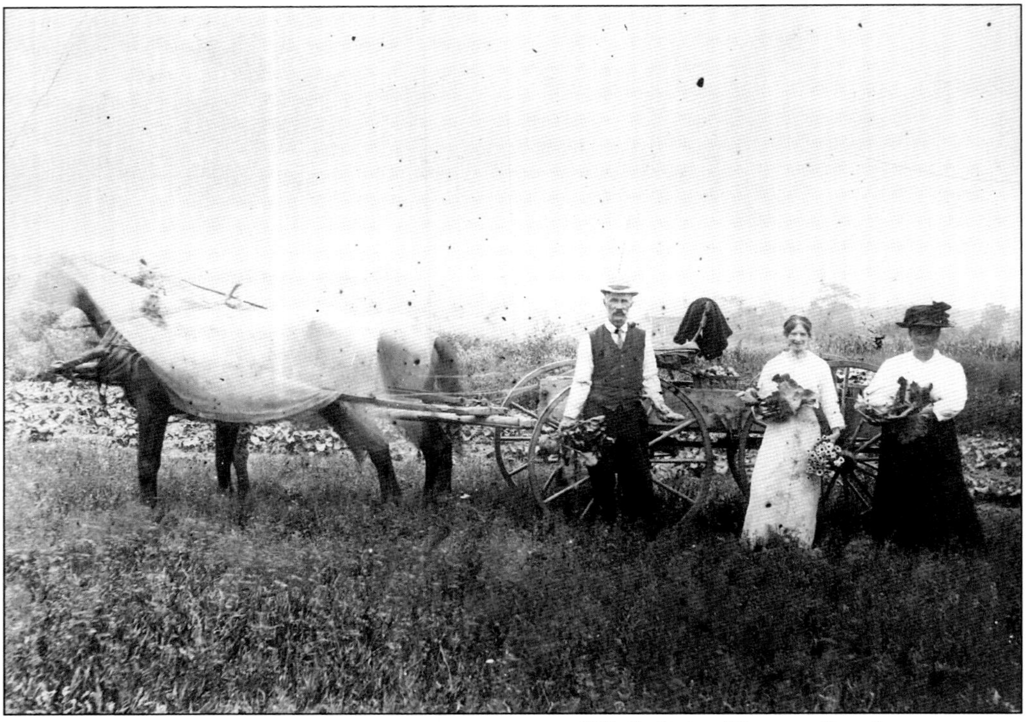

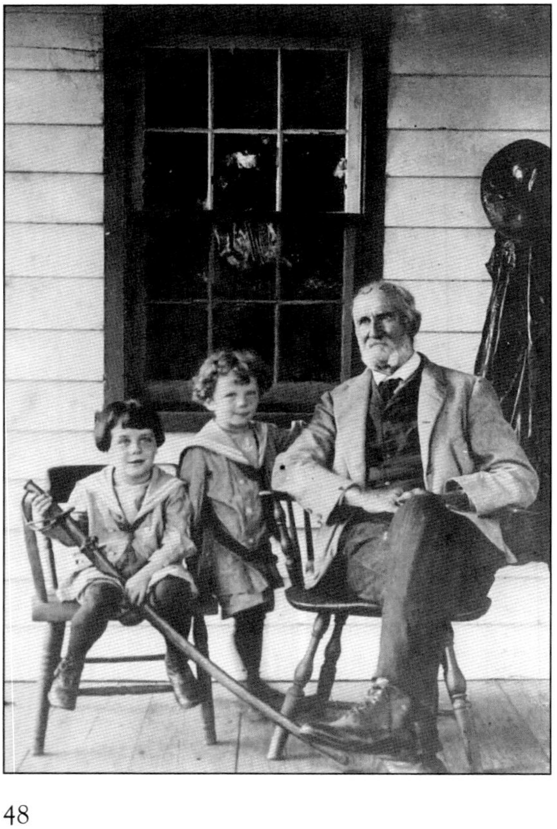

While Point Pleasant Beach was growing by leaps and bounds as a tourist mecca, West Point Pleasant retained its rural character with still extensive farm and woodlands. The Dorsett farm encompassed that part of Point Pleasant between Dorsett Dock and Beaver Dam Roads and south of Bridge Avenue. Here, potatoes are harvested in the early 1900s.

John Lott Dorsett takes a moment to pose with his grandchildren on the porch of the Dorsett Homestead around 1905. From the looks of that cutlass, he was probably in the middle of a good pirate story (for more on the Dorsett Homestead, see Vol. I, p. 22).

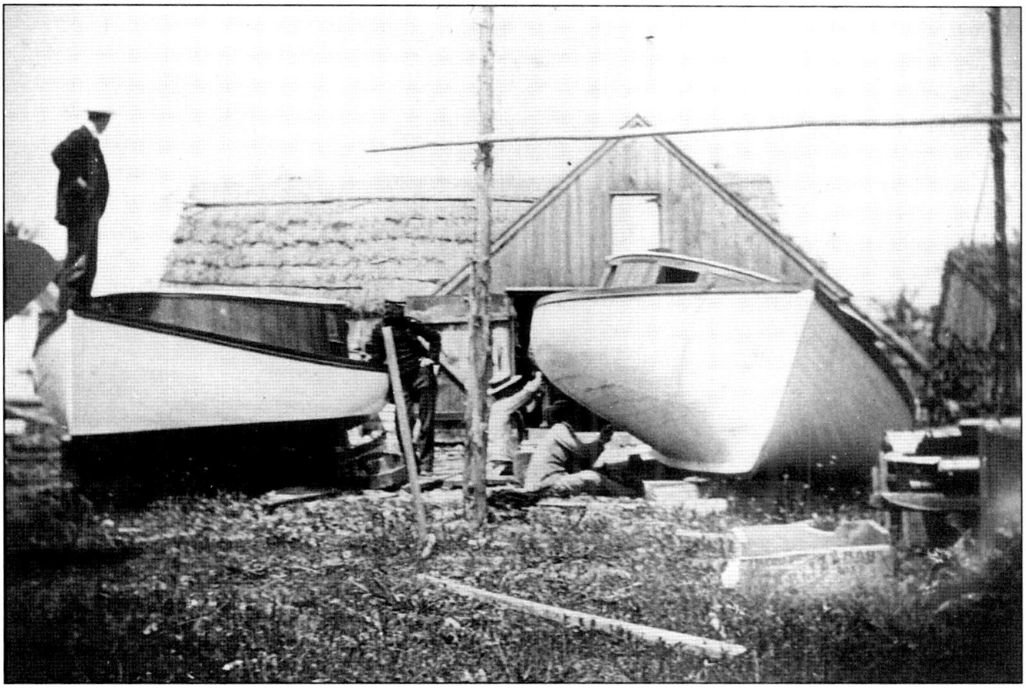

Barnegat Bay skiffs are prepared for launch at the Dorsett boatyard on the Beaver Dam Creek about 1910. Dorsett was a prolific boat builder, a trade he passed on to his son, John A. Dorsett.

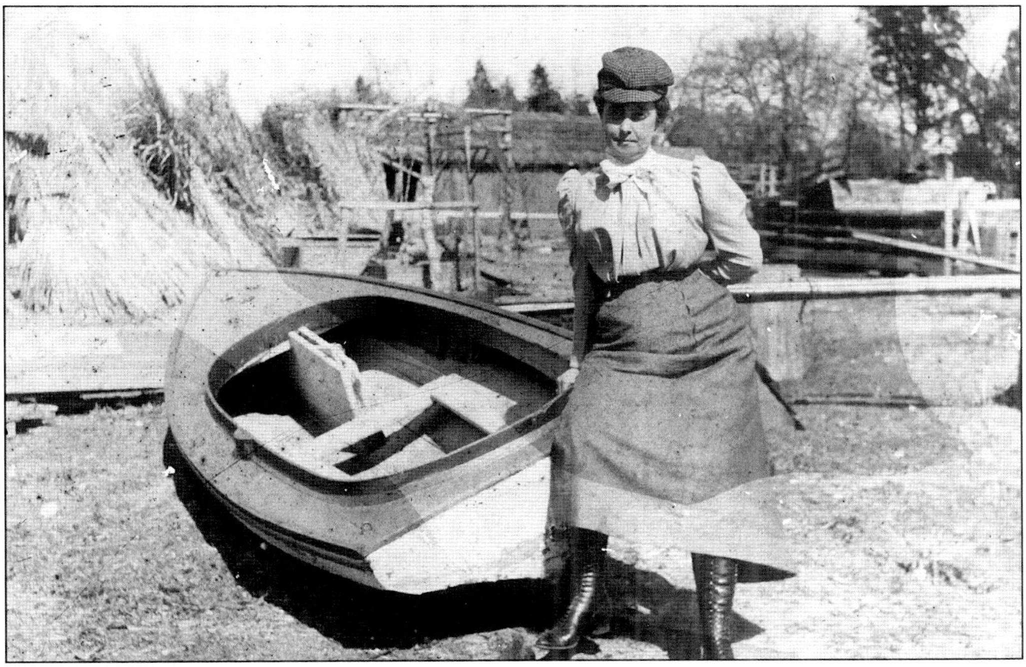

This young lady appears ready to take to the open seas as she stands next to a Dorsett sneak box. Dorsett Landing was an important sailing launch on Beaver Dam Creek; it eventually disappeared after the death of John L. Dorsett in 1910.

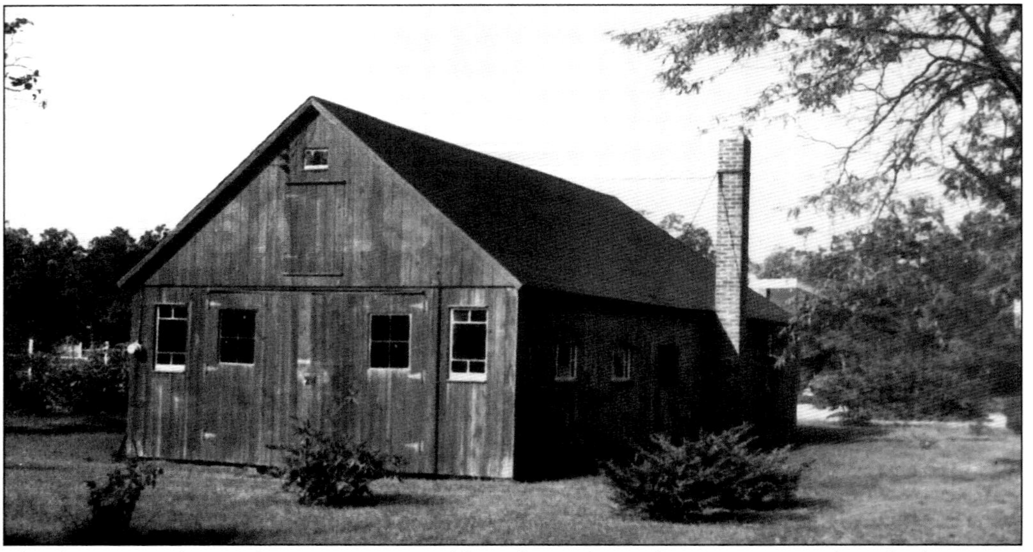

This barn was where John A. Dorsett and later his wife Sarah L. Dorsett made sails that many considered to be the finest available on the bay. The building was located on the southwest corner of Bridge Avenue and Dorsett Dock Road. A branch of the Ocean Federal Savings Bank is on the site today.

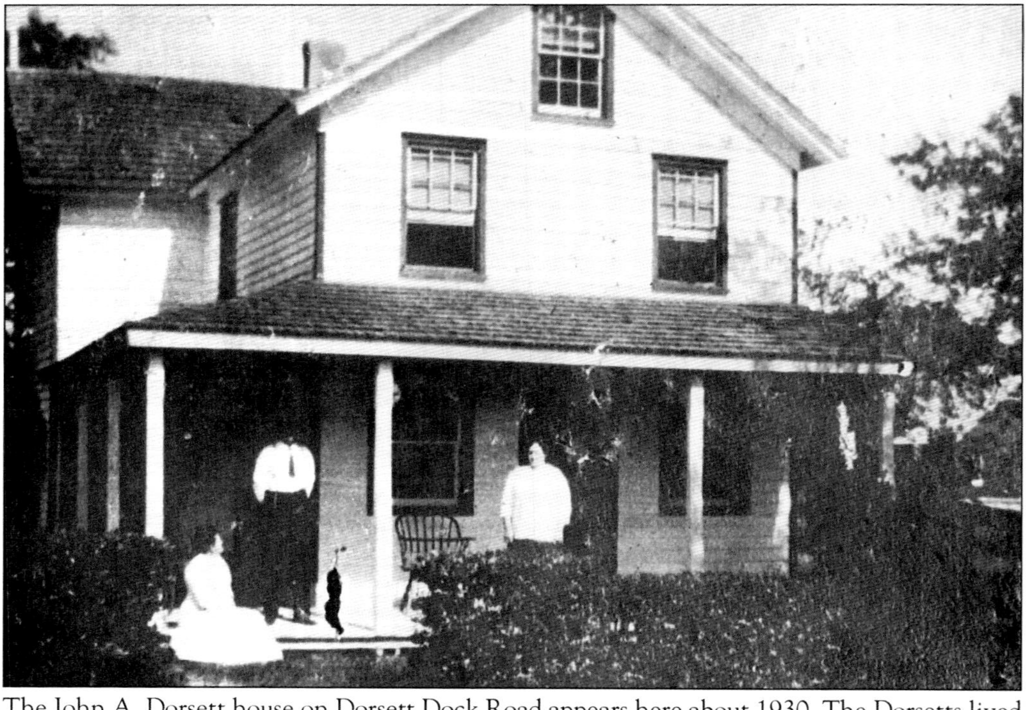

The John A. Dorsett house on Dorsett Dock Road appears here about 1930. The Dorsetts lived just a stone's throw away from their sail loft. After her husband's death, Sarah Dorsett advertised the business as "S. L. Dorsett, Sailmaker" and when once asked why she did not use her own full name, she replied that she feared when prospective customers saw a woman's name they would not entrust their work to her hands.

William Henry LeChard (left) and Miller Wilbert hold a huge goose shot while gunning. Barnegat Bay gunning was a major attraction at the Jersey Shore during the 1800s and early 1900s as many well-known sportsmen took advantage of the large numbers of waterfowl that stopped on the bay during their yearly migrations.

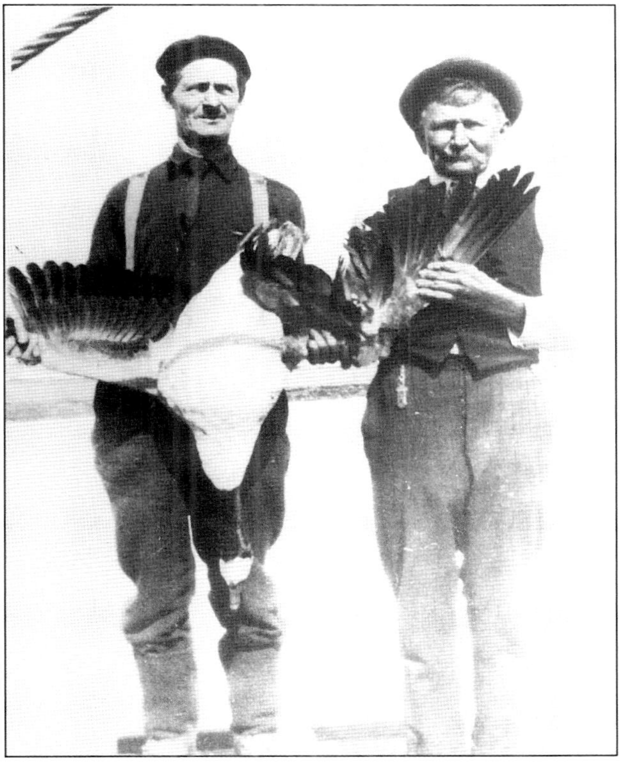

Of the many creeks that emptied into the Beaver Dam Creek in Point Pleasant, Herbert's Creek is the best known (below). It was up this creek that the government dug the Manasquan River-Bay Head Canal. Other creeks included Boat Point Creek and Certainty Creek.

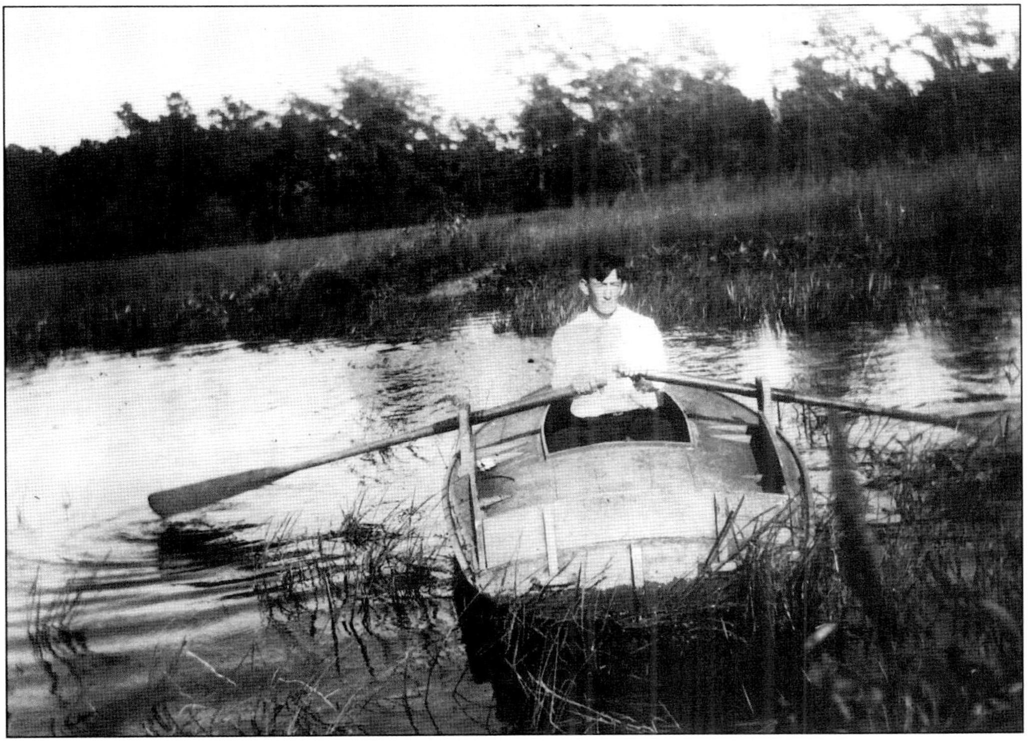

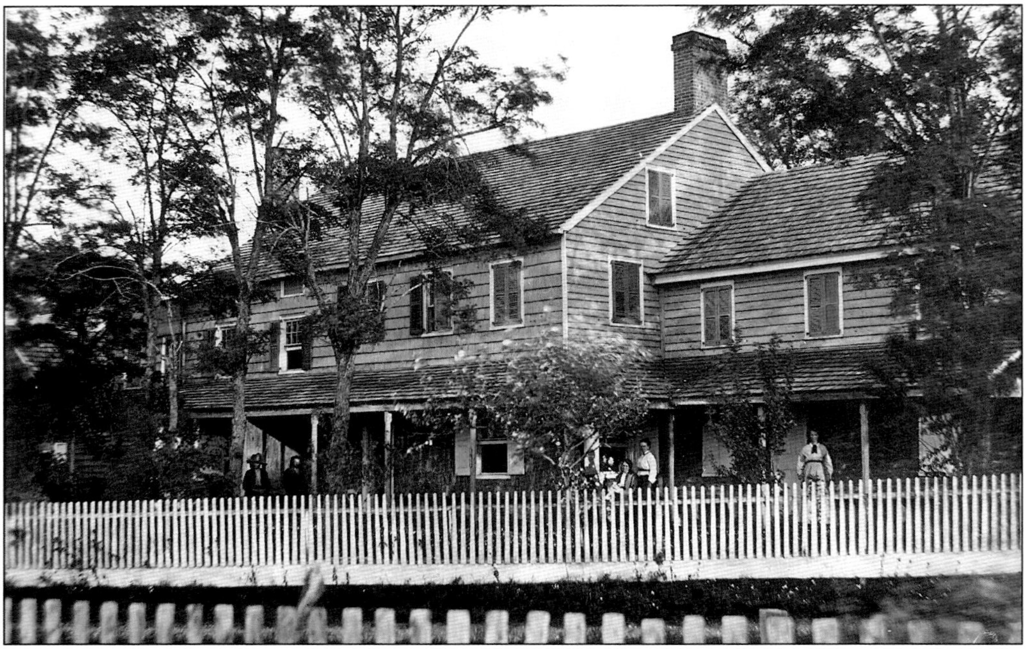

The Cook Homestead in Point Pleasant Beach was one of five farms during the 1800s that occupied the beachfront land from the Manasquan Inlet to Sea Avenue. It was also the only one to survive intact into the twentieth century. The main house is shown here in 1896. The Cook farm is perhaps best known from the numerous photographs taken in the 1890s by Charles C. Cook, son of Ebenezer Cook.

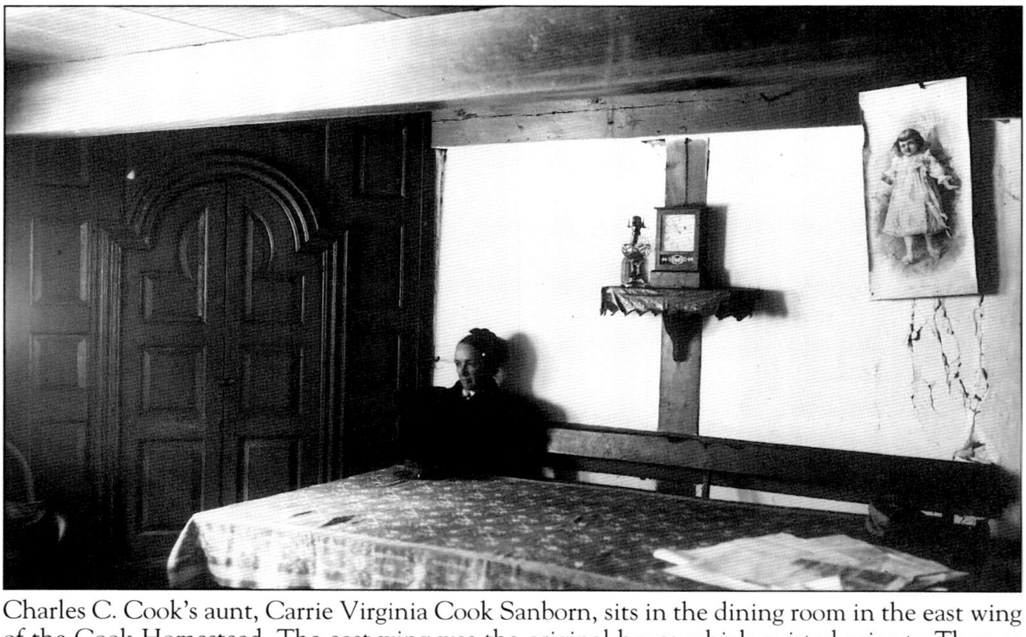

Charles C. Cook's aunt, Carrie Virginia Cook Sanborn, sits in the dining room in the east wing of the Cook Homestead. The east wing was the original house which existed prior to Thomas Cook Sr.'s purchase of the property from Walter and Mary Curtis in 1782. Several additions were built over the ensuing years. Note the large corner china closet.

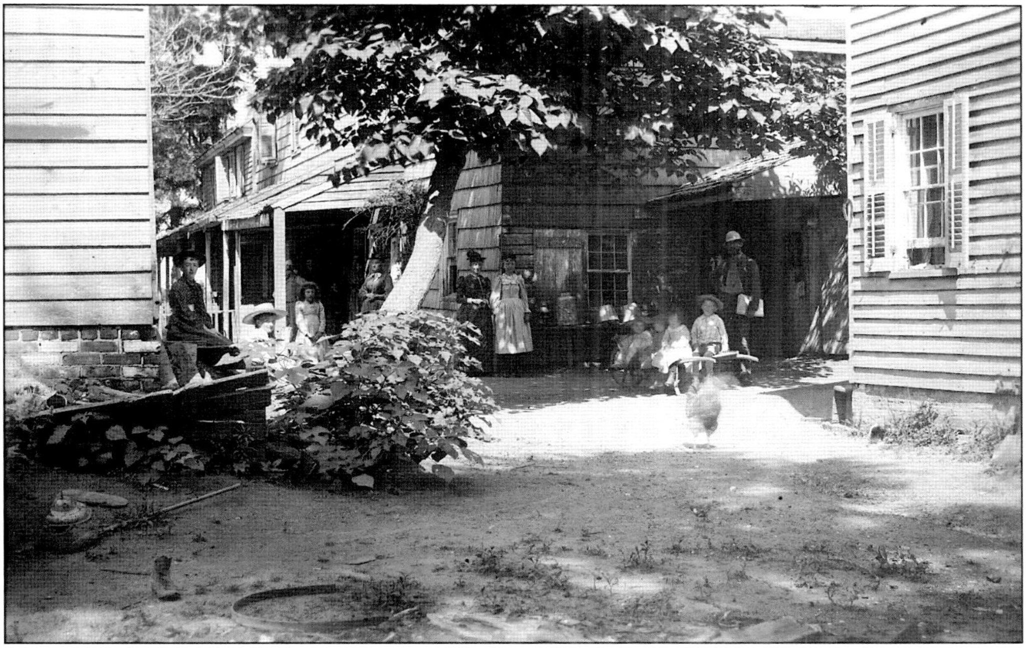

In addition to the main house, the Cook farm contained many additional buildings, all contributing to the success of the farm. Here, boarders pose at the east end of the house, flanked by the tenant house (right) and ice house. In front of the ice house was a pump that provided water described as "the source of an exquisite pleasure, the purest and sweetest that nature can yield as dripping with coolness as it rose from the well."

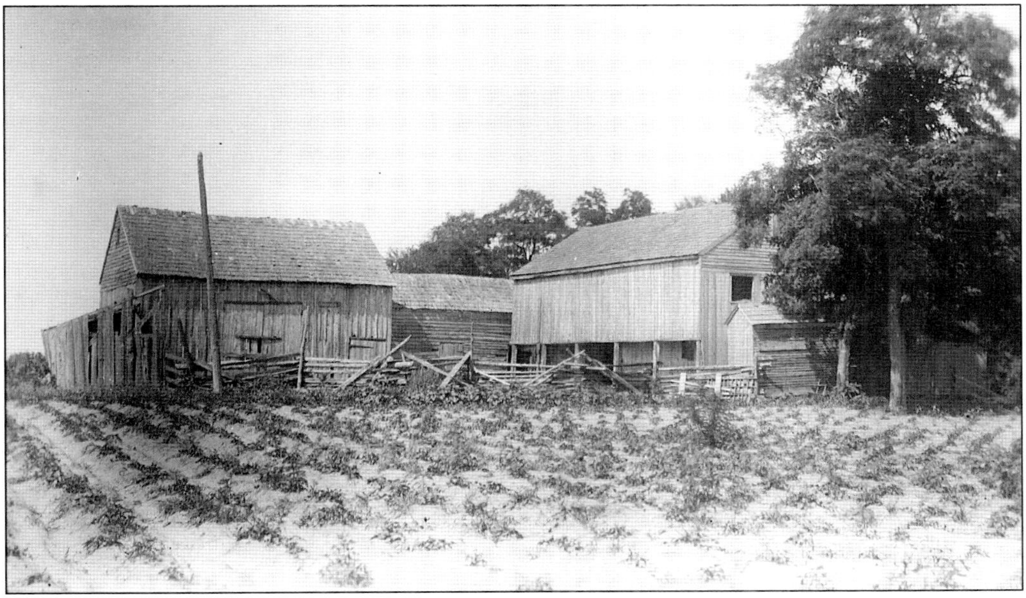

To the west of the Cook Homestead stood the barns and carriage house, shown here in 1897. Thomas Cook Sr. married Racheal Borden in 1783 and their son Thomas was born in 1792. Thomas inherited the farm, which grew to about 300 acres. He first married Rebecca Combs, who died, and then married Anne Williams Arnold, a widow whose son was John Arnold.

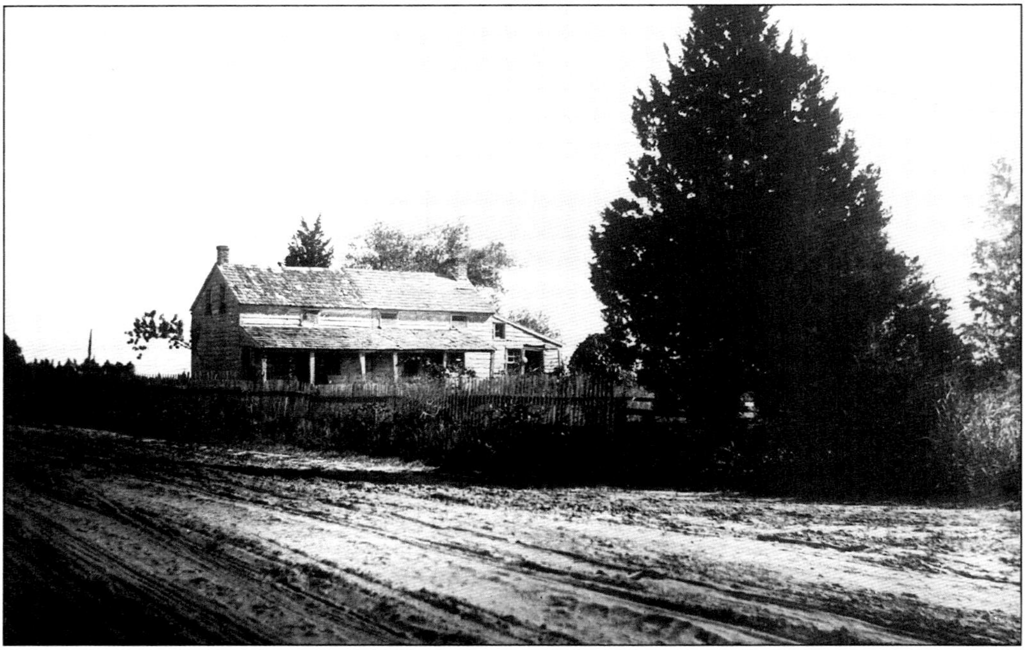

The western border of the Cook farm contained another tenant house, shown here in 1888. The rutted dirt road is River Avenue and to the right is North Avenue, which was later abandoned. The east end of North Avenue is today Arbutus Avenue. The view is north toward the Manasquan River.

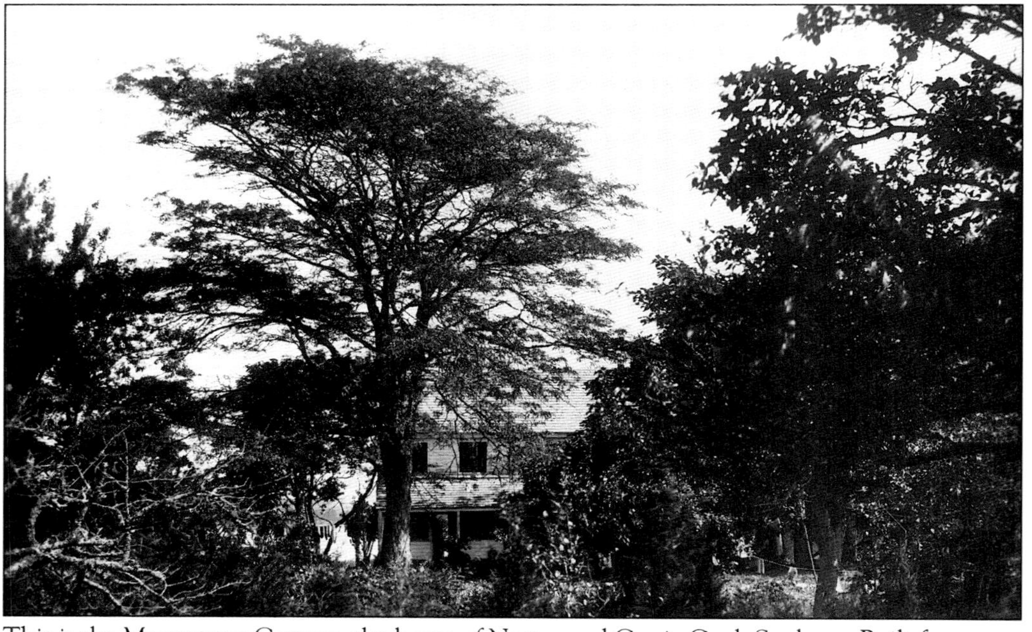

This is the Manasquan Cottage, the home of Nestor and Carrie Cook Sanborn. Built four years after their marriage in 1870, the cottage stood between River Avenue and the railroad near the Manasquan River on land that was given by Thomas Cook Jr. to his daughter. The Sanborn cottage was open to guests for nearly sixty years before it was destroyed by fire in 1932.

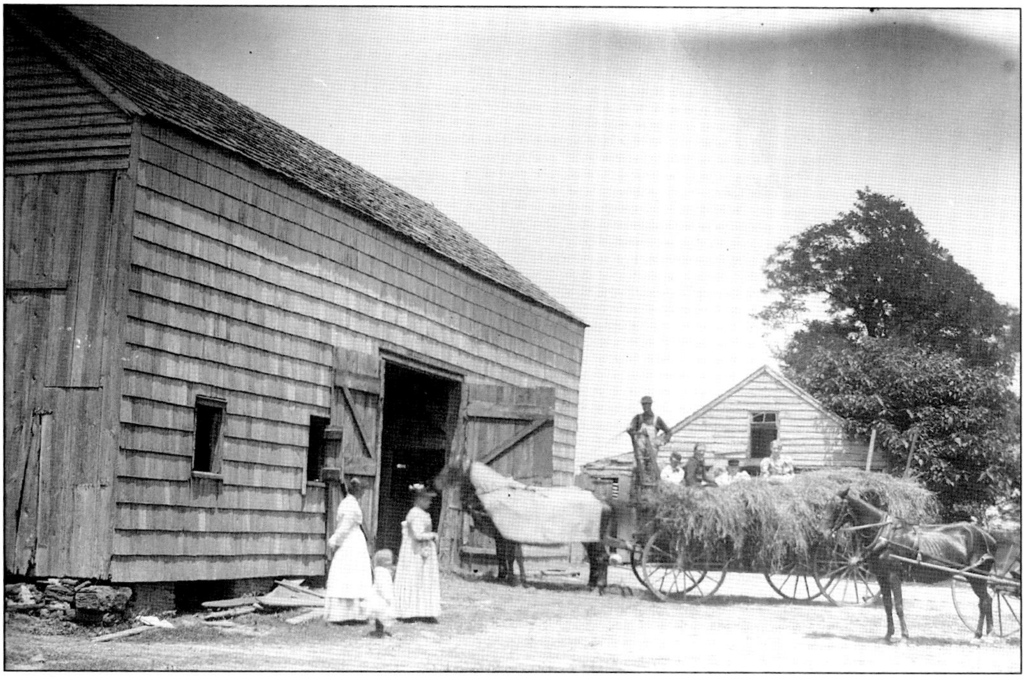

Cook Homestead guests board a hay wagon and prepare to journey across the farm for a rendezvous at the Manasquan Inlet. A barn and the carriage house round out the scene. Two paths led to the beach from the Cook Homestead. One ran due east along the present Niblick Street and the other ran generally north toward the river and then east. This is the route we're taking today.

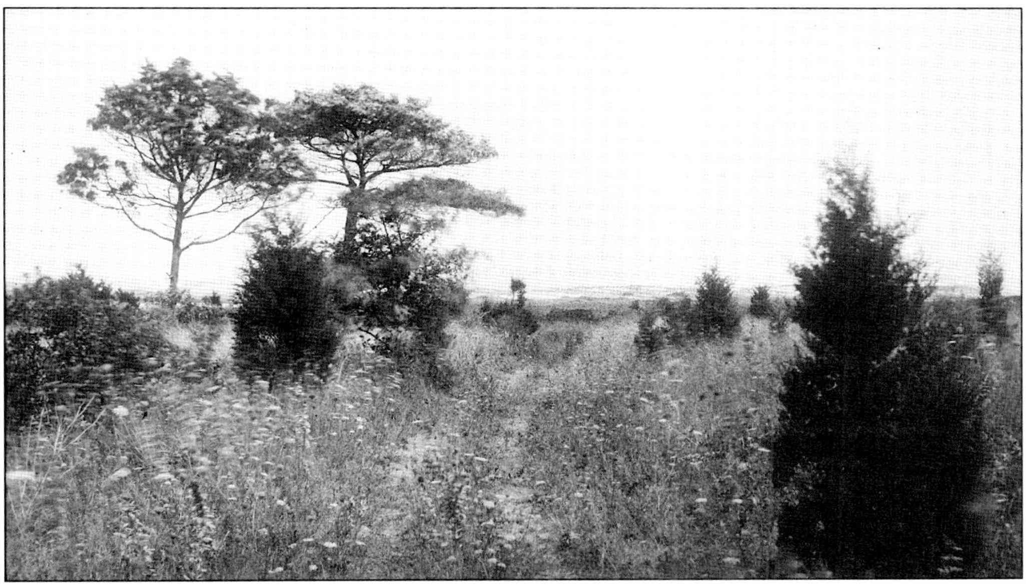

The lane heads northward across the present Antrim School field and then turns northeast at about the present intersection of Harvard and Chicago Avenues. This is the view eastward from that spot in 1898. Notice the 10- to 20-foot dunes in the distance.

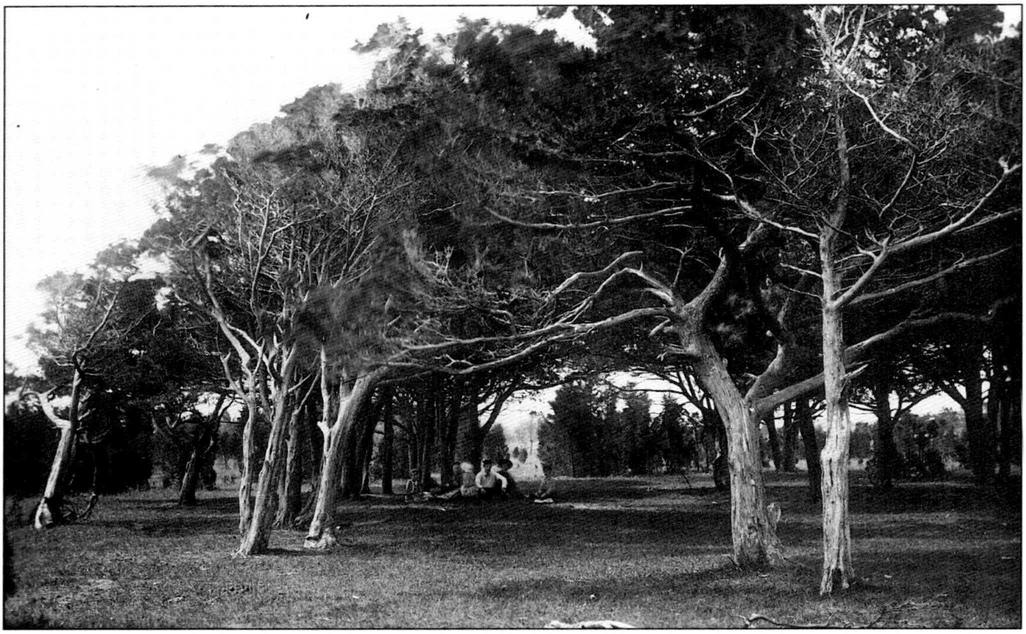

Along the way, our group stops at the cedar grove along Will's Hole Thorofare which today would be at the foot of Boston Avenue. This was the largest of several cedar groves that existed on the Cook property. Another large grove of cedars stood several hundred feet east of the homestead.

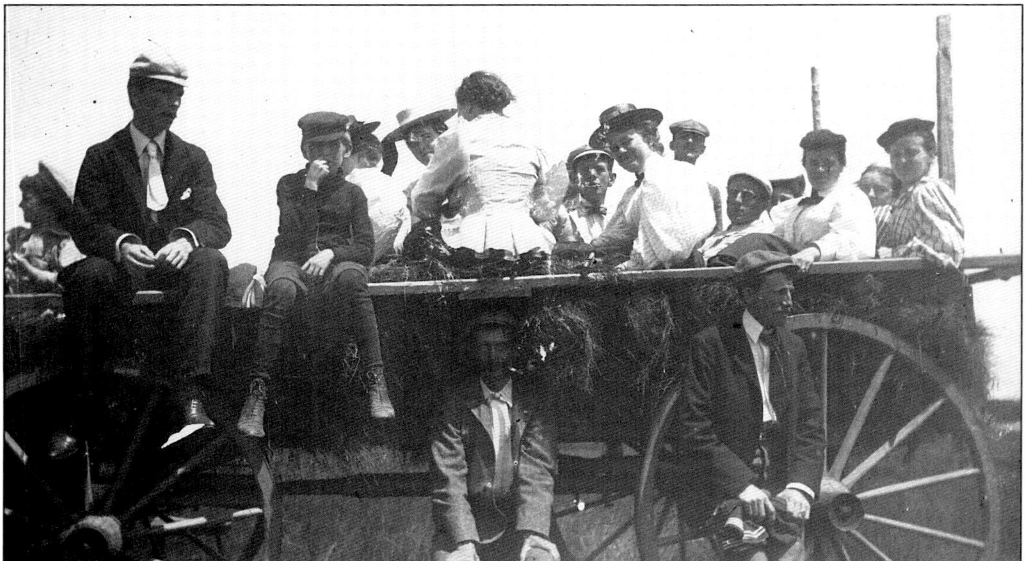

Resuming our journey, the hay ride crosses the small wooden trestle over Cook's Creek and reaches the Inlet Pavilion (see Vol. I, p. 114) and a row of crude changing houses. Bathing, fishing, and frolicking were then the order of the day under the able guidance of the Reed family, who were running the farm at this time. Five years later the Cook farm was sold and this simple way of life gradually ended (for more on the Cook farm, see Vol. I, pp. 12–13).

Three

Parading Across Town

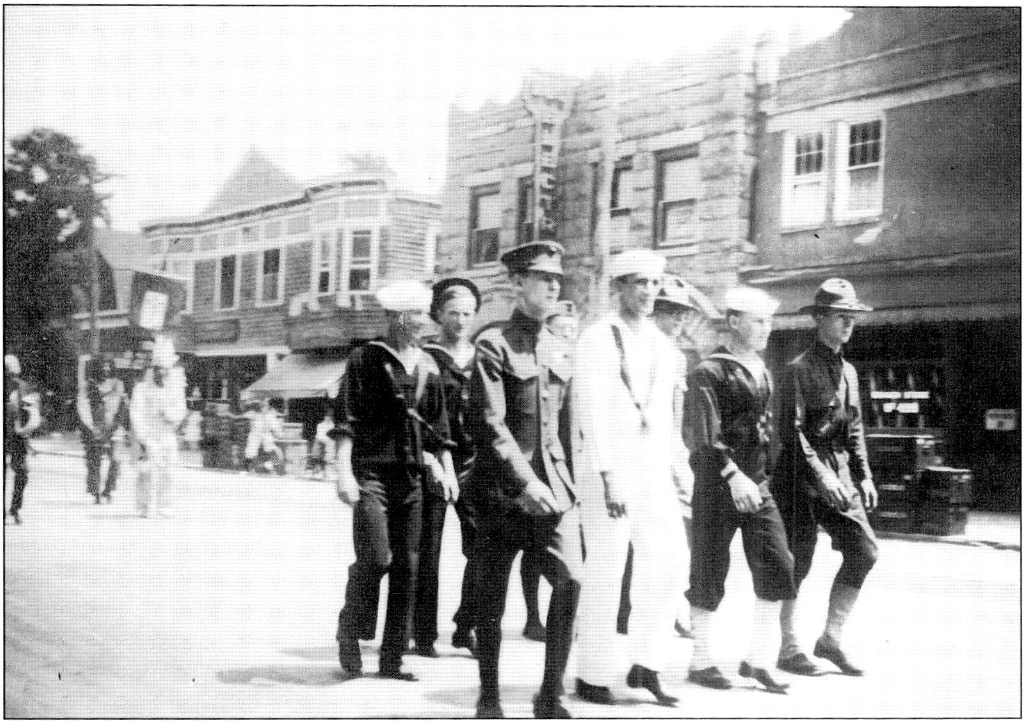

A welcome-home parade and celebration were given for Point Pleasant's soldiers and sailors who served in the first World War. The July 4, 1919 celebration spilled over into much of the following week with a luncheon at the Carrollton Hotel grill and tea room and dances at the Carrollton and the Pine Bluff Inn.

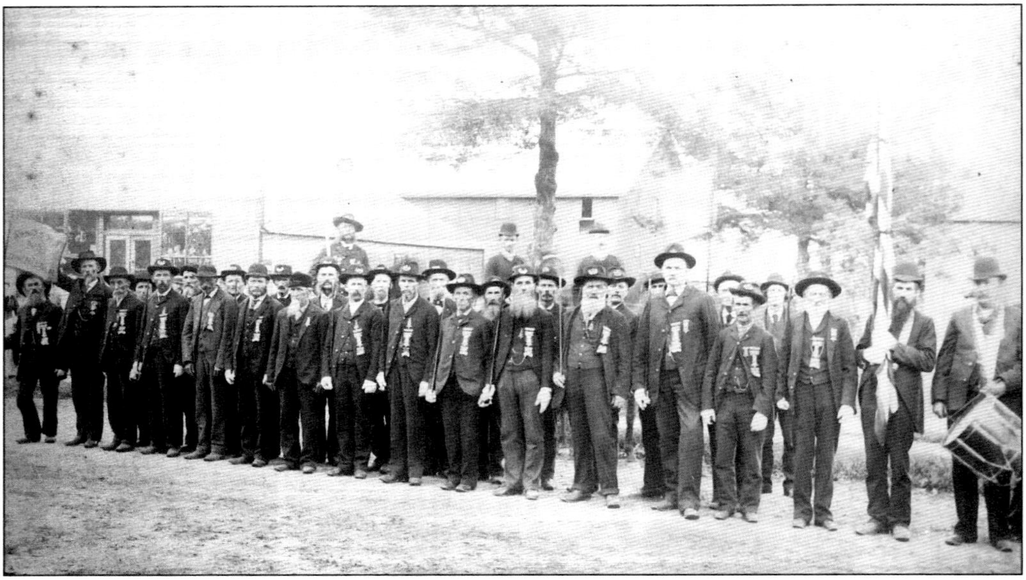

Members of the Elwood Arnold Post #37, Grand Army of the Republic (G.A.R.), stand at attention on Decoration Day *c.* 1895. Post Commander Roderick A. Clark, founder of Clark's Landing, is fifth from the right in the front row.

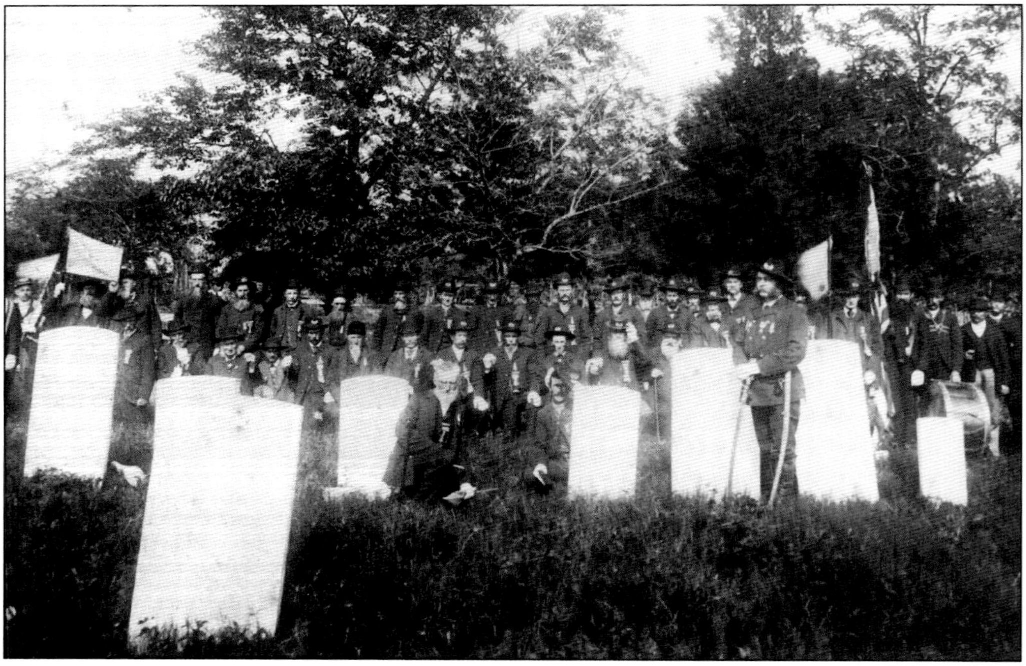

The Point Pleasant G.A.R. consisted mostly of members of Company F, 14th New Jersey Volunteers who were called to Toms River on August 20, 1862, and on into battle in the Civil War. Graves, such as these in the M.E. Cemetery on Lakewood Road, were decorated each year at the end of May (thus the term "Decoration Day"). The post was named in memory of John Arnold's son Elwood after he died in 1879. The Elwood Arnold Post G.A.R. was finally disbanded in 1918.

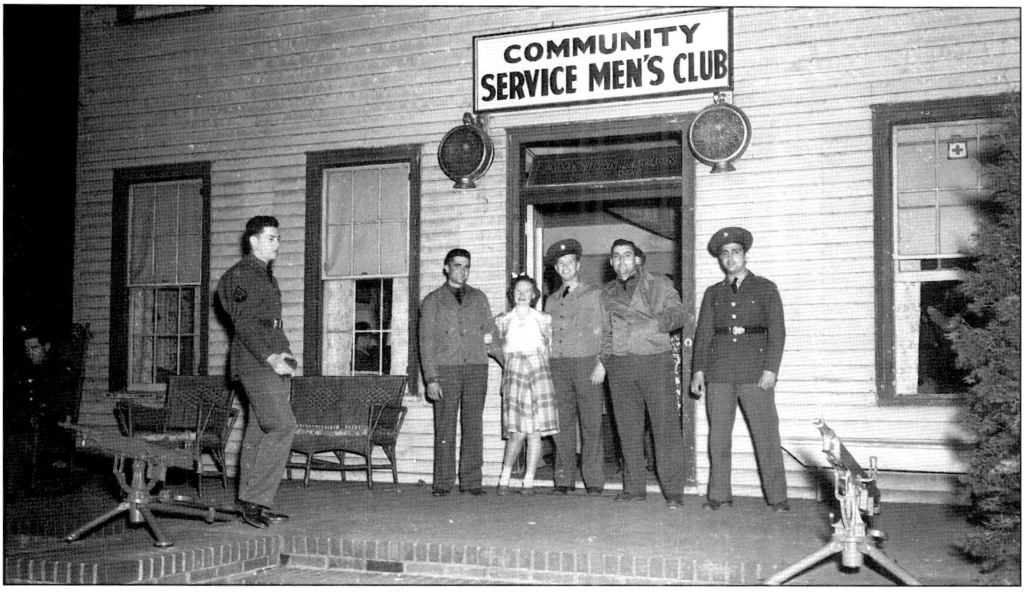

The American Legion Joseph J. Clifton Post #196 was organized in 1919. Point Pleasant resident Joseph Clifton had lost his life in the Meuse-Argonne drive in France during World War I. In 1930, the post bought the John Marshall house on Arnold Avenue (above), the site of the present Elks Club, and remained there until the present post building on American Legion Way was built in the early 1950s. The Community Service Men's Club met in the American Legion home during World War II.

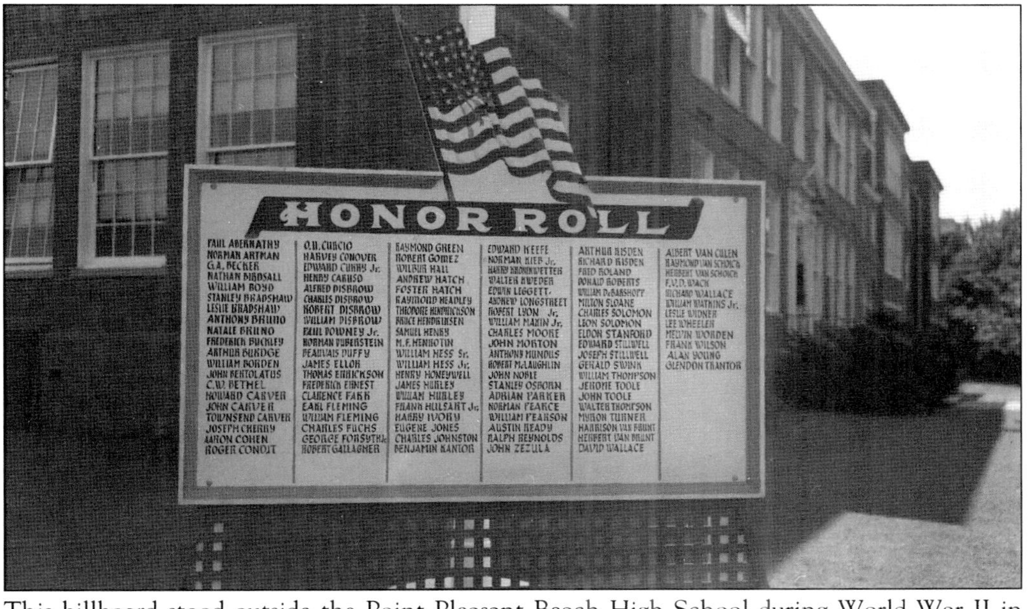

This billboard stood outside the Point Pleasant Beach High School during World War II in honor of those residents who were defending their country. The original listing of one hundred and eleven names on the Honor Roll began with Paul Abernathy and ended with Alan Young in the summer of 1942. Names were added as the war went on; over 260 were eventually placed on the Honor Roll.

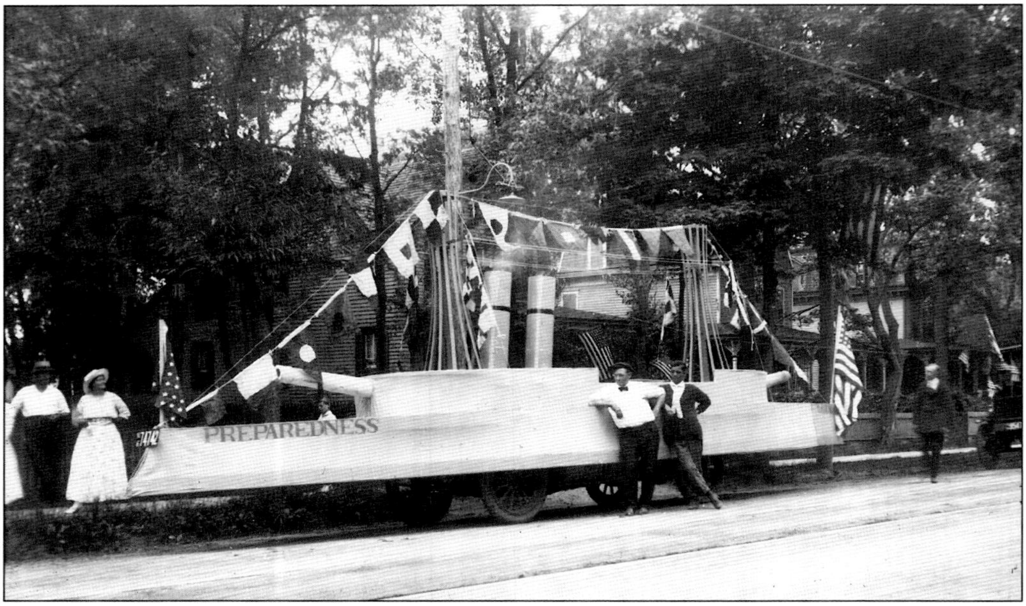

During the 1920s, the second week of August was a special time in Point Pleasant with the annual staging of the Mid-Summer Frolic. The first frolic was held in 1923 with over $900 in proceeds donated to the Paul Kimball Hospital in Lakewood. The Mid-Summer Frolic included an annual baby parade and a procession of creative floats, such as this one depicting a battleship in 1928.

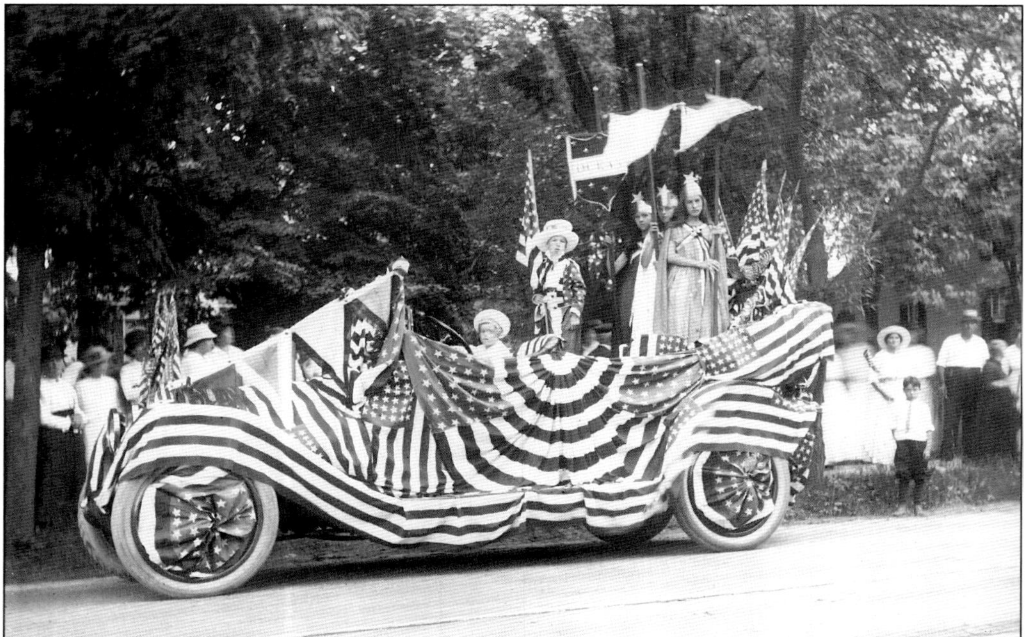

While the marching bands and parade floats became more exotic as each Mid-Summer Frolic passed, it was the baby parade and crowning of Queen Iris that took center stage. The proceeds from the second and third frolics in 1924 and 1925 went to the three local fire companies.

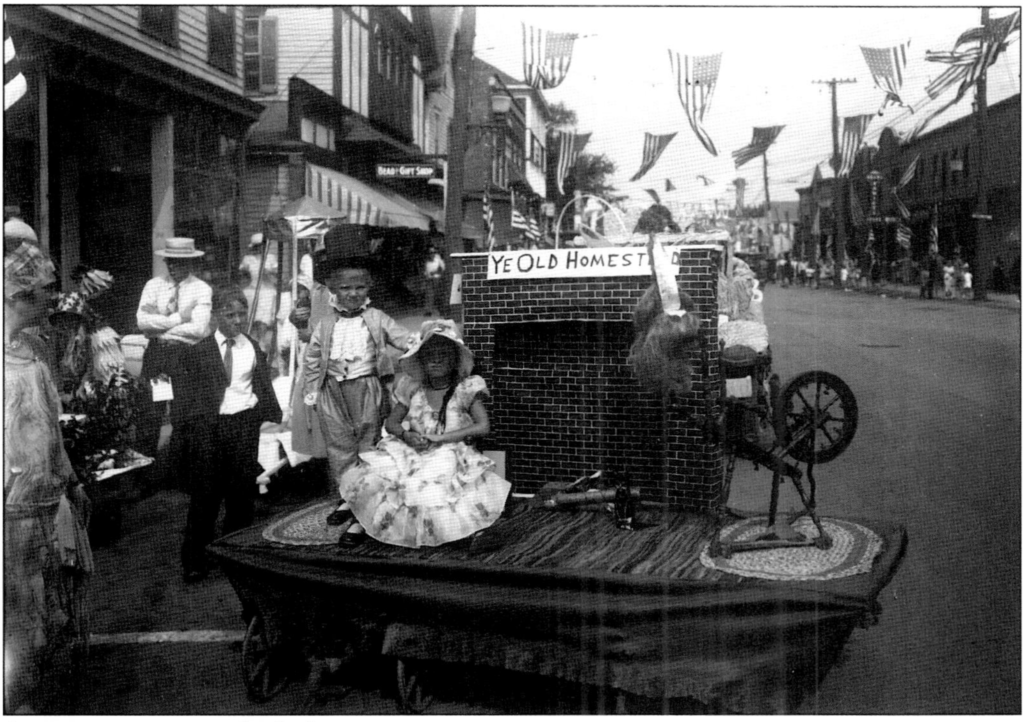

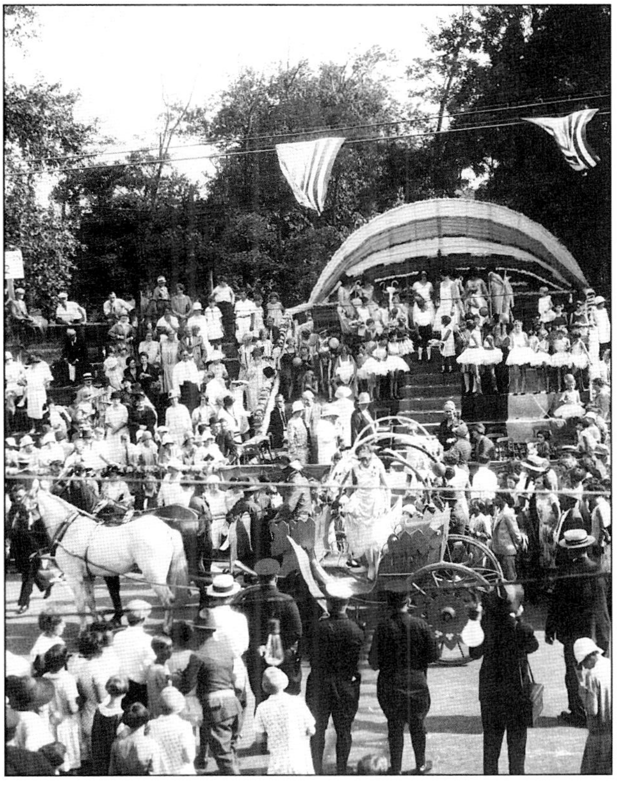

Community spirit ran high during the week of frolic festivities. Block parties were held all over town, as well as charity balls at the hotels, a firemen's parade, charity events, baseball games, and water sports at Clark's Landing. No wonder the Mid-Summer Frolic was held over the span of an entire week.

Queen Iris's throne and the spectator grandstands were erected each summer along Arnold Avenue in Brisbane Park, the site of the present Woolworth building. Progress forced the relocation of the reviewing stands to Richmond Avenue where Foodtown presently stands in 1929. Here, Queen Iris III, DeMora Barber, exits her coach on Arnold Avenue in 1925.

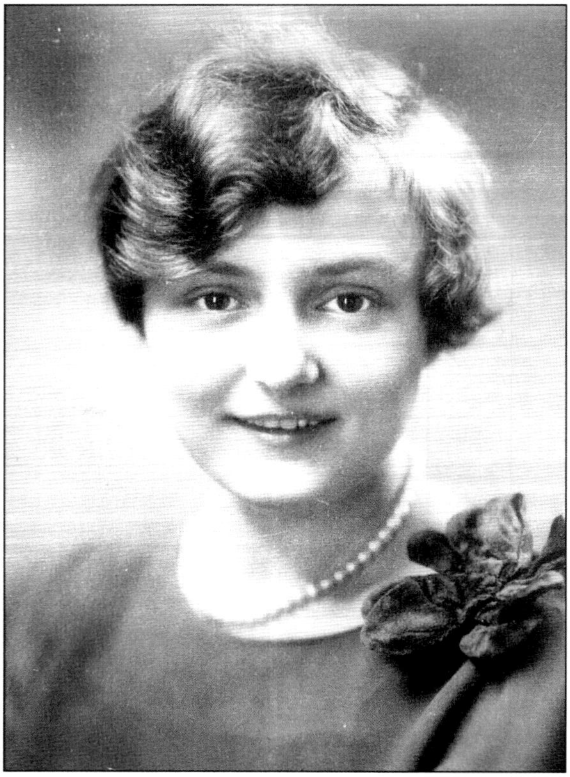

Queen Iris VII, Miss Marjorie Leward of Brooklyn, appears here in 1929. There were eight queens presiding over the Mid-Summer Frolic between 1923 and 1930. The first was Edith Lane, followed by Ida Shinn, DeMora Barber, Elizabeth Bills, Isabel Seymour, Marjorie Leward, and Doris Stromberg.

In 1928 the staging area for the baby parade floats was at the Red Men's Hall on Arnold Avenue (below). The parade drew over two thousand entrants. That year saw the crowning of a baby parade princess, Jean Ballard Errickson. Alice Cherry was Princess Alice II in 1929 and Rose Stone was Princess Rose III in 1930.

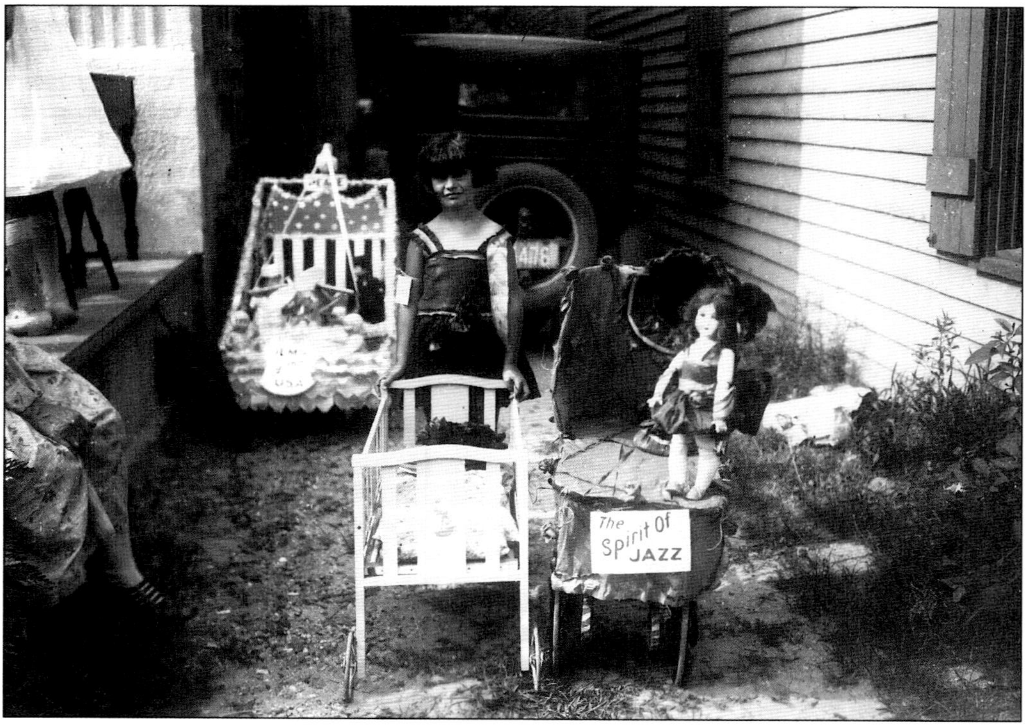

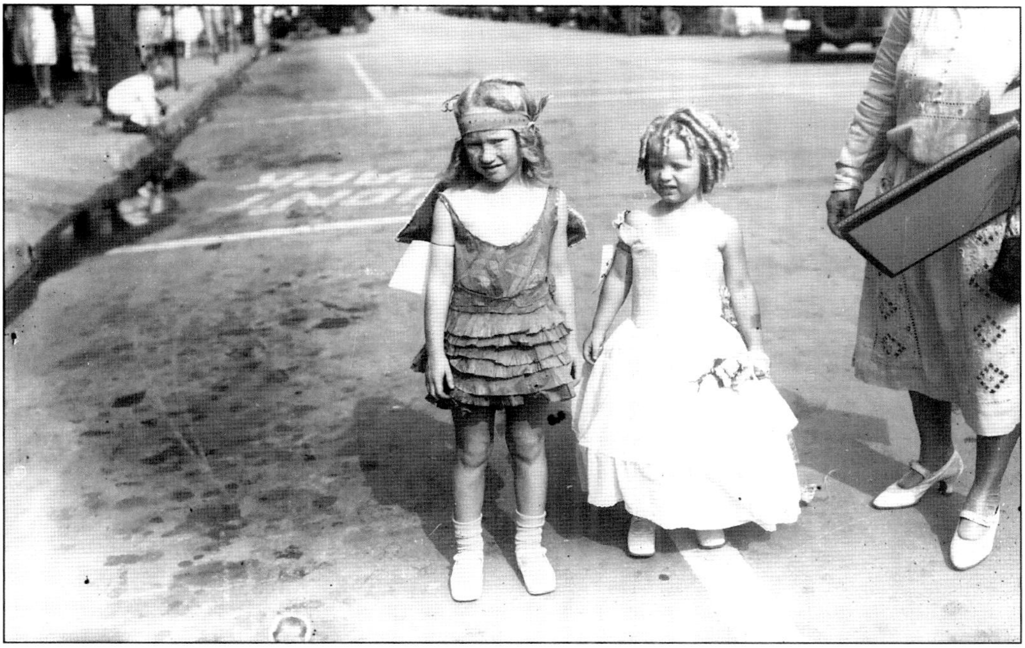

With the baby parade drawing attention on Arnold Avenue, the water sports events went on simultaneously at Clark's Landing. These events included canoe races, bateau races, canoe tilting, tub racing, outboard-motor boat racing, a criss-craft race, a tomato race, and a watermelon scramble.

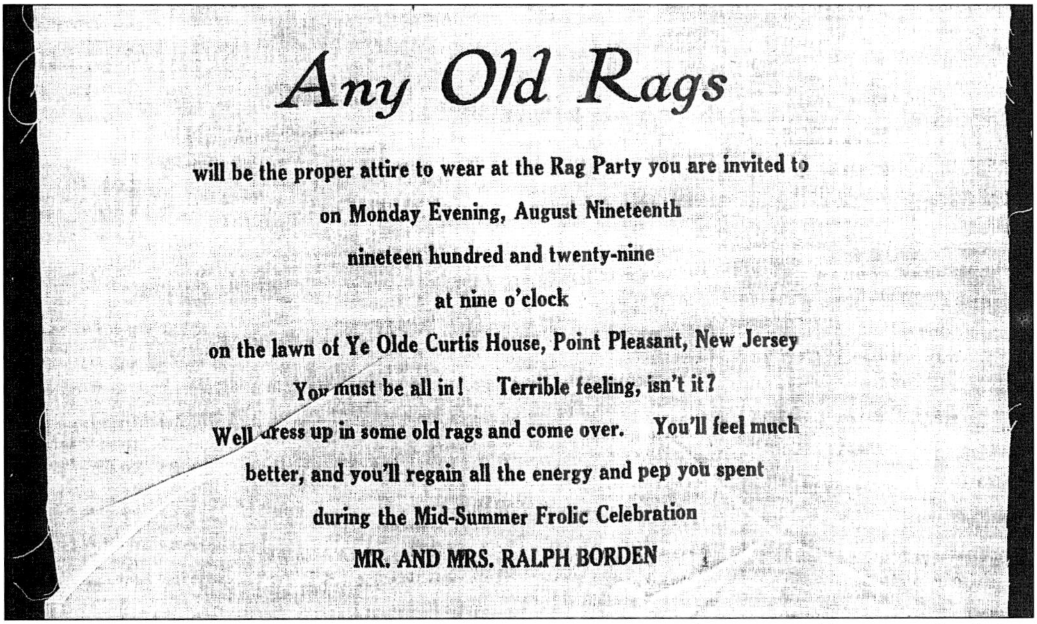

Any Old Rags

will be the proper attire to wear at the Rag Party you are invited to
on Monday Evening, August Nineteenth
nineteen hundred and twenty-nine
at nine o'clock
on the lawn of Ye Olde Curtis House, Point Pleasant, New Jersey
You must be all in! Terrible feeling, isn't it?
Well dress up in some old rags and come over. You'll feel much
better, and you'll regain all the energy and pep you spent
during the Mid-Summer Frolic Celebration
MR. AND MRS. RALPH BORDEN

In 1926, New Jersey Governor and Mrs. A. Harry Moore were the guests of honor at the baby parade . . . a tradition that continued through the 1930 frolic with Governor Morgan F. Larson. The John Wanamaker Girl Cadets of Philadelphia appeared yearly at the parades starting in 1925.

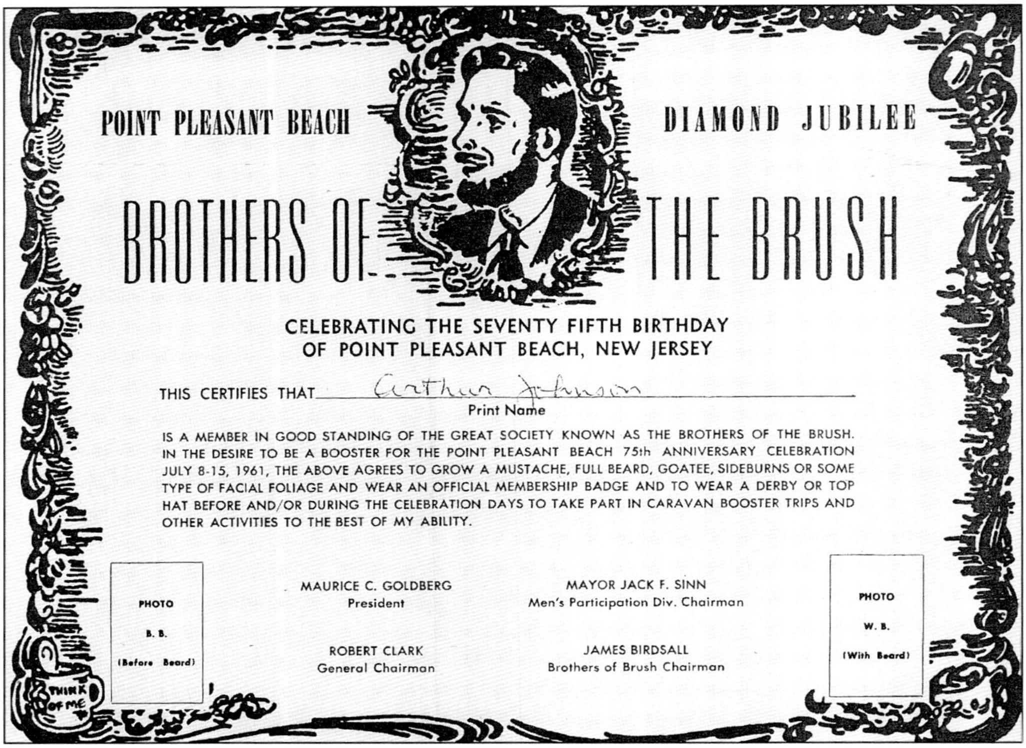

POINT PLEASANT BEACH DIAMOND JUBILEE

BROTHERS OF THE BRUSH

CELEBRATING THE SEVENTY FIFTH BIRTHDAY
OF POINT PLEASANT BEACH, NEW JERSEY

THIS CERTIFIES THAT Arthur Johnson
Print Name

IS A MEMBER IN GOOD STANDING OF THE GREAT SOCIETY KNOWN AS THE BROTHERS OF THE BRUSH. IN THE DESIRE TO BE A BOOSTER FOR THE POINT PLEASANT BEACH 75th ANNIVERSARY CELEBRATION JULY 8-15, 1961, THE ABOVE AGREES TO GROW A MUSTACHE, FULL BEARD, GOATEE, SIDEBURNS OR SOME TYPE OF FACIAL FOLIAGE AND WEAR AN OFFICIAL MEMBERSHIP BADGE AND TO WEAR A DERBY OR TOP HAT BEFORE AND/OR DURING THE CELEBRATION DAYS TO TAKE PART IN CARAVAN BOOSTER TRIPS AND OTHER ACTIVITIES TO THE BEST OF MY ABILITY.

PHOTO
B. B.
(Before Beard)

MAURICE C. GOLDBERG
President

MAYOR JACK F. SINN
Men's Participation Div. Chairman

ROBERT CLARK
General Chairman

JAMES BIRDSALL
Brothers of Brush Chairman

PHOTO
W. B.
(With Beard)

THINK OF ME

In 1961, Point Pleasant Beach celebrated its 75th anniversary in a big way. The events of July 10 through 15 included the historic spectacle "Sands of Time" each evening at the Niblick Street Athletic Field, a pirate treasure hunt for the kids, the New Jersey Seafood Princess Contest, and the annual Big Sea Day Parade and its related activities. This was an application for the Brothers of the Brush, a beard-growing contest.

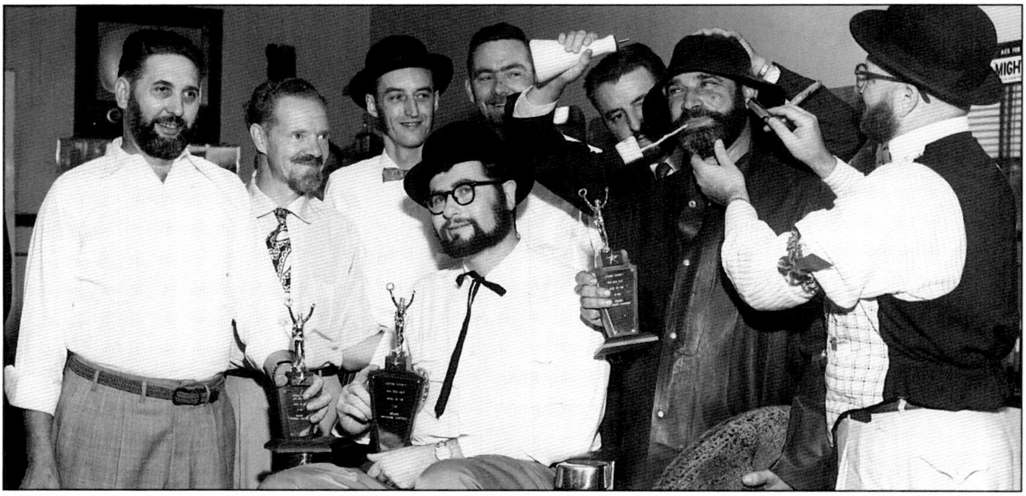

The beard-growing contest, part of the Big Sea Day celebration in Point Pleasant Beach, was always good for a few laughs. The contest winners in 1955 (above) were Nathan Cotler (seated center), Ray Stieger (left), and Sal Maraziti (with rain slicker and corn-cob pipe), who is about to get a close shave from Maurice Goldberg.

Municipal Engineer Andy Handzo drives an antique automobile on Arnold Avenue during the 1954 Big Sea Day Parade. Handzo chaired the antique auto committee for Big Sea Day and was the first president of the North Shore Antique Auto Club. The building in the background still stands at 1009 Arnold Avenue.

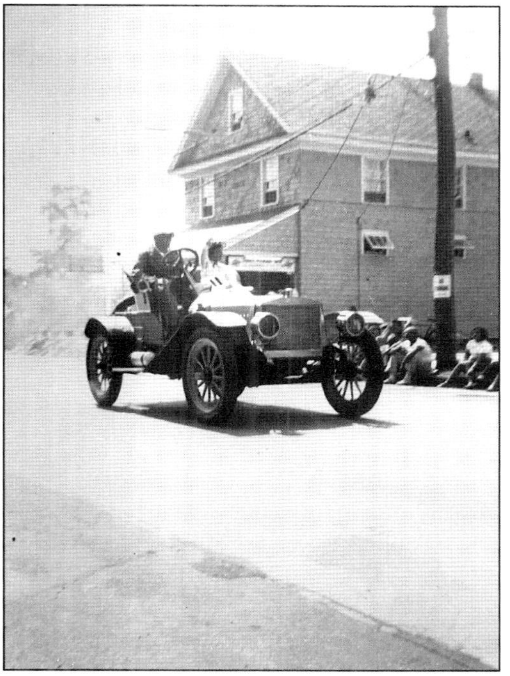

A Big Sea Day Parade makes its way down Ocean Avenue in 1959. This Seacoast Oil Company float commemorated the addition of Hawaii as the 50th state in the union. Such beautiful floats were common during Big Sea Day.

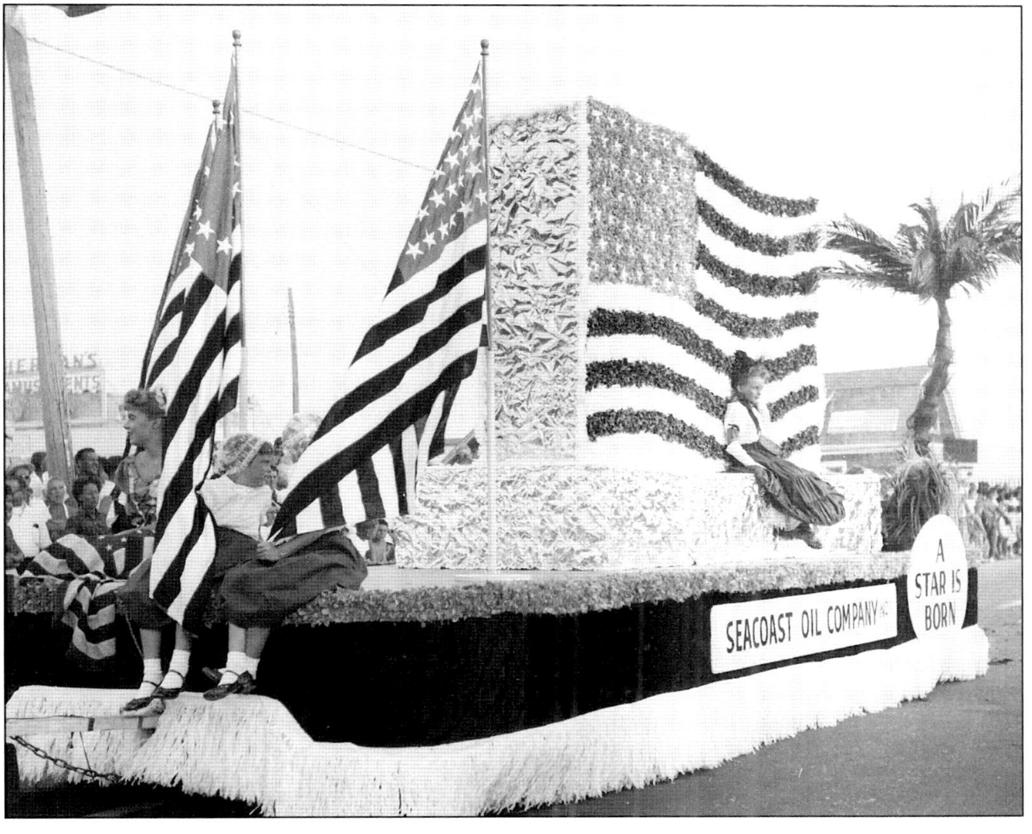

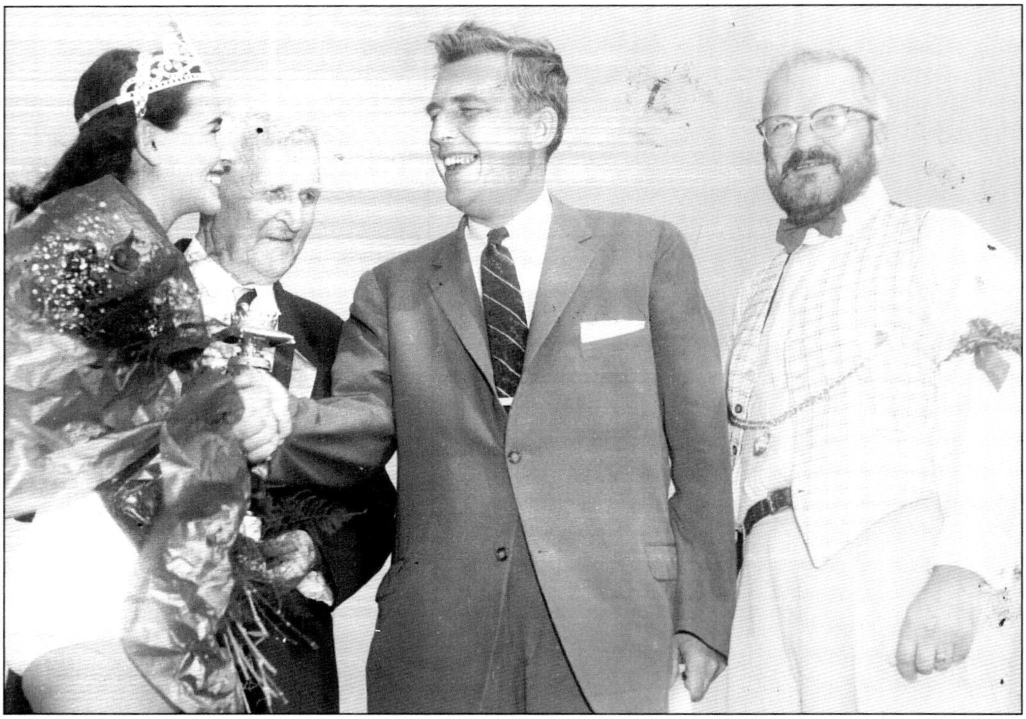

New Jersey Governor Robert B. Meyner congratulates the 1956 Miss Seafood Princess, Rosina Guadagnino of Plainfield, as Axel Carlson and Maurice Goldberg (right) look on.

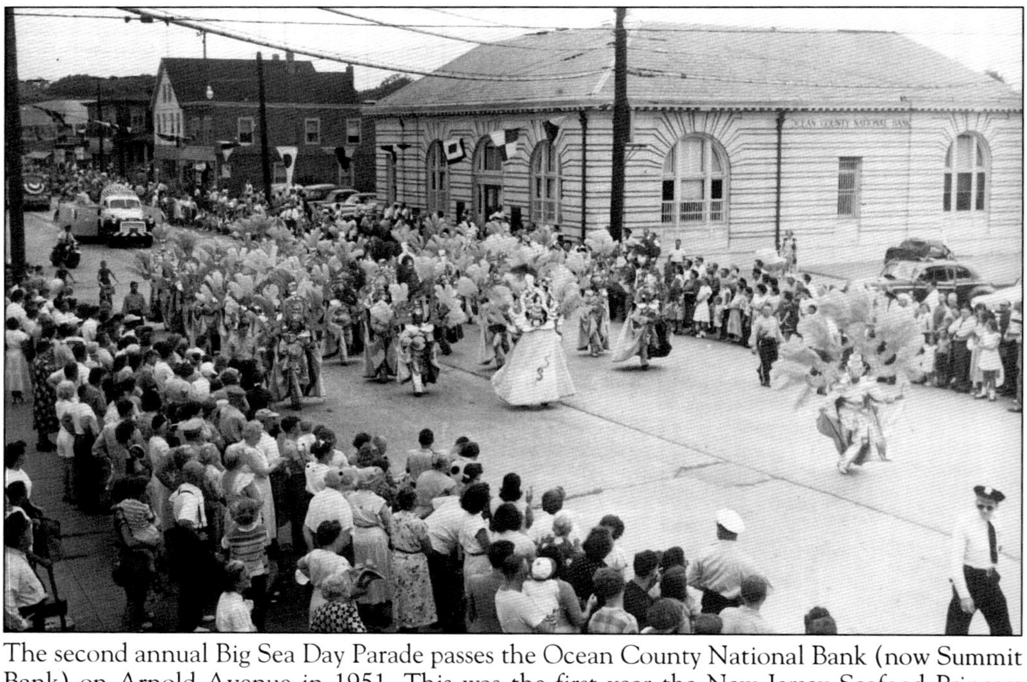

The second annual Big Sea Day Parade passes the Ocean County National Bank (now Summit Bank) on Arnold Avenue in 1951. This was the first year the New Jersey Seafood Princess Contest was held here; the first two were staged in Atlantic City.

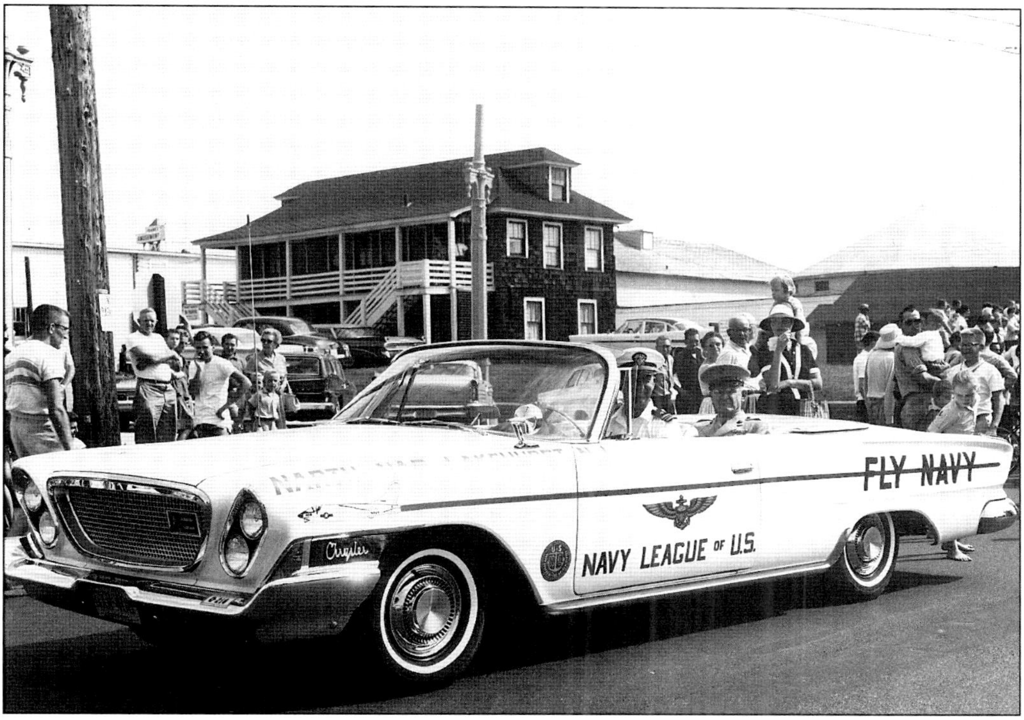

The Lakehurst Naval Air Station joins in the 1962 Big Sea Day Parade on Ocean Avenue. In the back seat of this Chrysler convertible is Ret. Col. William M.E. Hess, noted author and local historian.

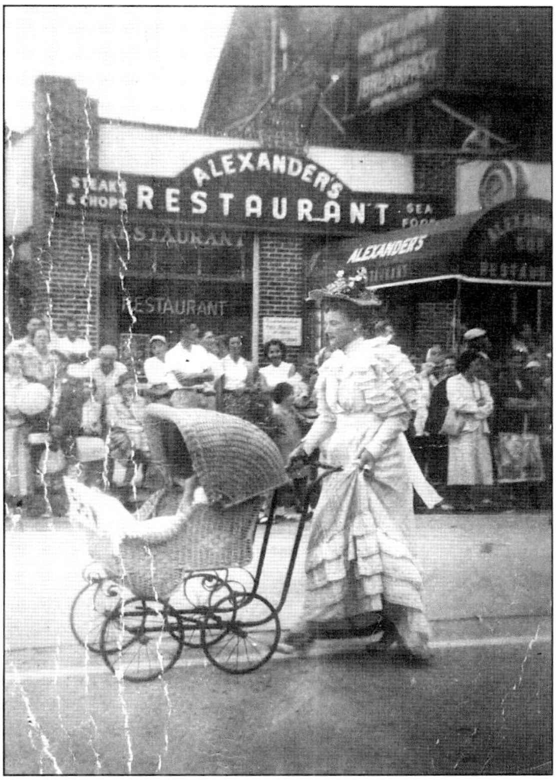

The first Big Sea Day was held in conjunction with Ocean County's centennial celebration on August 12, 1950. More than fifty units representing every phase of early American history were represented in the parade. Horse-drawn carriages and floats, early automobiles, and people dressed in costumes from long ago (right) lent a note of color and gaiety seldom seen in parades outside that of the Mummers Parade in Philadelphia or the New York Christmas parades.

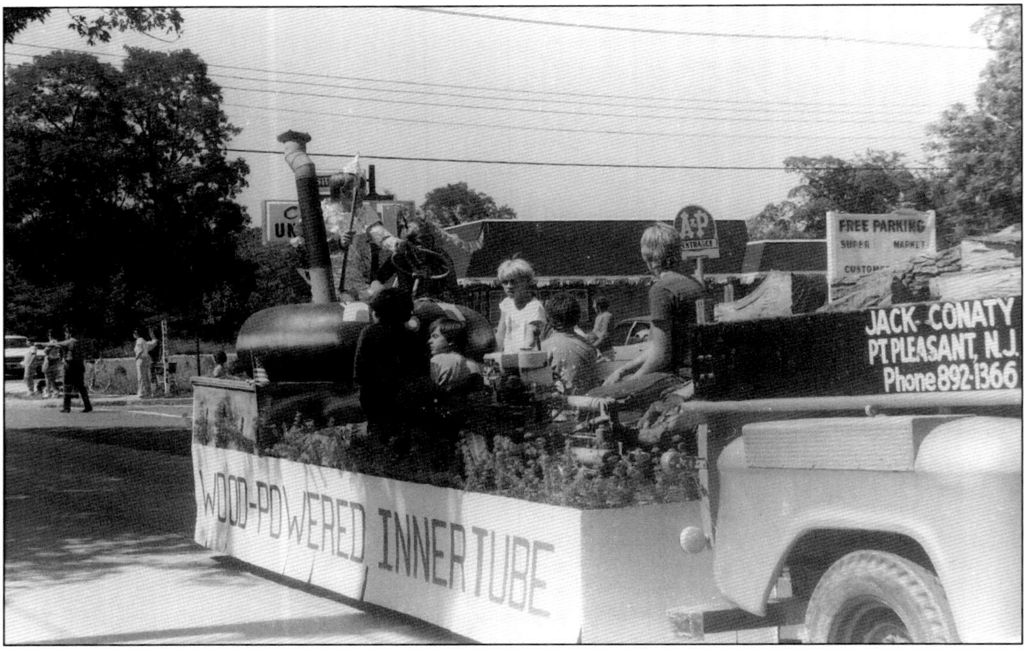

By 1965, Big Sea Day had finished its annual run in Point Pleasant Beach. But it wasn't long before a new summer tradition began in the form of the Grand Inner Tube Race. Known by various names over the years, the first tube race was held on Risden's Beach in September 1968. Festivities included a parade with hilarious floats, such as this one on Arnold Avenue in 1972.

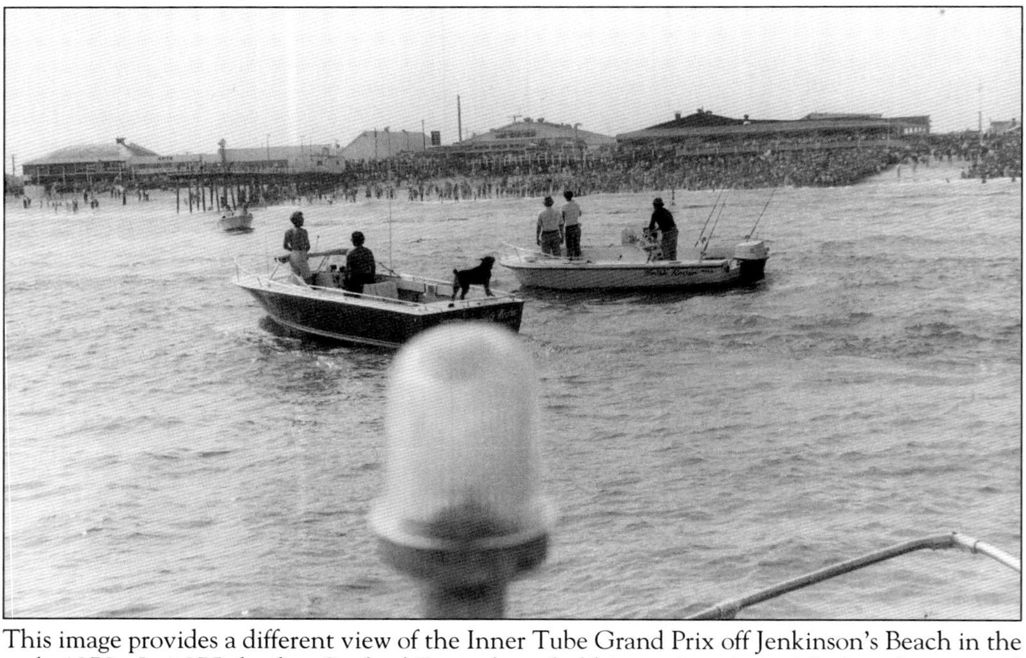

This image provides a different view of the Inner Tube Grand Prix off Jenkinson's Beach in the early 1970s. In 1975 the first Seafood Festival was held in conjunction with the tube race and the two events have shared the gala weekend ever since. Soon the Point Pleasant Lions Club began sponsoring the tube race and today it has become a major fund-raising event.

Four

The Social Scene

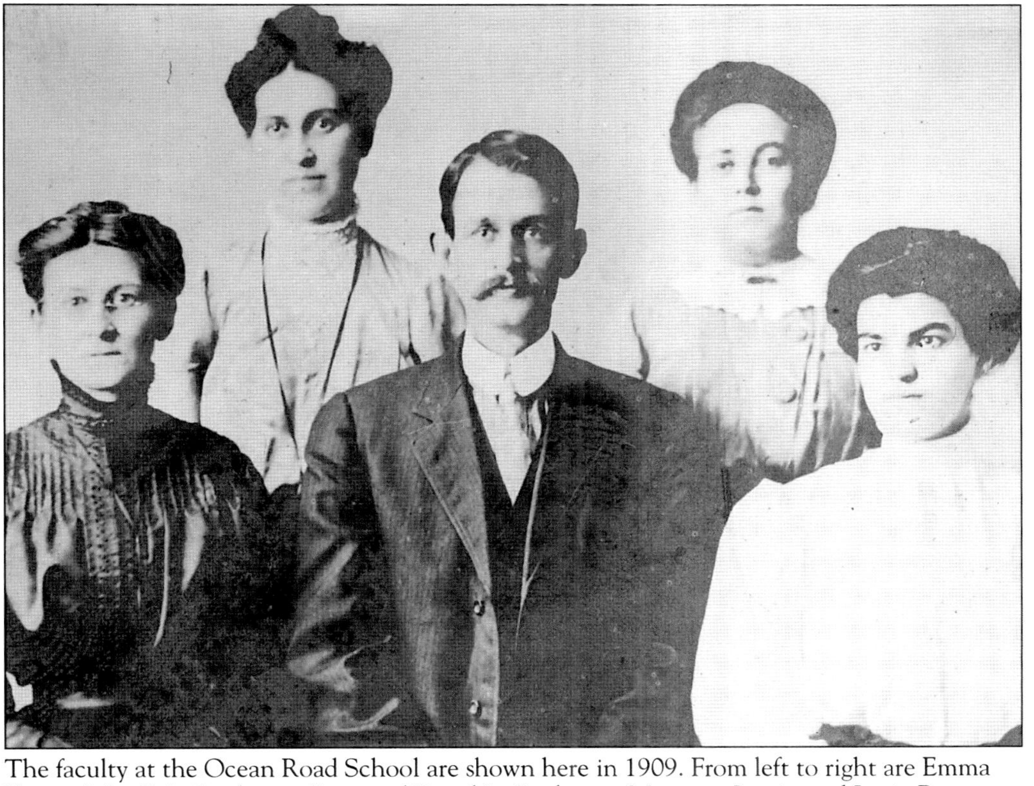

The faculty at the Ocean Road School are shown here in 1909. From left to right are Emma Young, Mrs. R.L. Predmore, Principal Royal L. Predmore, Margaret Lewis, and Jessie Ransom.

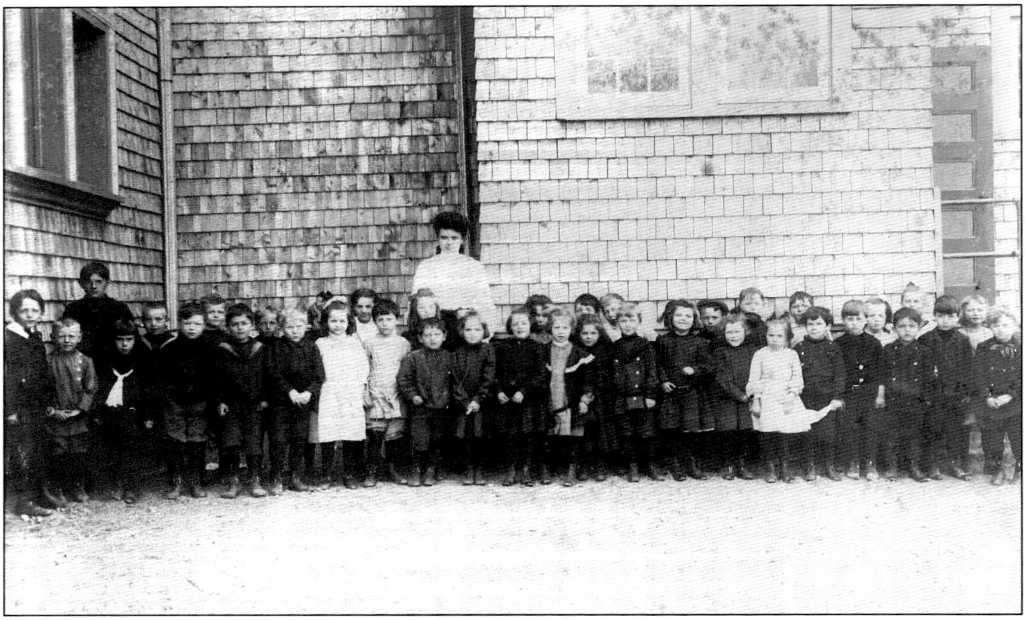

Kindergarten and first grade classes line up outside the original wooden Point Pleasant Beach School in 1905. Watching over the kids is teacher Helen Waller.

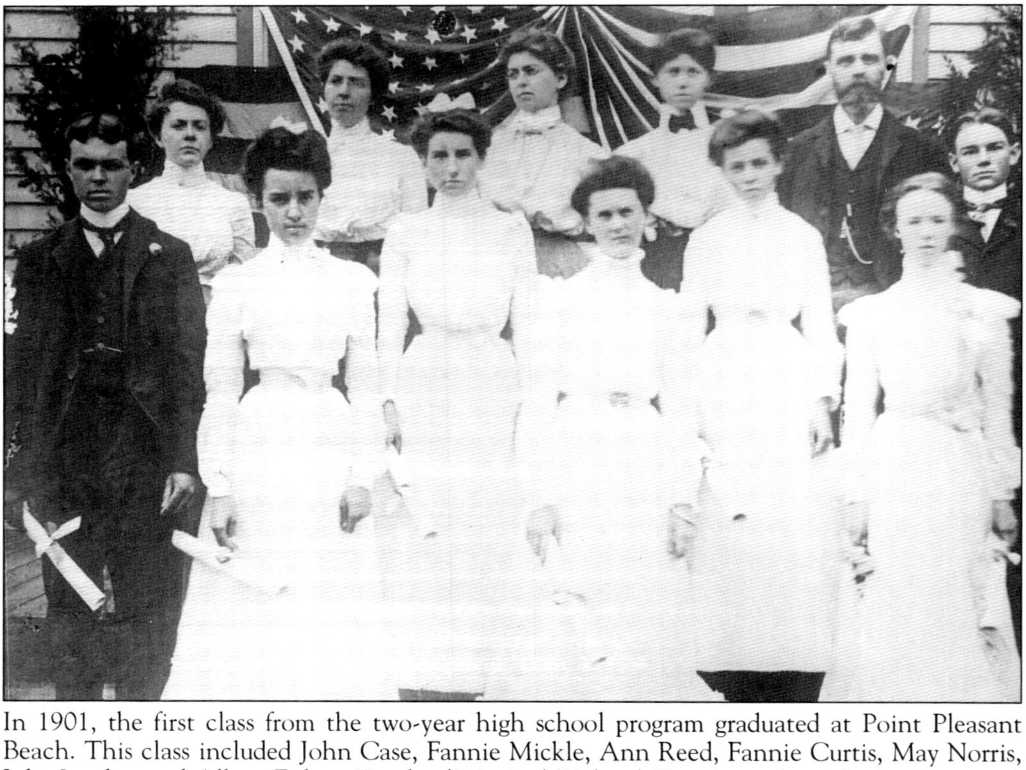

In 1901, the first class from the two-year high school program graduated at Point Pleasant Beach. This class included John Case, Fannie Mickle, Ann Reed, Fannie Curtis, May Norris, Julia Lawler, and Albert Fisher. Teacher/Principal Richard Case is on the right in the second row, along with the school faculty.

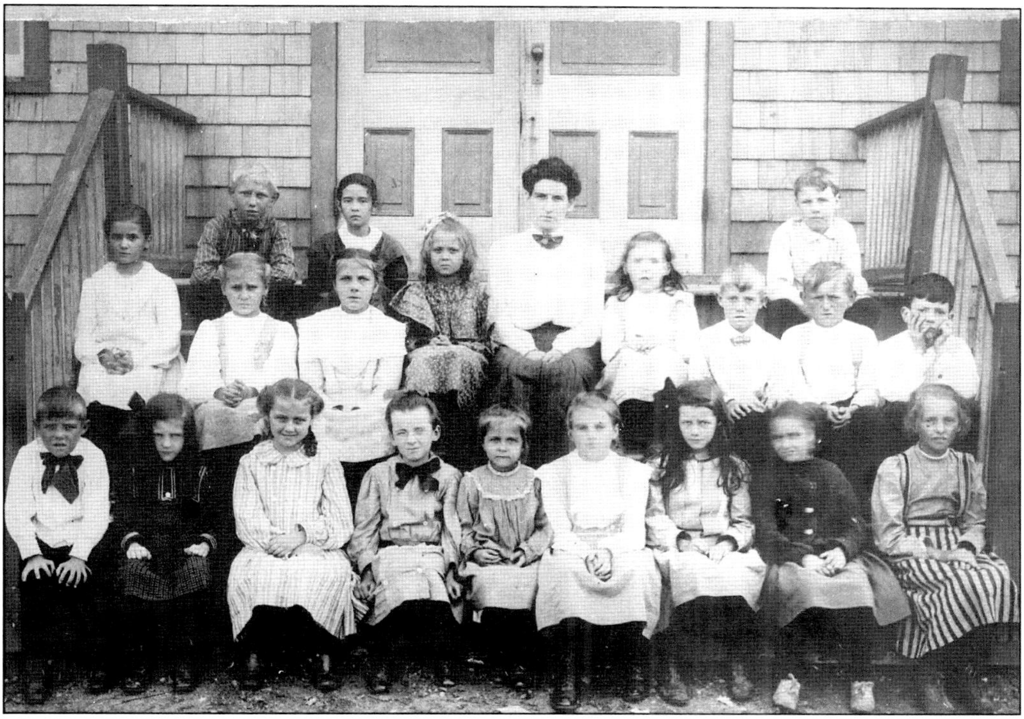

The first and second grade classes at Ocean Road School appear here in 1903. This photograph was taken on the front steps of the school two years after it was built and prior to the addition of a vestibule. Third from the left in the front row is longtime resident and future Ocean Road School teacher Maude Holman.

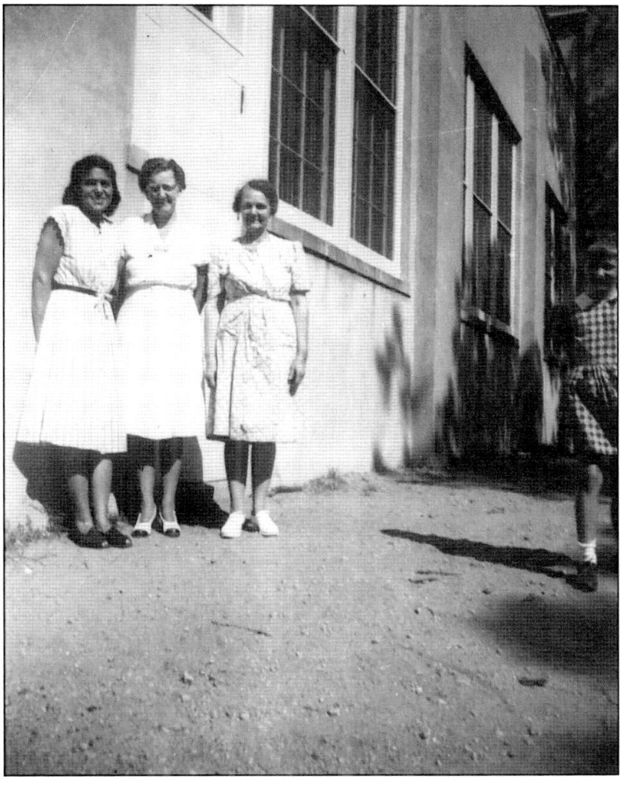

These teachers were on duty at the Ocean Road School about 1948. Standing from left to right are first-grade teacher Stella Gottlieb and third-grade teachers Maude Holman Young and Esther Mangold. In the background is the school auditorium, built in 1930. Maude Young retired from full-time teaching in 1958.

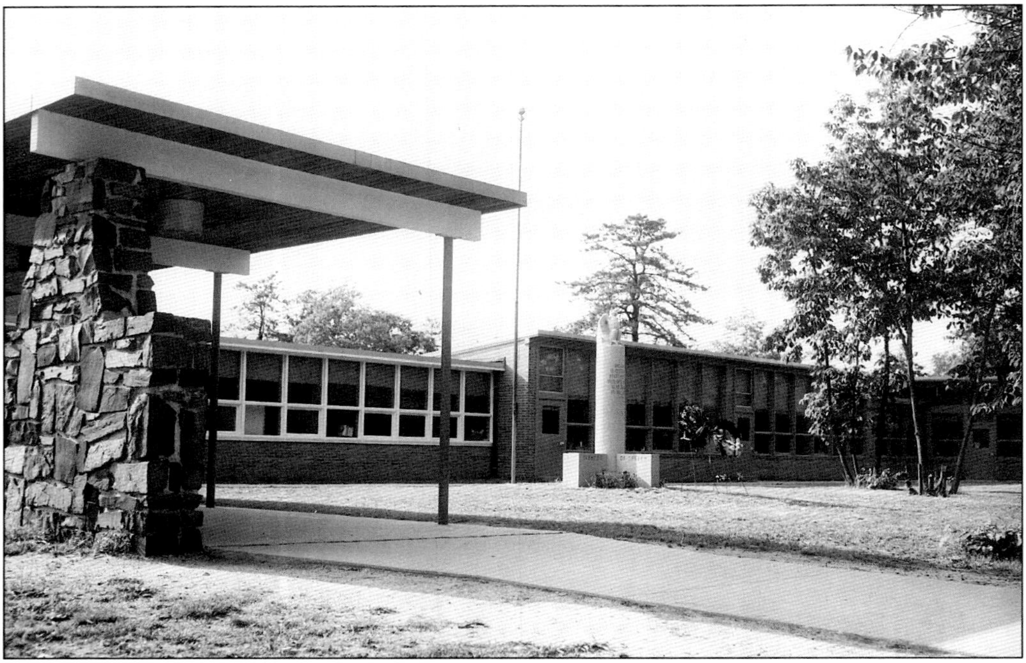

The Memorial Middle School was built between Florence and Taylor Avenues in Point Pleasant in 1957. The un-named street in front of the school was dedicated that same year as Laura Herbert Drive. Laura Herbert taught second grade at Ocean Road School for more than forty years, retiring in 1960.

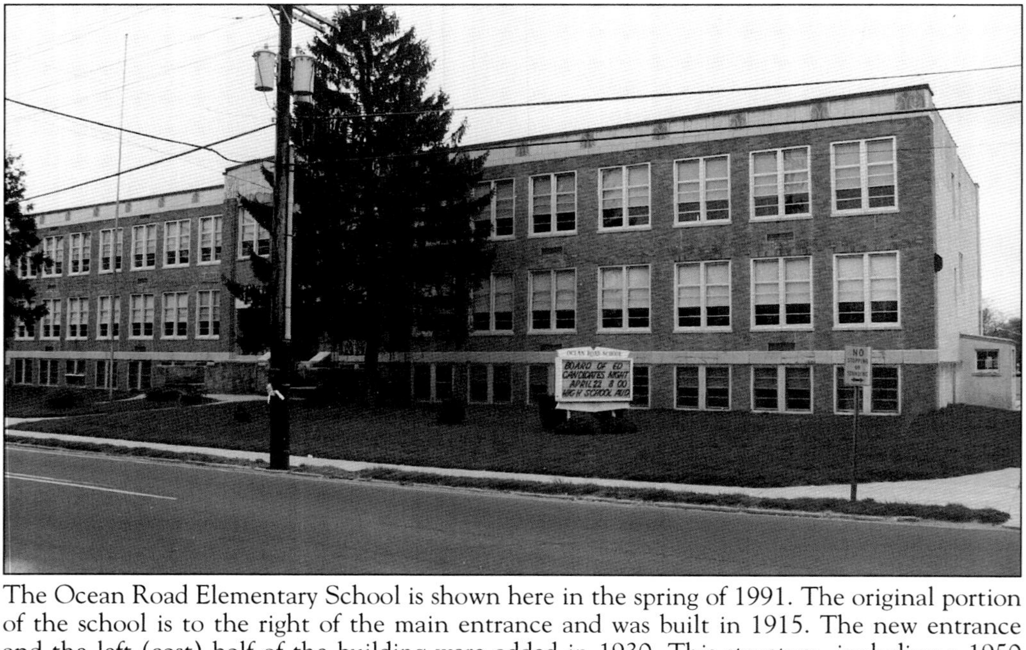

The Ocean Road Elementary School is shown here in the spring of 1991. The original portion of the school is to the right of the main entrance and was built in 1915. The new entrance and the left (east) half of the building were added in 1930. This structure, including a 1950 addition, was torn down in 1992 and replaced with the present Ocean Road School.

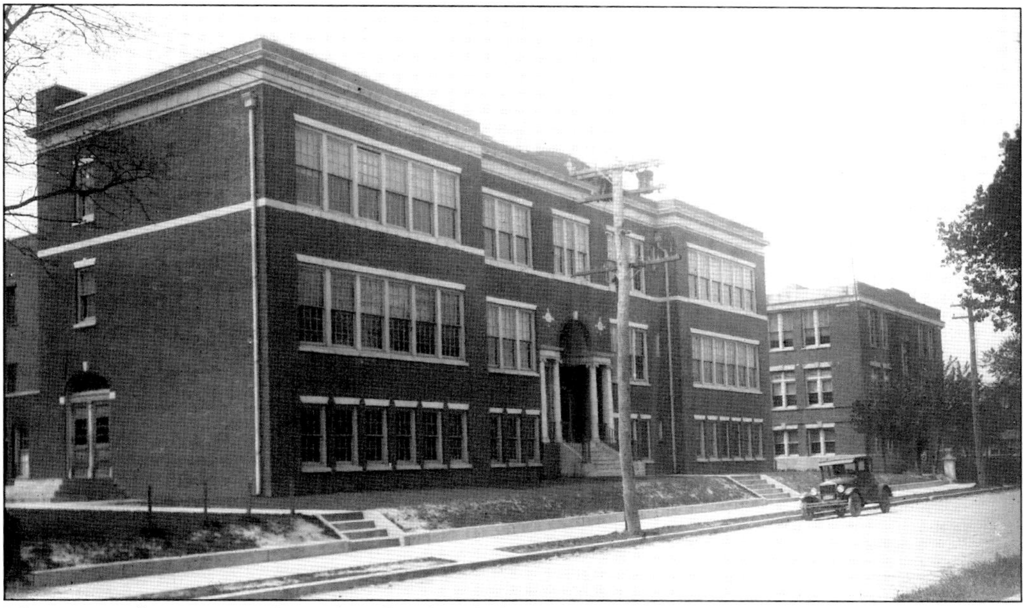

The Point Pleasant Beach High School and elementary school (on the right) appear together in 1923. Grades kindergarten through 12 were held in the elementary school, or annex as it was later called, until the present high school was completed in 1922. Preceding this date, classes were occasionally held in local storefronts because of severe overcrowding.

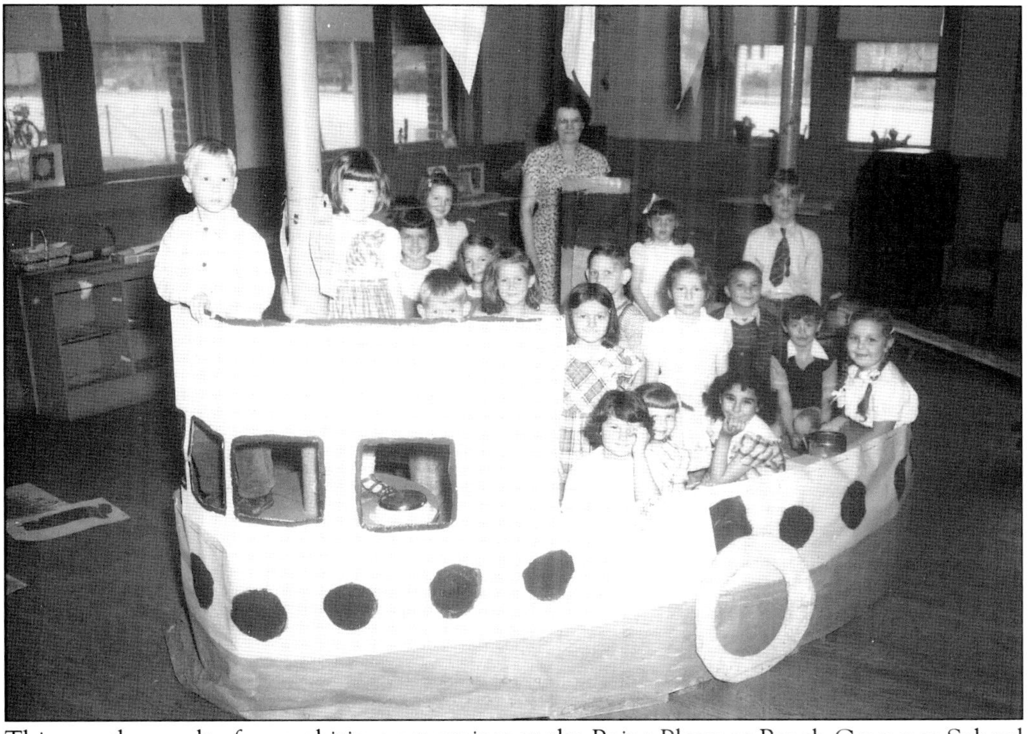

This was the result of an ambitious art project at the Point Pleasant Beach Grammar School in 1948.

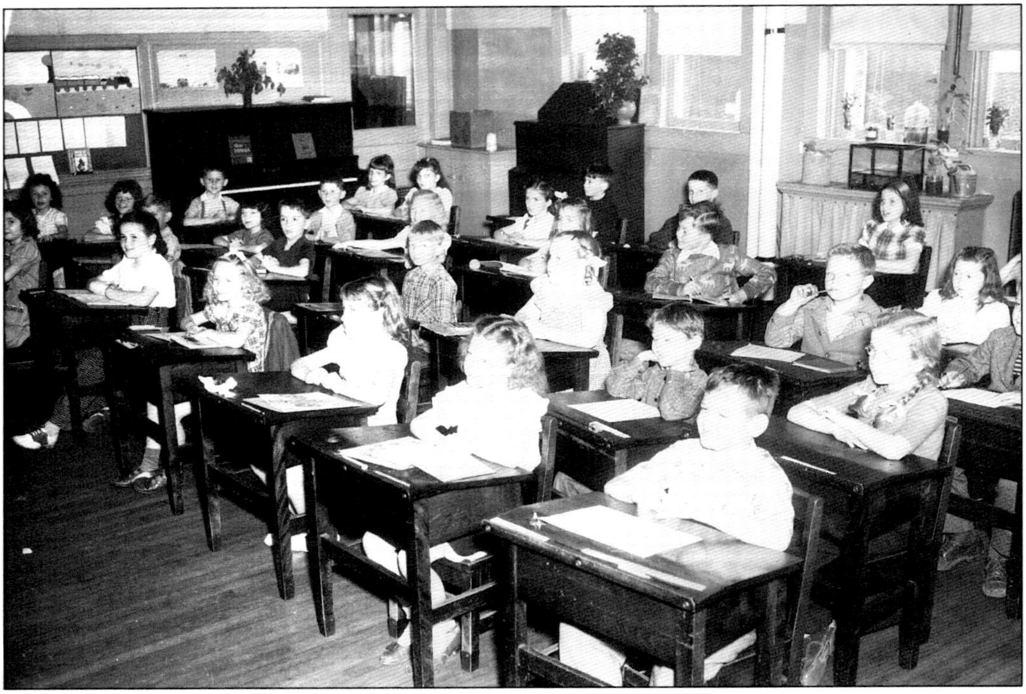

This is how a typical classroom appeared on the second floor of the "annex" in 1948. The aging heavy oak chairs and desks with the old-fashioned inkwell holes were still in use.

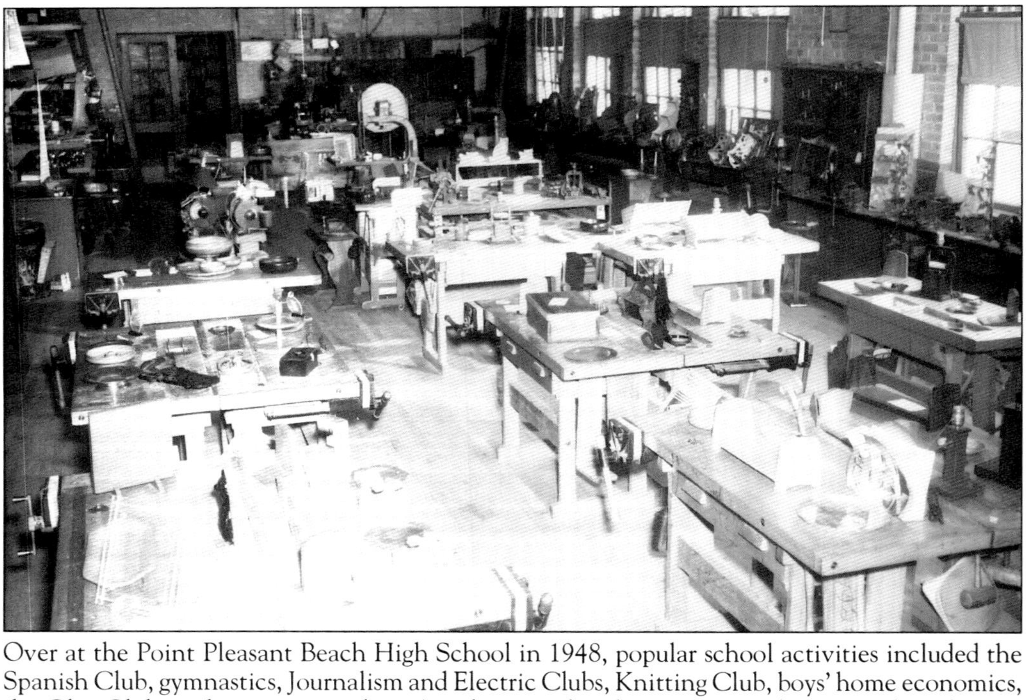

Over at the Point Pleasant Beach High School in 1948, popular school activities included the Spanish Club, gymnastics, Journalism and Electric Clubs, Knitting Club, boys' home economics, the Glee Club, and aeronautics class. Another popular class was manual training, later known as shop class, shown here in 1948.

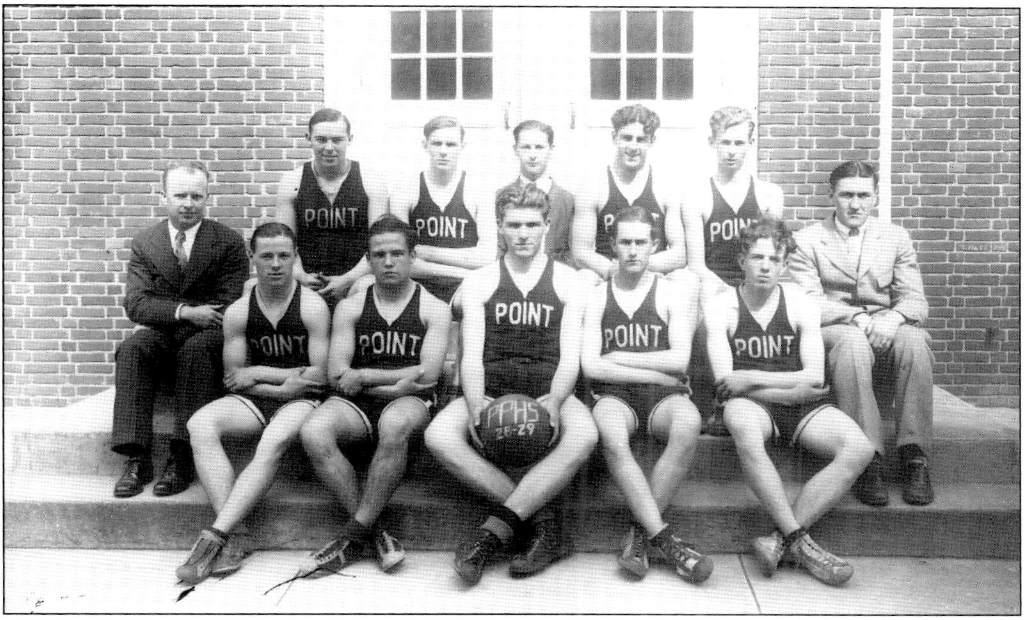

The 1928–29 Point Pleasant Beach High School basketball team is lined up for this photograph. In the front row from left to right are Joe Regan, Dale Bissey, Ben Turner, John Mason, and Sam Britton. In the second row from left to right are Principal Galloway, ? Harrison, Alex Henry, Dick Cottrell, unknown, Frank Britton, and Buddy Baer.

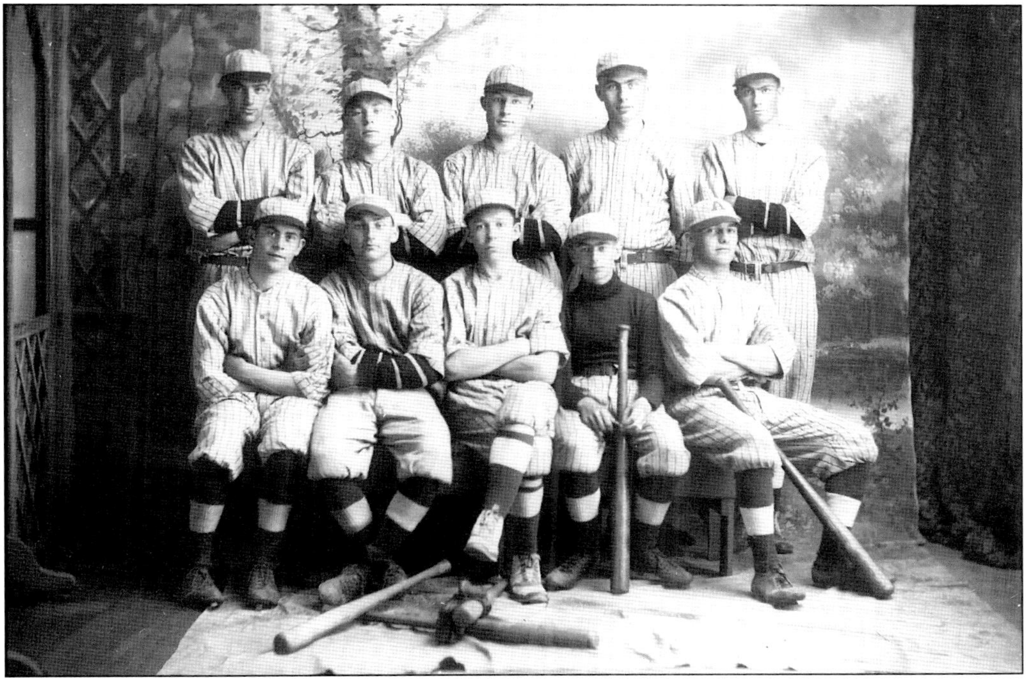

This formidable bunch made up a mid-1920s Beach High School baseball team. Games were played at the Clark's Landing field. By 1928, this site was replaced by bungalows and games were moved to the new Clayton Field at the south end of town (see Vol. I, p. 89).

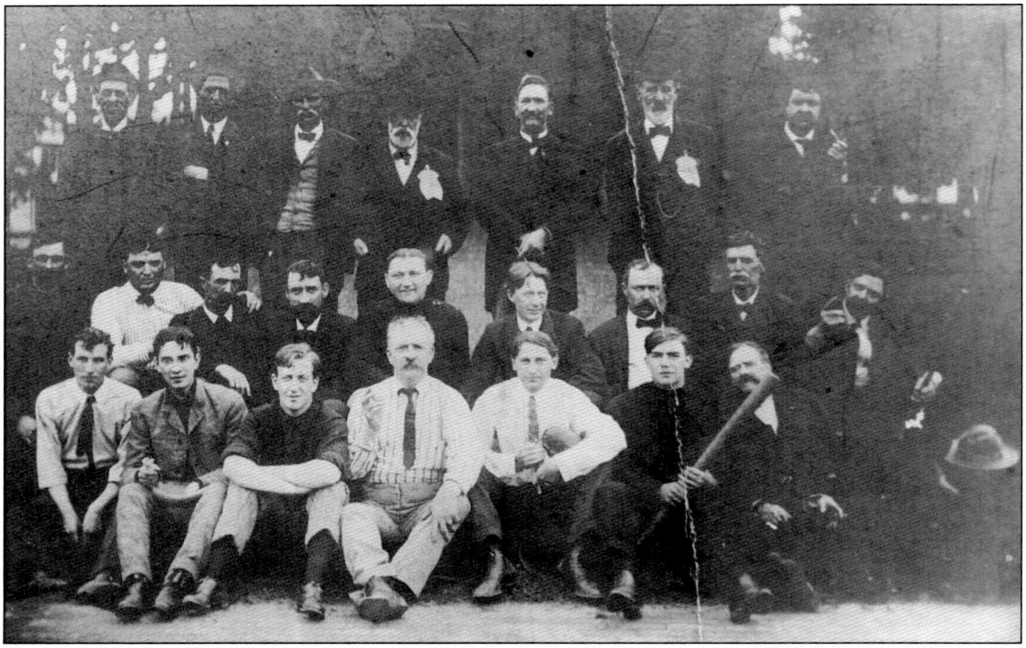

One of Point Pleasant's champion baseball teams of the early 1900s posed for this photograph. From left to right are: (front row) Mike Hurley, Dr. Howard Tindell, Marion VanNote, Larry VanNote, Arthur Zimmerman, Joe Martin, and Fred Makin; (center row) Dick Johnson, Jack Mondie, Wm. Ferguson, Wyckoff Applegate, Jack Siebert, George Osborn, Joseph Vannote, Henry Pearce, and Spike Hanley; (back row) T.A. Zimmerman, Clarence Hardy, B.L. Garrison, Elijah Chadwick, Abe Lower, John Osborn, and Jean Lott.

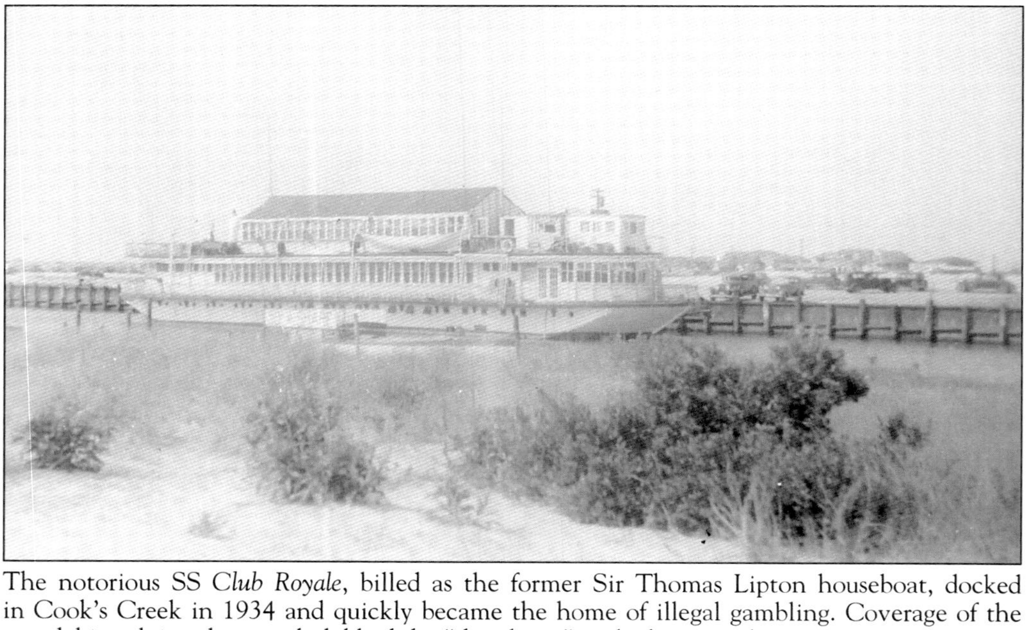

The notorious SS *Club Royale*, billed as the former Sir Thomas Lipton houseboat, docked in Cook's Creek in 1934 and quickly became the home of illegal gambling. Coverage of the scandal involving the vessel, dubbed the "showboat," ranked among the top ten news stories of 1934 in New Jersey.

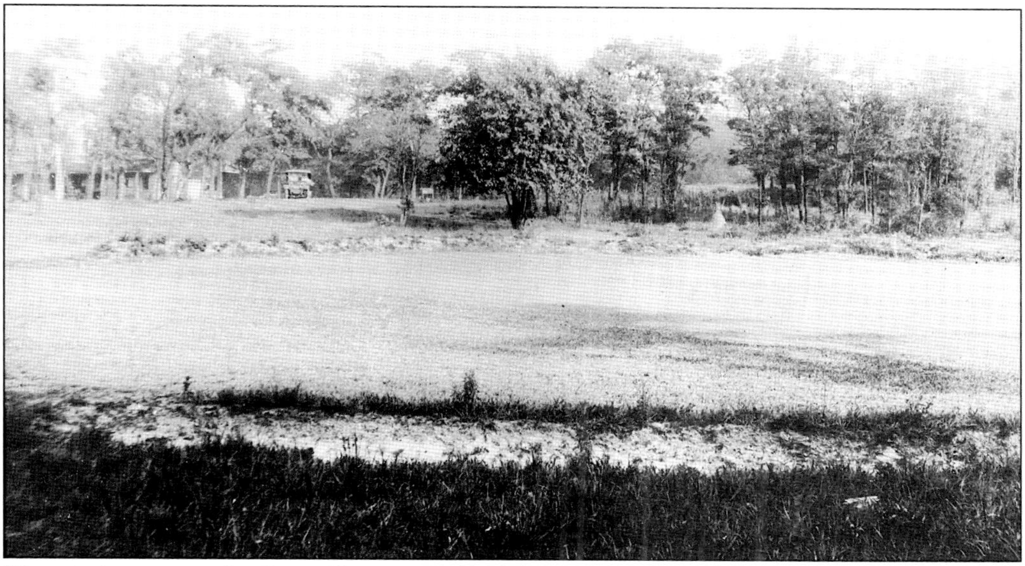

The ninth green at the Point Pleasant Golf Club course is shown here *c.* 1920. The nine-hole course was located on that part of the former Cook farm west of Baltimore Avenue and north of Niblick Street. The old Cook Homestead, serving as the clubhouse, is in the left background. Remnants of the golf links were still visible into the early 1950s.

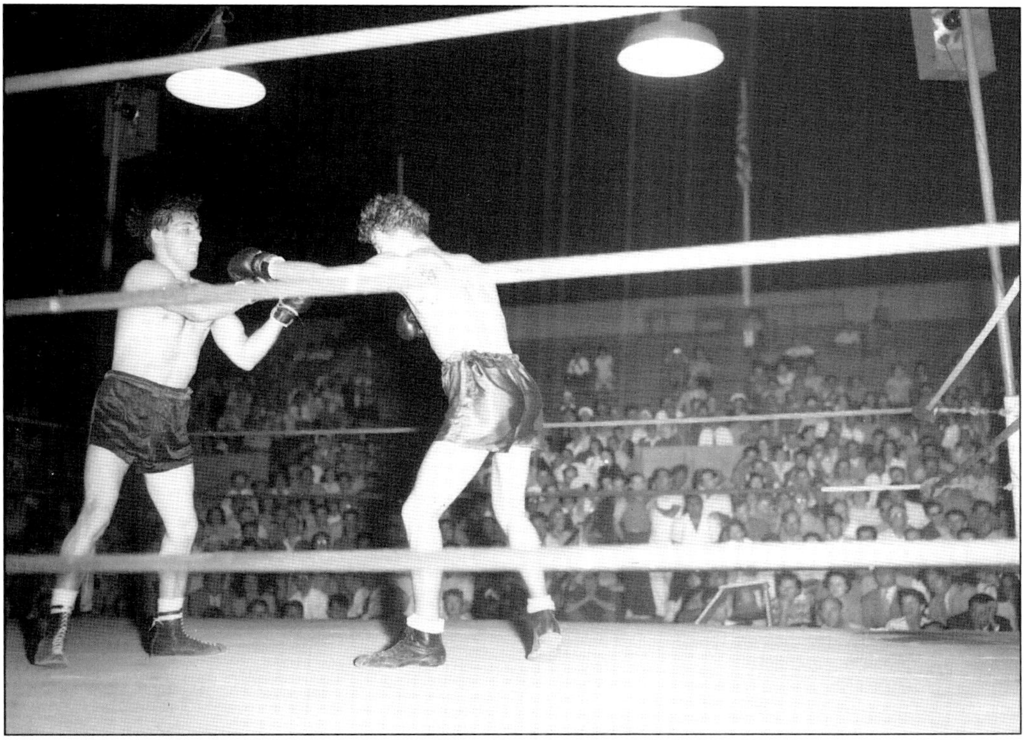

About 1932 an outdoor sports arena was built on Richmond Avenue near Clayton Field. The Point Pleasant Arena featured amateur and professional boxing and wrestling into the early 1940s. This boxing match was captured on film at the arena in 1941.

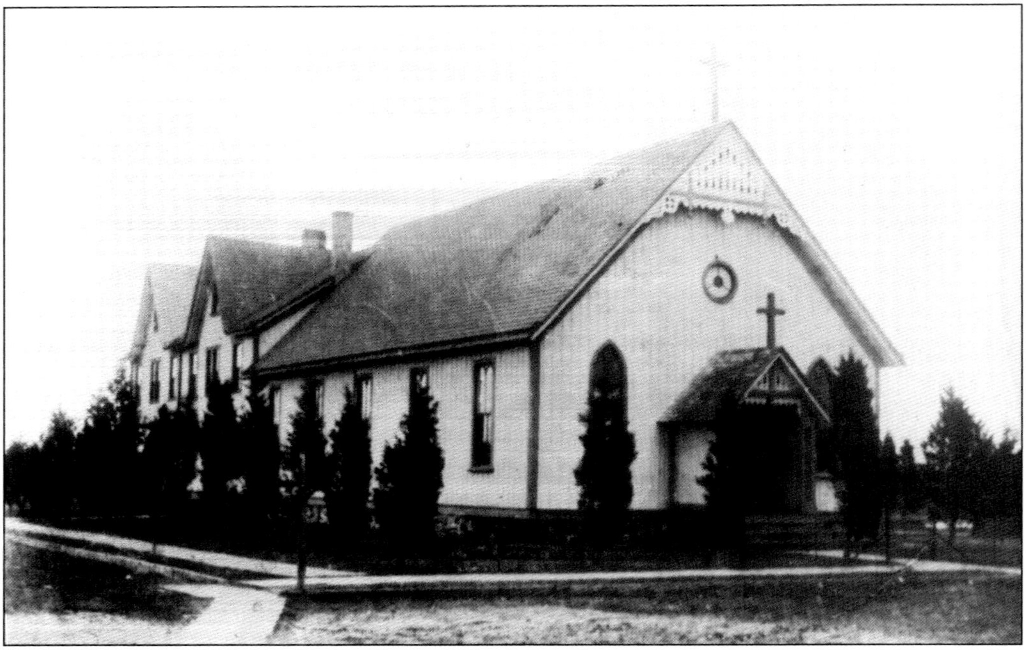

The first Saint Peter's Catholic Church was built on the southeast corner of Richmond and Washington Avenues. The church and attached rectory were built in 1882 by Manasquan contractor J.B. Sherman at a cost of $5,000.

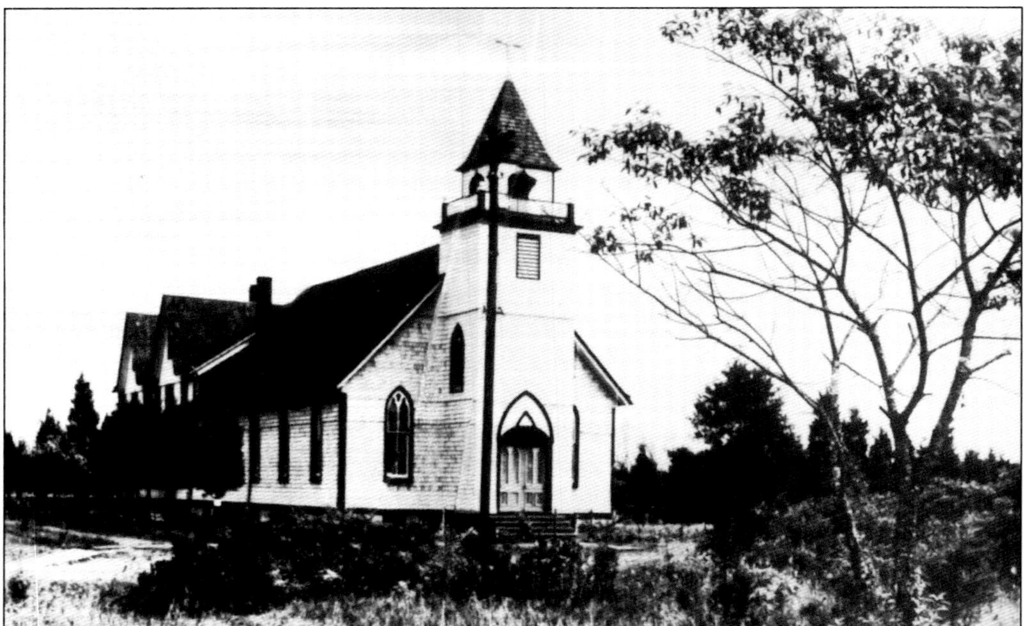

In 1899, the church steeple was added and other improvements were made to Saint Peter's under the direction of Father Daniel Lutz, OMC. These efforts were short-lived, however, as the church and rectory were destroyed by fire in January 1901. Four lots were quickly purchased at the church's present site with the new church building completed in 1902.

The interior of Saint Mary's-by-the-Sea Episcopal Church is shown (right) as it looked in 1951. This church was moved to its present site at Bay and Atlantic Avenues in 1889 from its original location in White Lawn Cemetery. The church building was moved on rollers and placed atop the old underground ice house, which belonged to the Resort House Hotel down the street.

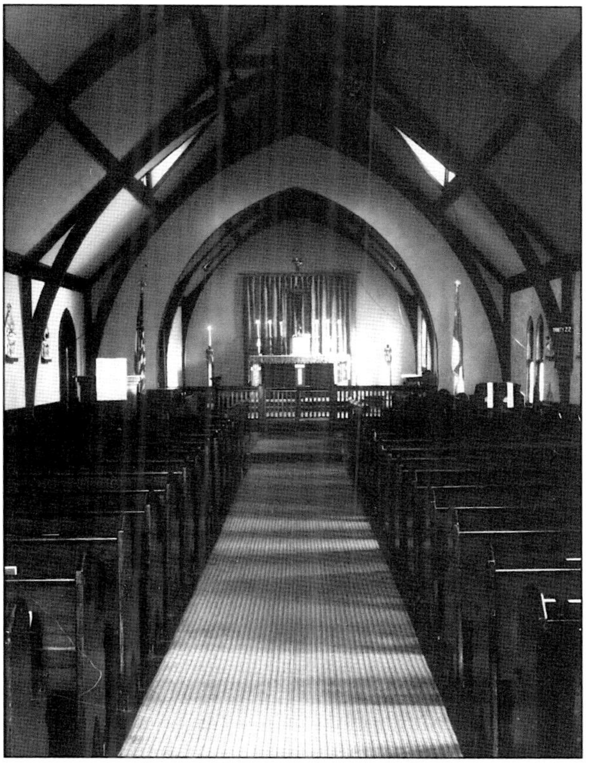

It's five days before Christmas in 1943 and the choir at the Central United Methodist Church on Arnold Avenue concludes the Sunday service with a procession. Following on the heels of Bay Head Methodists separating from the Harvey Memorial Church in Point Pleasant, Point Beach Methodists built their own church in 1922 after holding services for several years in the nearby Rogers Building on Arnold Avenue.

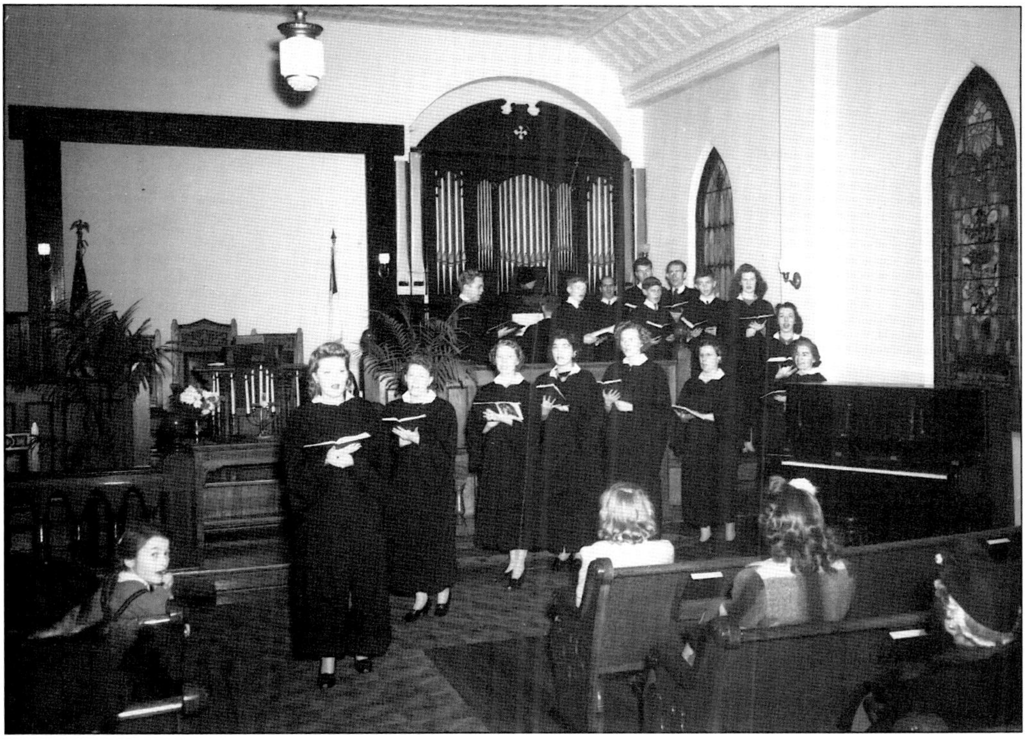

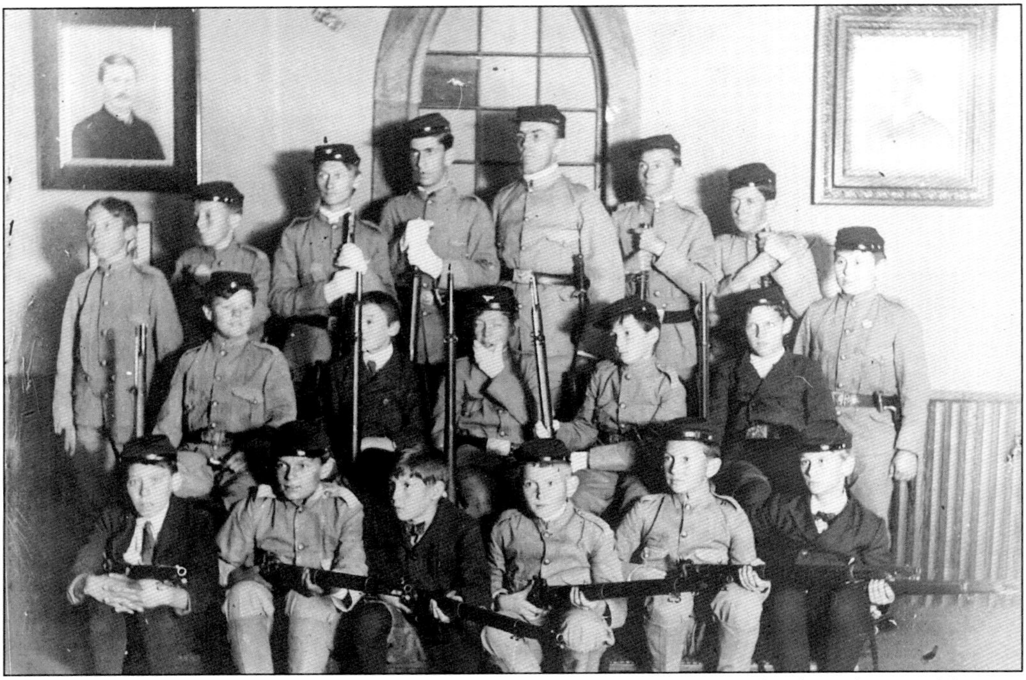

The Boy's Brigade was an organization of local youths who were taught discipline and honor. This early 1900s photograph of the Point Pleasant Boy's Brigade shows an abundance of uniforms, rifles, and enthusiasm.

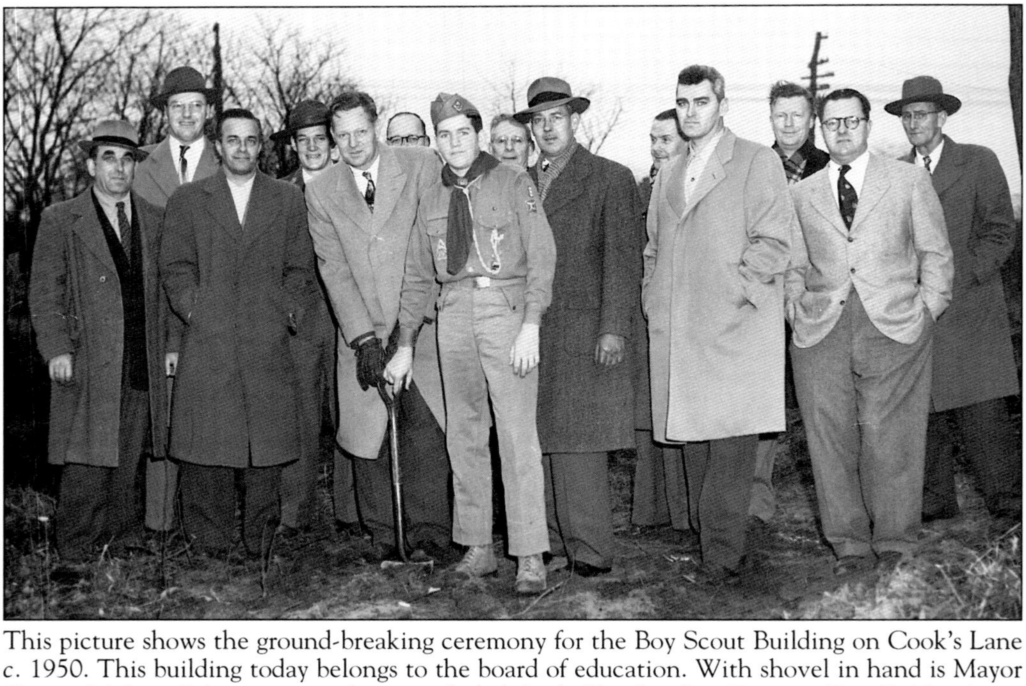

This picture shows the ground-breaking ceremony for the Boy Scout Building on Cook's Lane c. 1950. This building today belongs to the board of education. With shovel in hand is Mayor George Makin. Others in attendance included Andy Handzo, Les Genung, Ben Goble, Arnie Lane, Reverend John Townley, Dr. Bruce Hendrickson, and Norm Shoemaker.

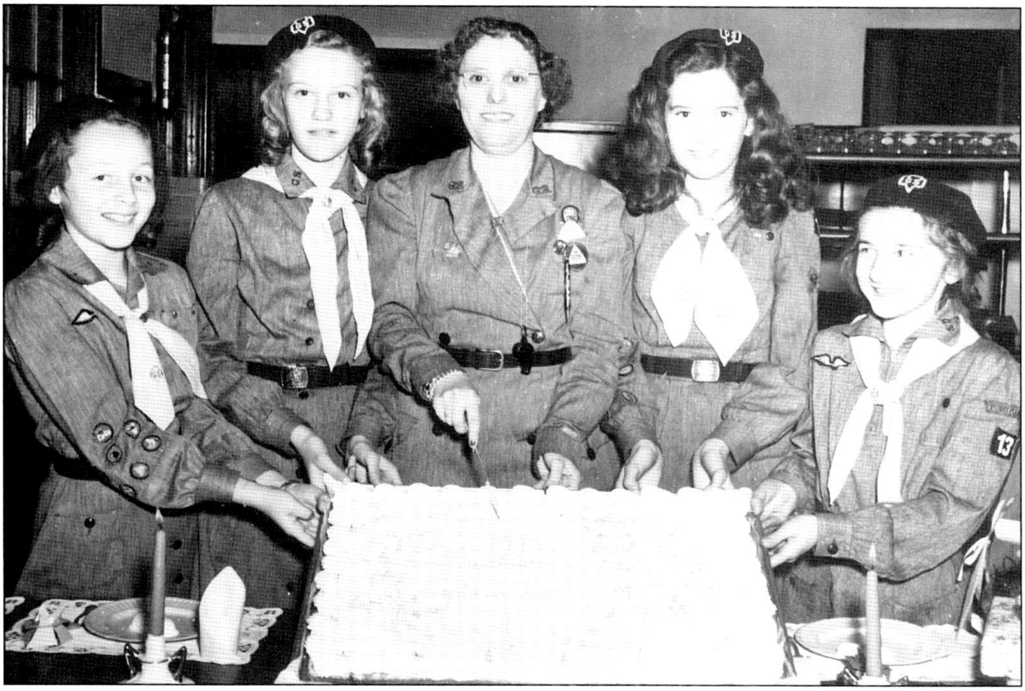

Members of Point Pleasant Girl Scout Troop #13 celebrate the birthday of their leader, Captain Ruth Coe, in 1946. Standing from left to right are Jill Lockwood, Beatrice Poland, Captain Coe, Ethel Mae Smetts, and Betty Lou Carson.

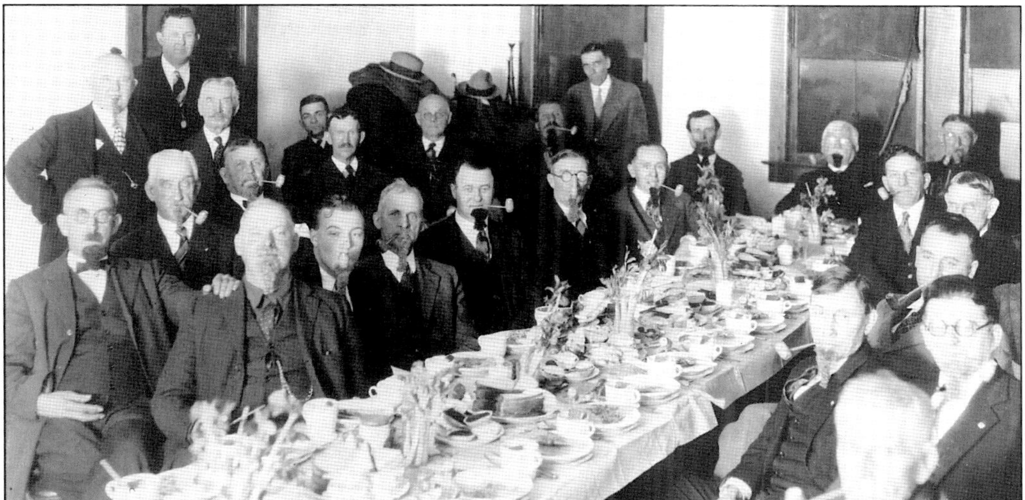

Members of the Citizen League organization gather in borough hall in 1930. Members from left to right are Elmer Errickson, Bill Stanford, Charles Imlay, Allie Pearce, Joe Elberson, unknown, Frank Shoemaker, Bill Errickson, Captain Robotham, Ralph Bruno, Albert Britton, George McGirr, Claude Saunders, Zeb VanNote, Harry Jacques, Frank Imlay, Vice President Harold Christie, Bill Boyd, President Dr. C.H. Grube, Clarence Lovell, Morris Nelson, Robert Thompson, Dewitt Ricketts, Secretary Asher Estelle, Harry Shoemaker, Reed Gager, and Henry Pearce.

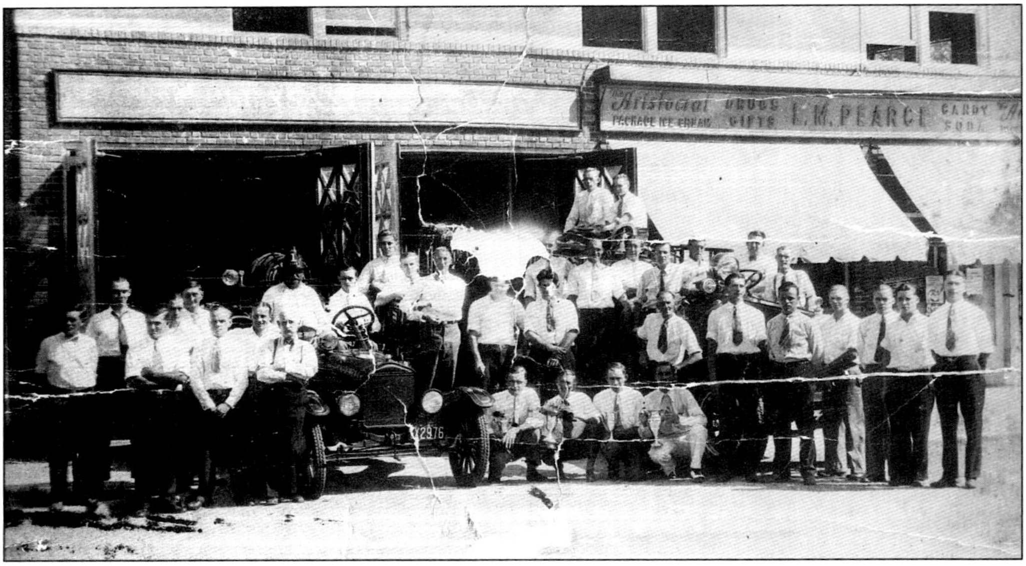

Members of the Point Pleasant Fire Company No. 1 show off their fire-fighting apparatus outside the firehouse in the original borough hall in 1931. This fire company was established in 1920 with the original engine house located on the north side of Lakewood Road between Arnold Avenue and the canal.

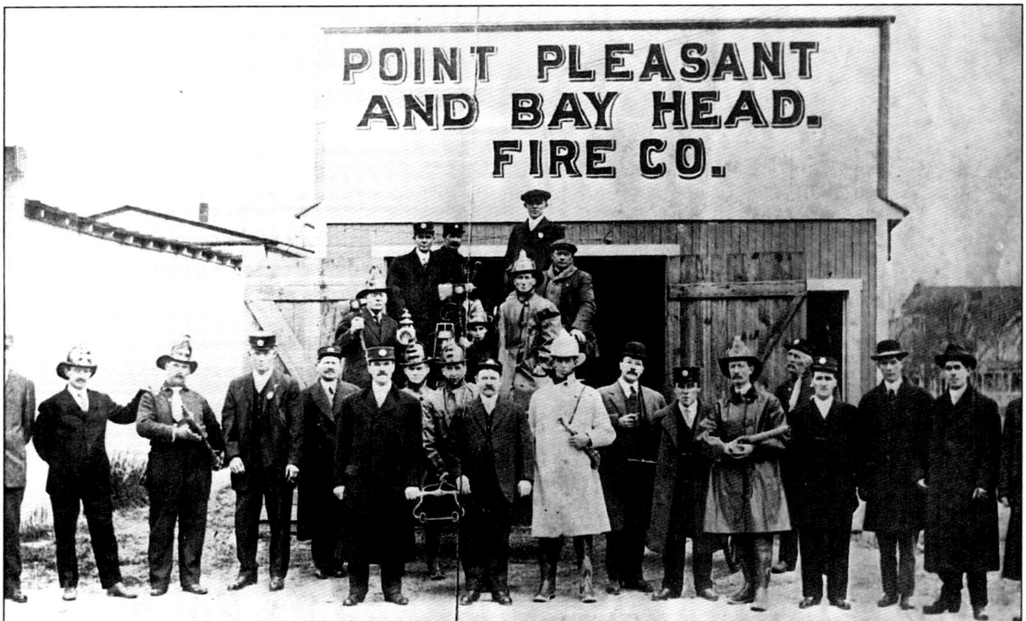

The Point Pleasant and Bay Head Fire Co. headquarters at Bay and Laurel Avenues is shown here in 1911. Standing from left to right are Joe Lynch, John Hawkins, Charlie Wolf, John Johnson, Dave Abromowitz, Roland Hatfield, Joe Vetrini, George Lewis, Chief Dory Pearce, John Laug, Garfield Birdsall, Joe Platt, Sam Chafey, Fred Pearce, Bill Smith, Ed Burge, and Jim Fitzgibbons. To the rear are John Phifer, Albert Fleming, Al Perry, John Callagan, Marty Hyers, and Arthur Birdsall.

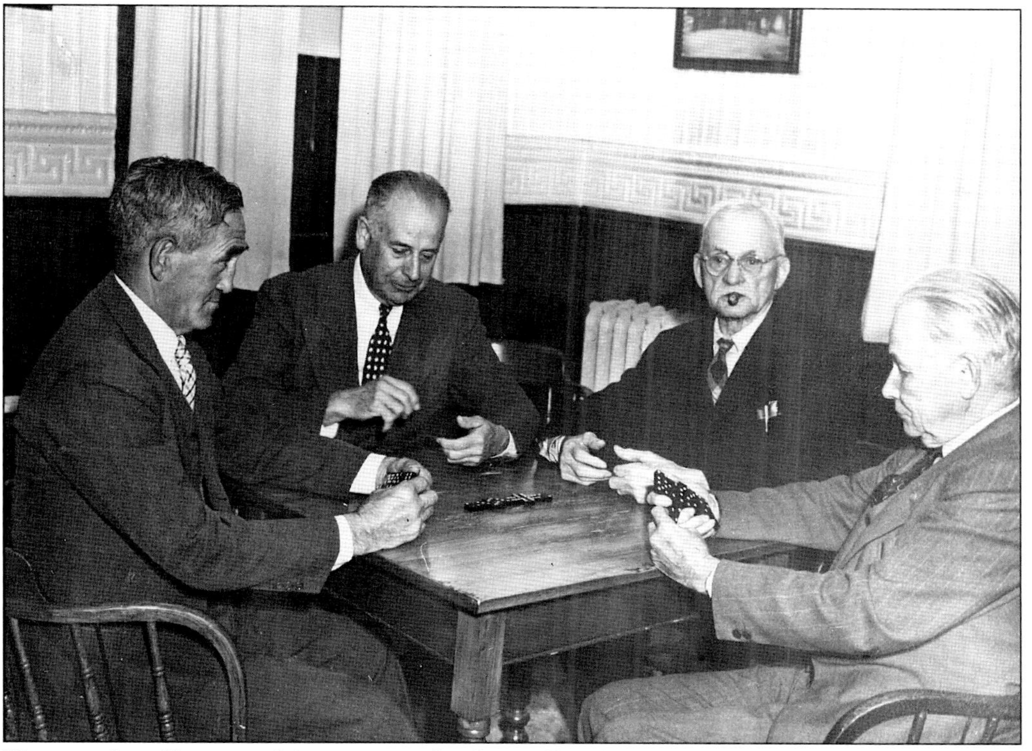

Playing a friendly game of dominoes in the Ocean Fire Company River Avenue station *c.* 1938 are Thad Havens, Dewitt Ricketts, Zeb VanNote, and Harry Shoemaker.

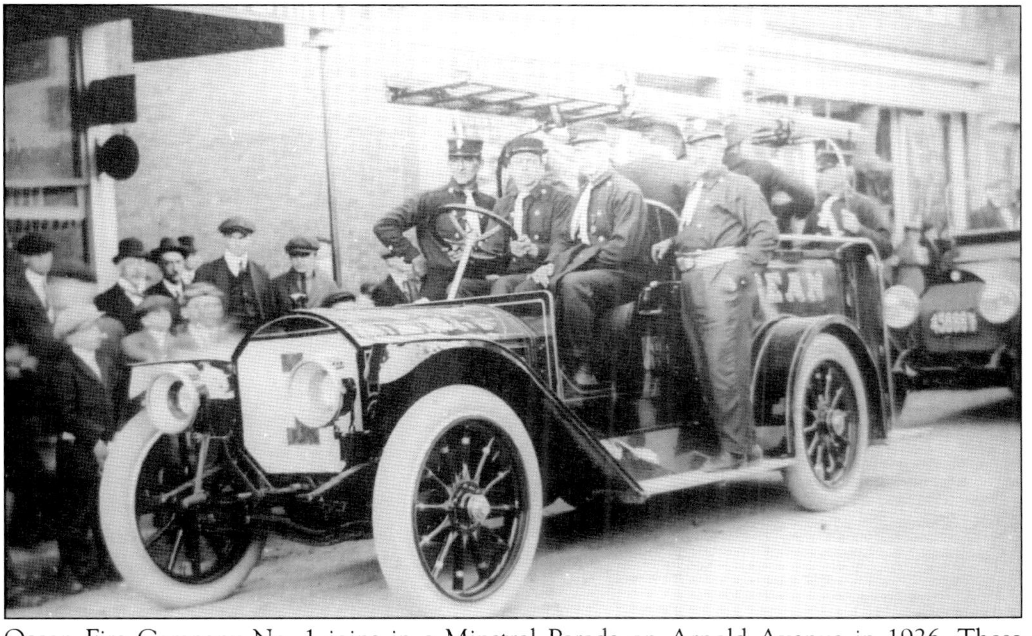

Ocean Fire Company No. 1 joins in a Minstrel Parade on Arnold Avenue in 1926. These events were held for the benefit of the local fire companies.

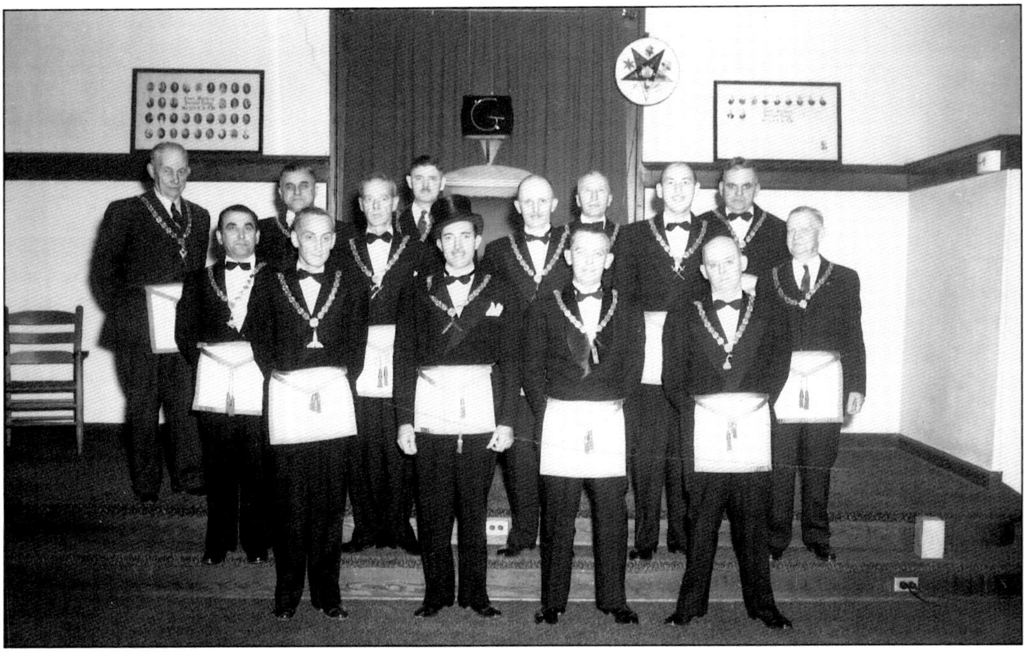

The Durand Masonic Lodge No. 179 - F. & A.M. was organized in Point Pleasant in 1904 and is now in its ninety-third year. The lodge members had met for many years in the Red Men's Hall on Arnold Avenue (above) before purchasing the present lodge at Richmond and New Jersey Avenues in 1951.

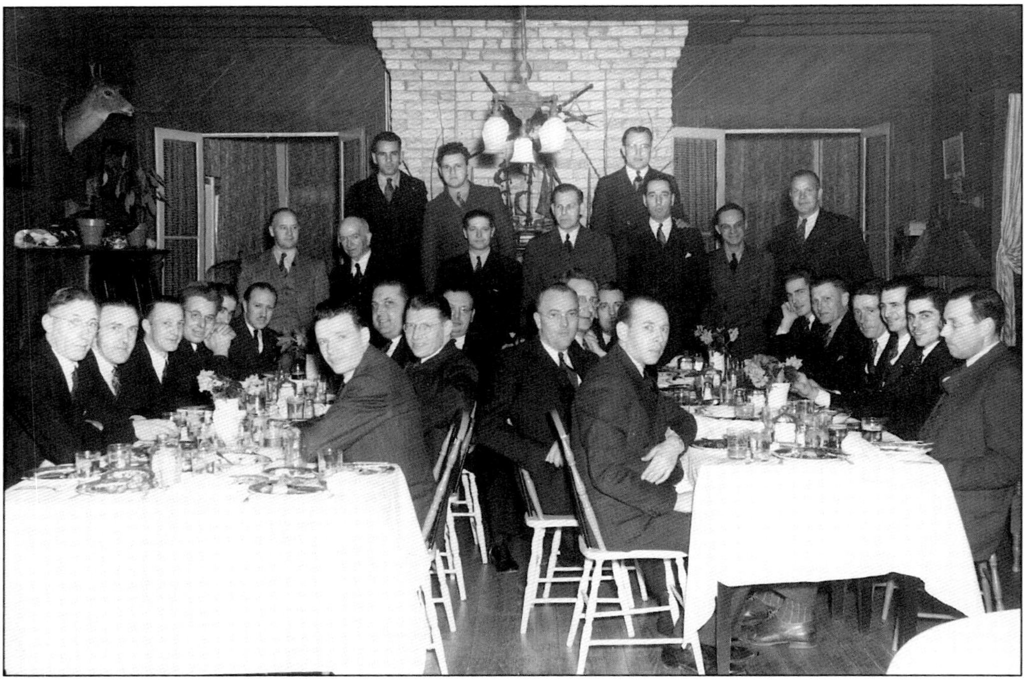

Many familiar faces can be seen here at a function for the Point Pleasant First Aid Squad in 1940. Can you name them?

Five

Let's Tour Point Pleasant

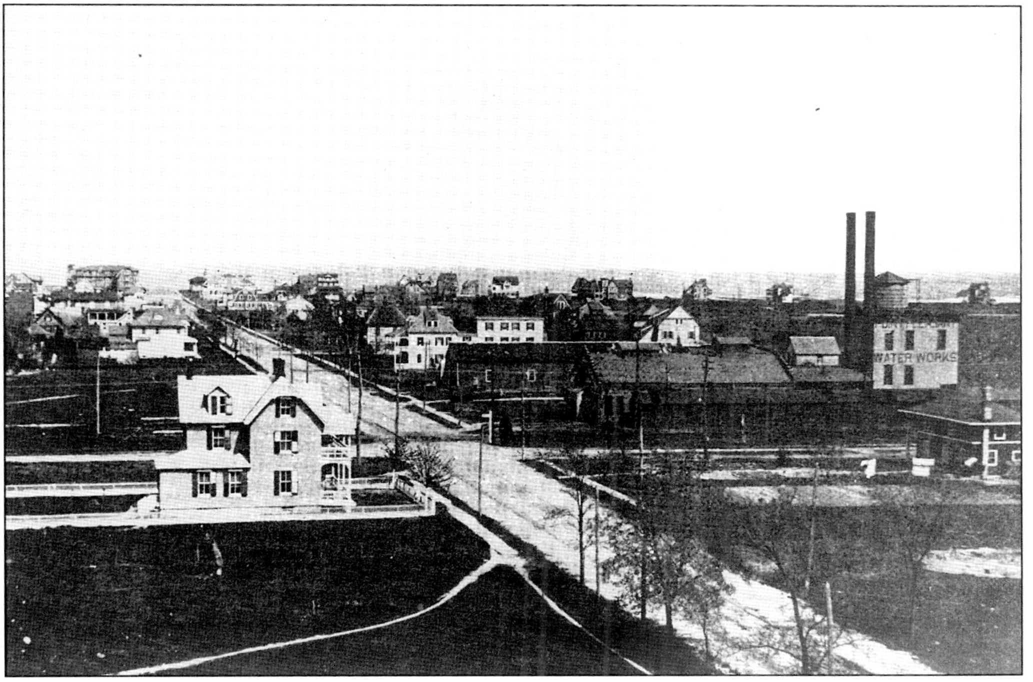

This was the view east from the tower of the Warwick Arms Hotel on Richmond Avenue in 1908. Trolley poles line Atlantic Avenue, and the trolley car barn and powerhouse—with its two 90-foot smoke stacks—are in the center of the photograph. The original waterworks is to the rear of the powerhouse on the right.

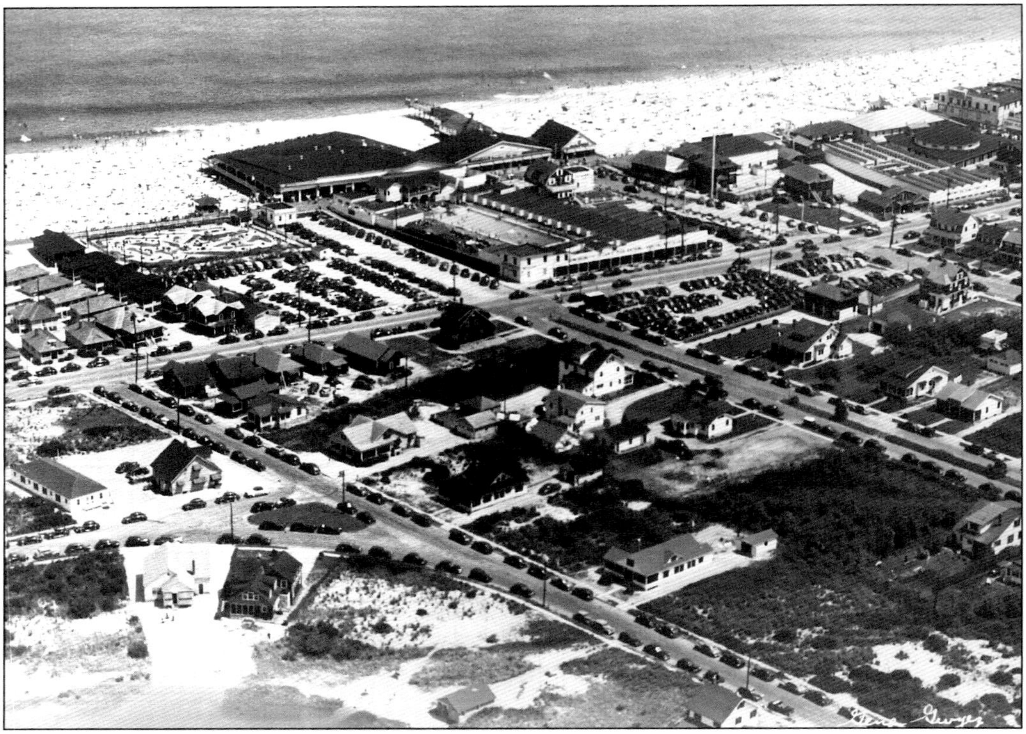

The beachfront between Niblick Street and Arnold Avenue is shown here as it looked in 1946.

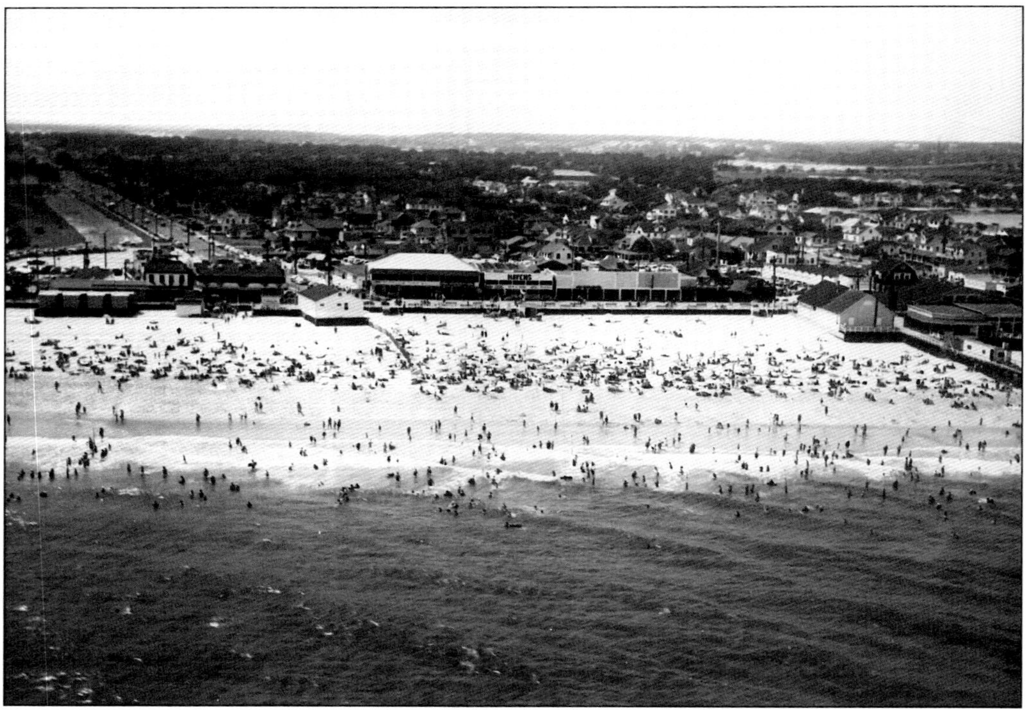

Summertime crowds enjoy the fresh sea breezes on Havens and Holiday Beaches in July 1956.

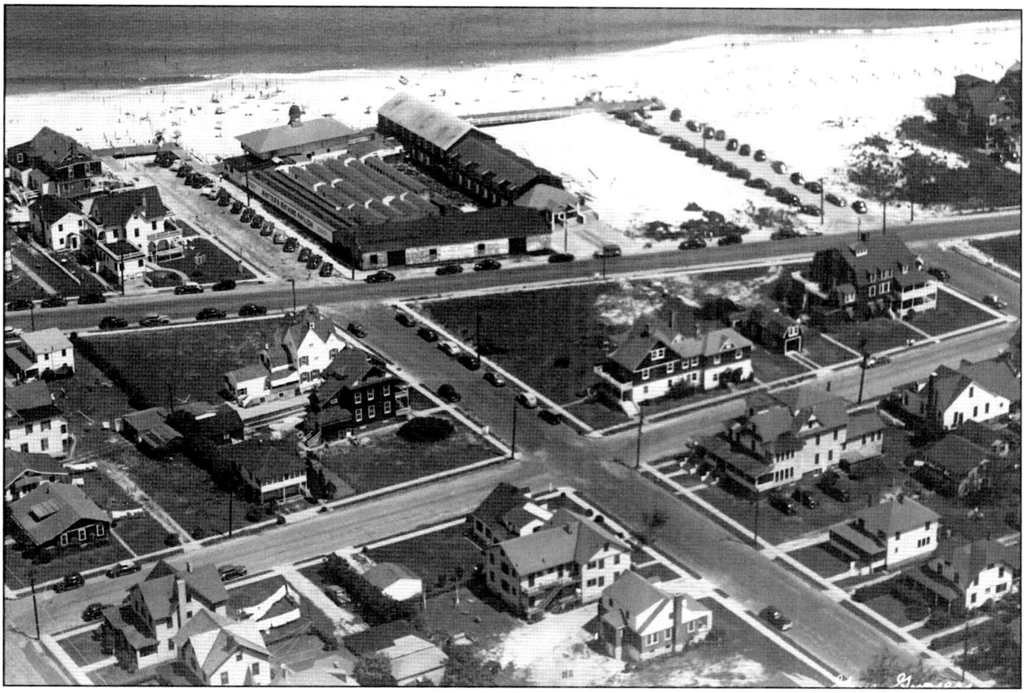

The beachfront resort business began at the old Resort House Pavilion with its familiar cupola and adjacent bathhouses at the foot of Atlantic Avenue in 1946. Adjacent to the south (right) is Risden's Casino.

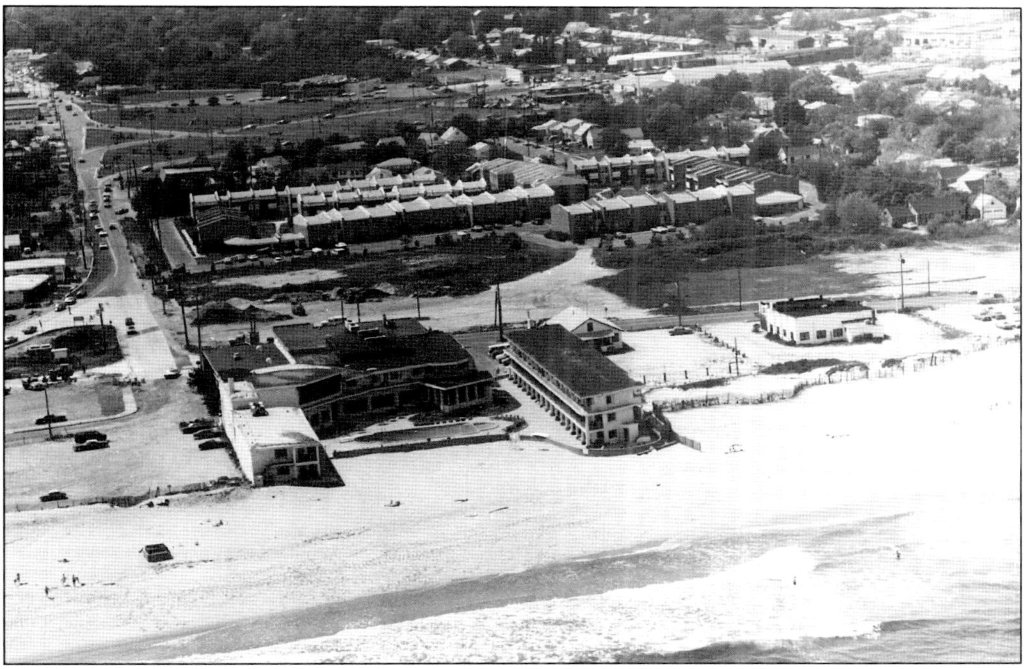

The Beacon Manor Motel and Beacon Garden Apartments at Ocean and Sea Avenues are shown here in 1977. The old O.B. Diner is visible in the distance.

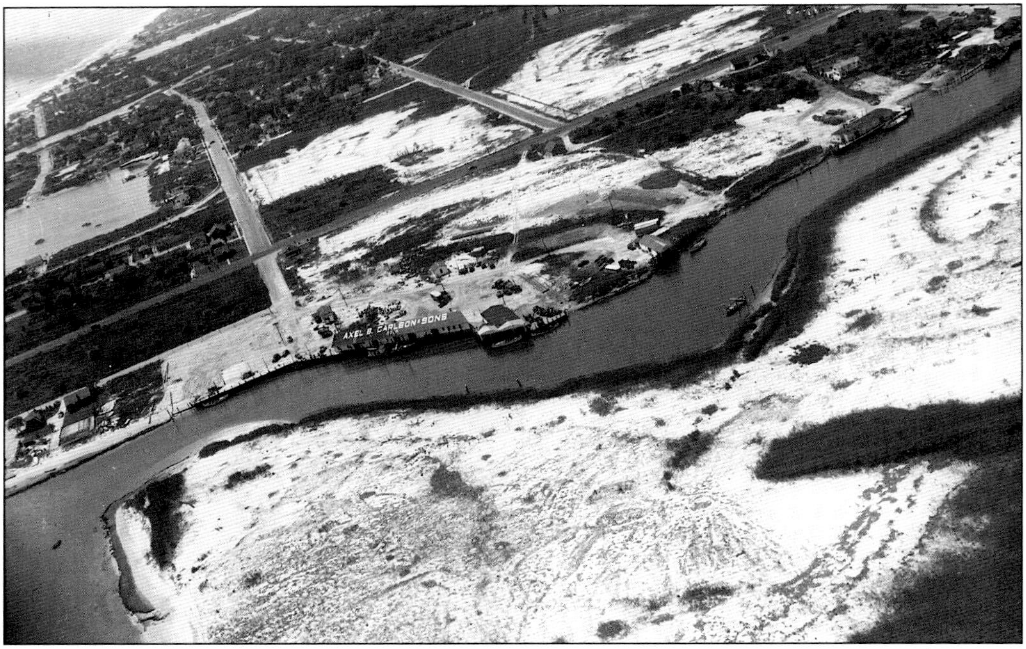

Will's Hole Thorofare and adjacent fisheries appear in this 1946 photograph. At this time, Channel Drive ended at Baltimore Avenue. Gull Island dominates the lower half of the photograph. Originally a mud flat and sedge in the Manasquan River, it was built up in the 1920s and '30s from dredging of the inlet, river, and Lake Louise.

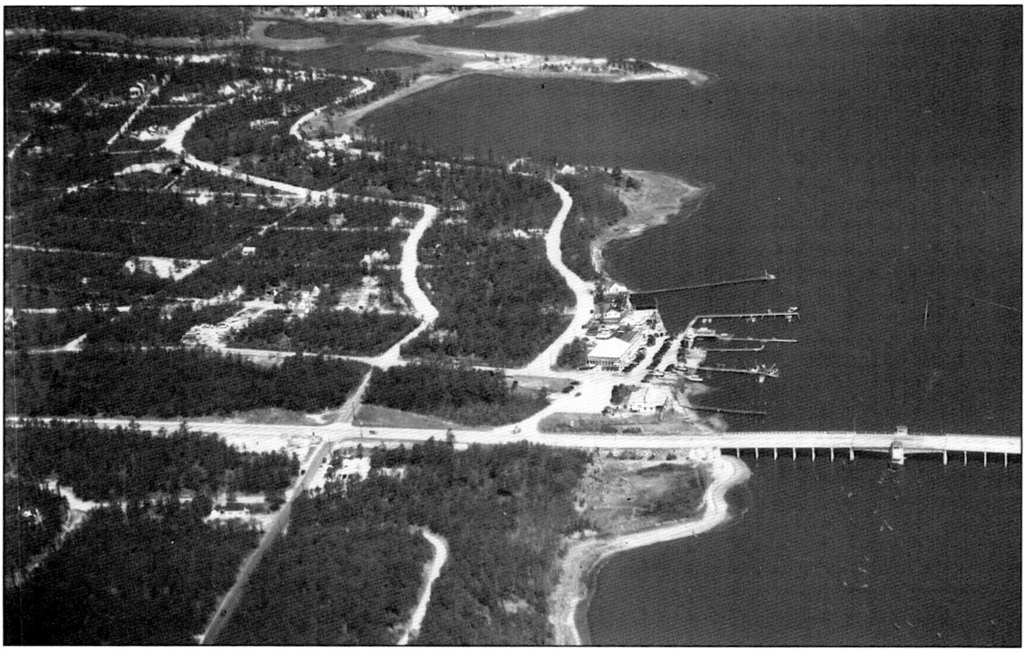

Shown here are the Route 70 bridge over the Manasquan River and the view west toward Riviera Beach in Brick Township in 1948. The woods to the east of Route 70 in the lower center is the present site of the Crystal Point Inn and marina.

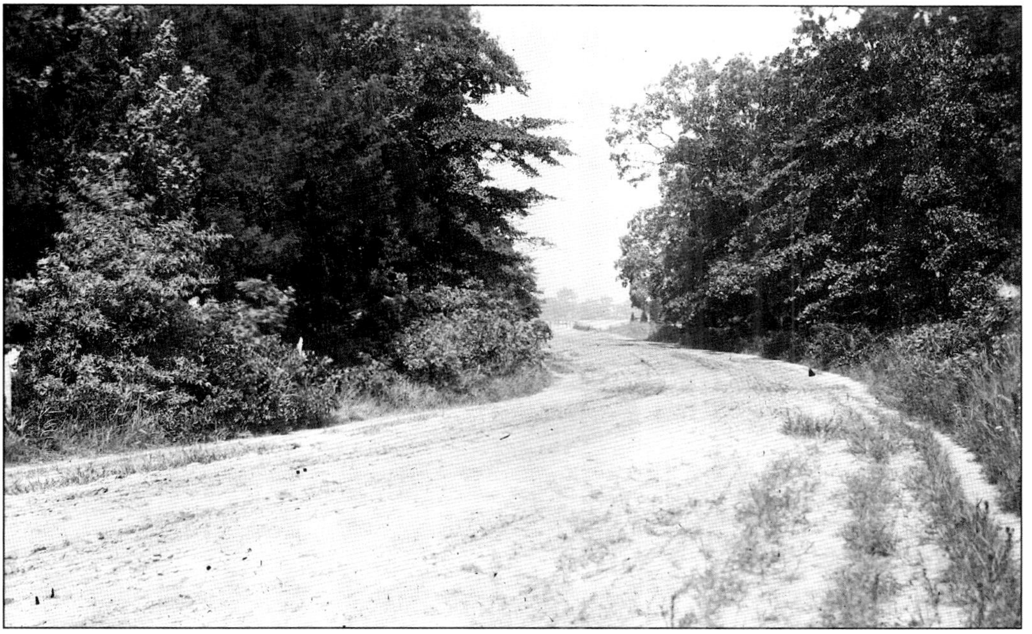

River Avenue approaches the Manasquan River bridge in 1896. Nestled in the woods to the right is Nestor and Carrie Sanborn's Manasquan Cottage (see p. 54). This site today is the intersection of Broadway and Route 35.

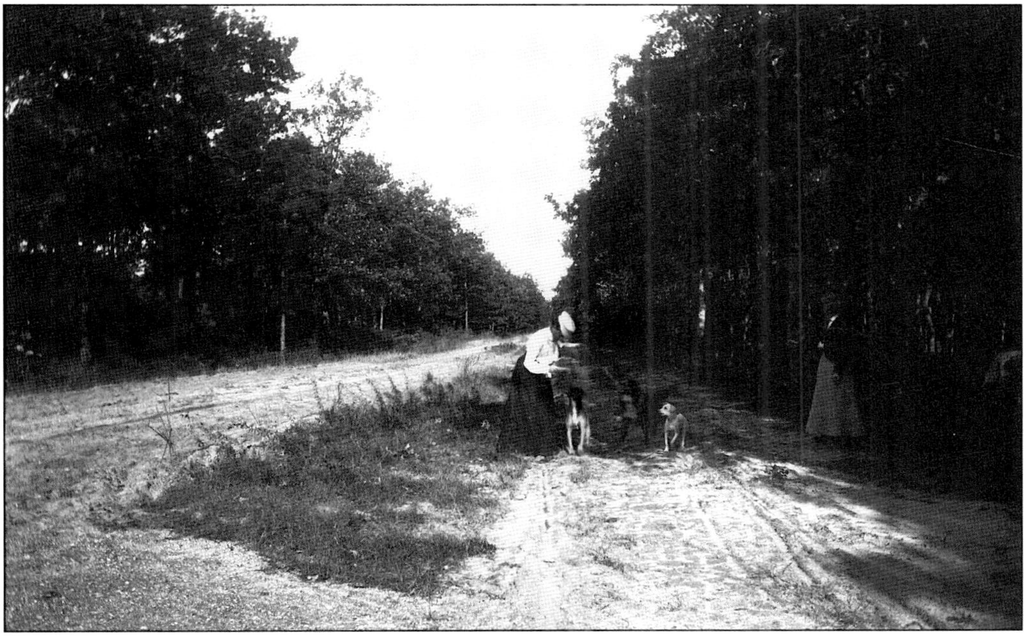

This view looks east on Herbertsville Road near the present Jaenel Parkway in Point Pleasant about 1899. According to records in Monmouth County, Herbertsville Road in Point Pleasant (originally Burnt Tavern Road) was laid out at a width of 3 rods (50 feet) in 1804. The upper portion of Herbertsville Road leading through Brick Township was recorded in the *Monmouth County Book of Roads* in 1822.

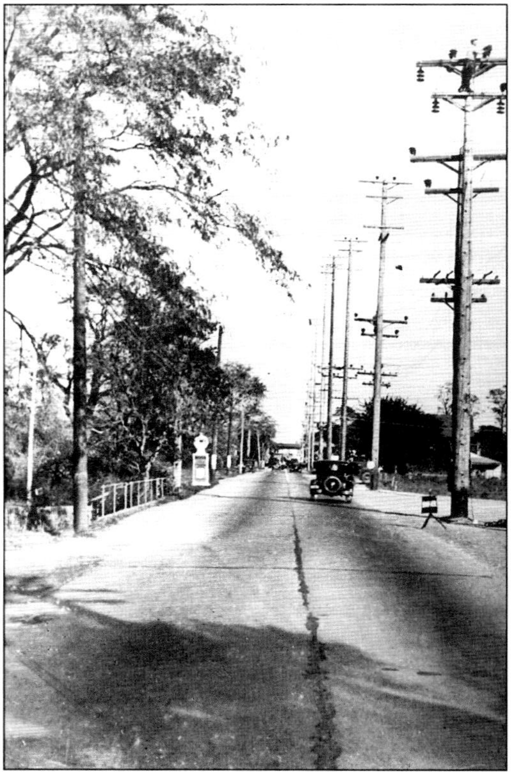

Lakewood Road (Route 88) is shown looking east from Herbertsville Road about 1925. New power poles over 100 feet in height are shown being installed to span the new Manasquan River-Bay Head Canal. These poles caused such hazardous conditions during lightning storms that they were later shortened.

This view looks north on Maxson Road at the intersection with Herbertsville Road in Point Pleasant in 1952. This area was part of the John Maxson farm and was laid out with streets and lots in the 1880s. Point Pleasant's first try at incorporation under the name Point Pleasant Heights in 1911 included this area between Lakewood Road and the Manasquan River.

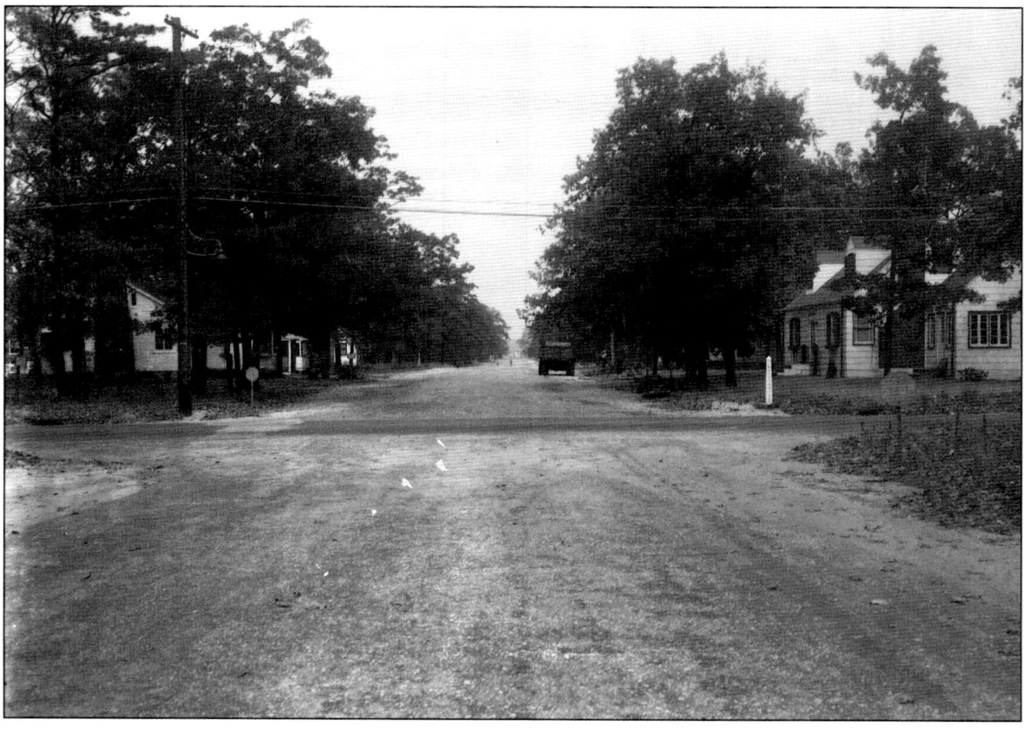

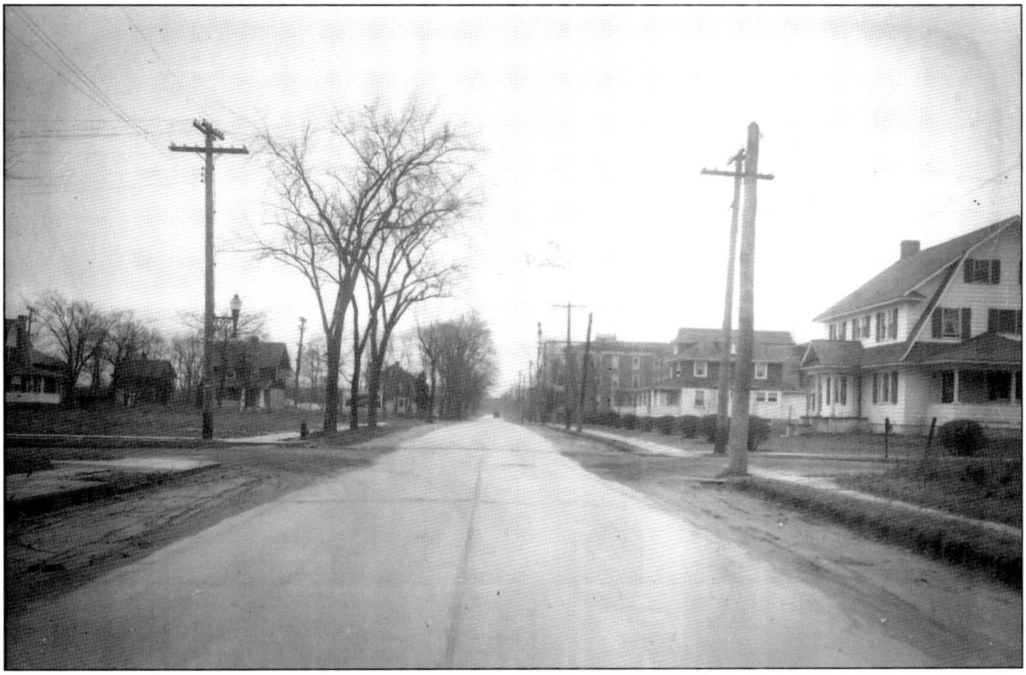

In this view, we are heading south on Richmond Avenue at the intersection with Forman Avenue in 1924. Richmond Avenue was opened from this point south to Sea Avenue in 1914. The house on the extreme right is today the chiropractic office of Dr. Steven Lenahan. Fifteen years earlier this property was the site of the Resort House/Warwick Arms Hotel.

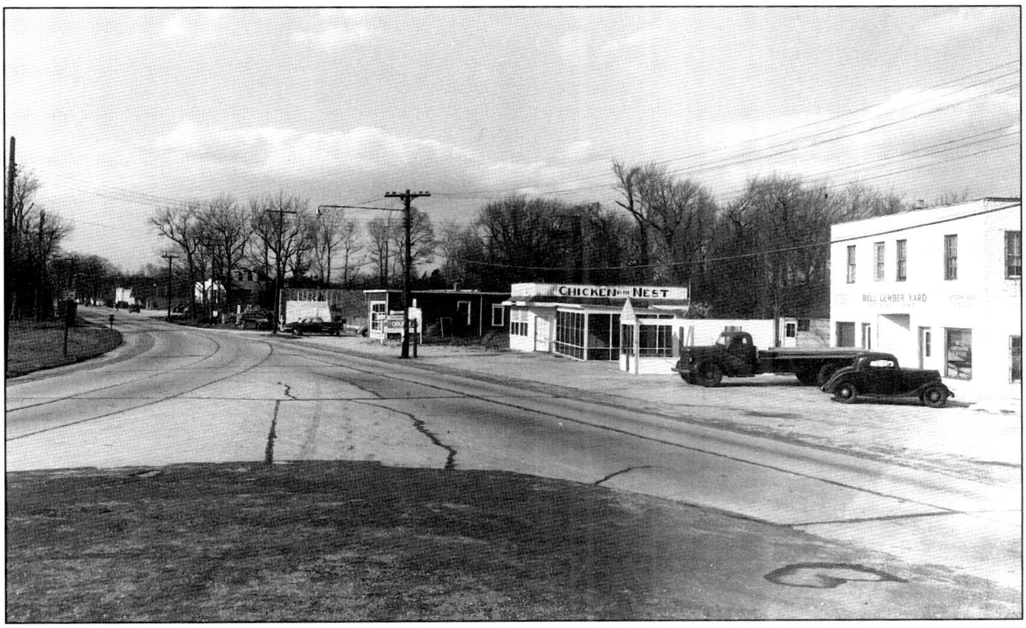

The south end of Richmond Avenue (shown here in 1946) was referred to through the 1950s as the "Million Dollar Mile." The view is toward the north. The Bell Lumber Yard on the extreme right is today the site of Surf Chevrolet.

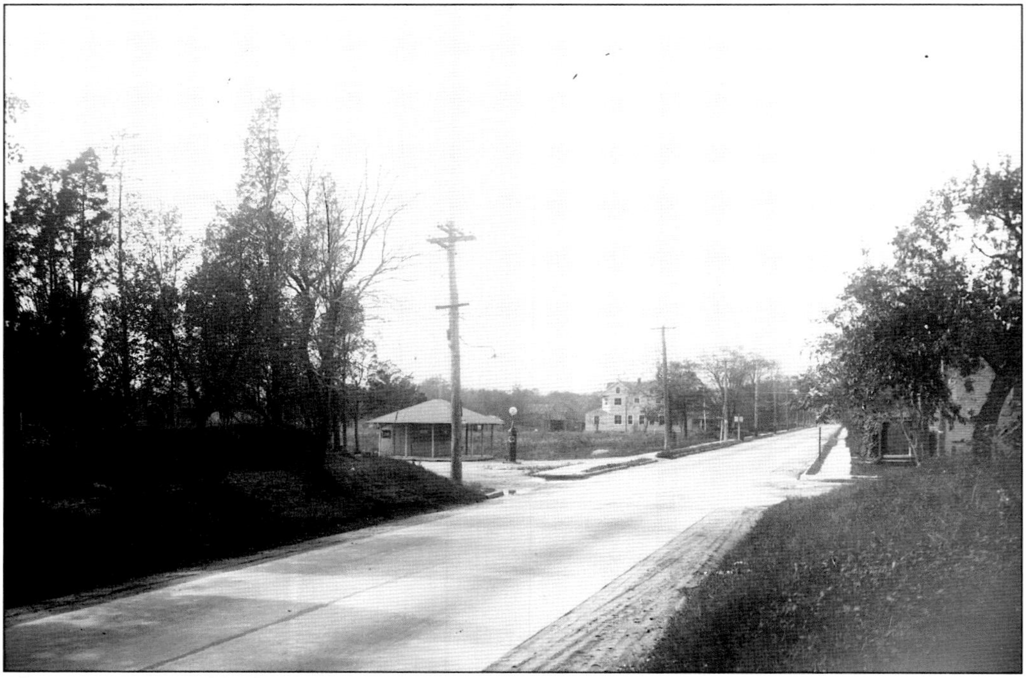

This is Ocean Road looking west at the intersection of Bay Avenue in 1924. Early records show that Ocean Road was originally known as the "Road to the Sea" and also provided access to an early sportsman's club on the beach, later to become the Beacon Hotel.

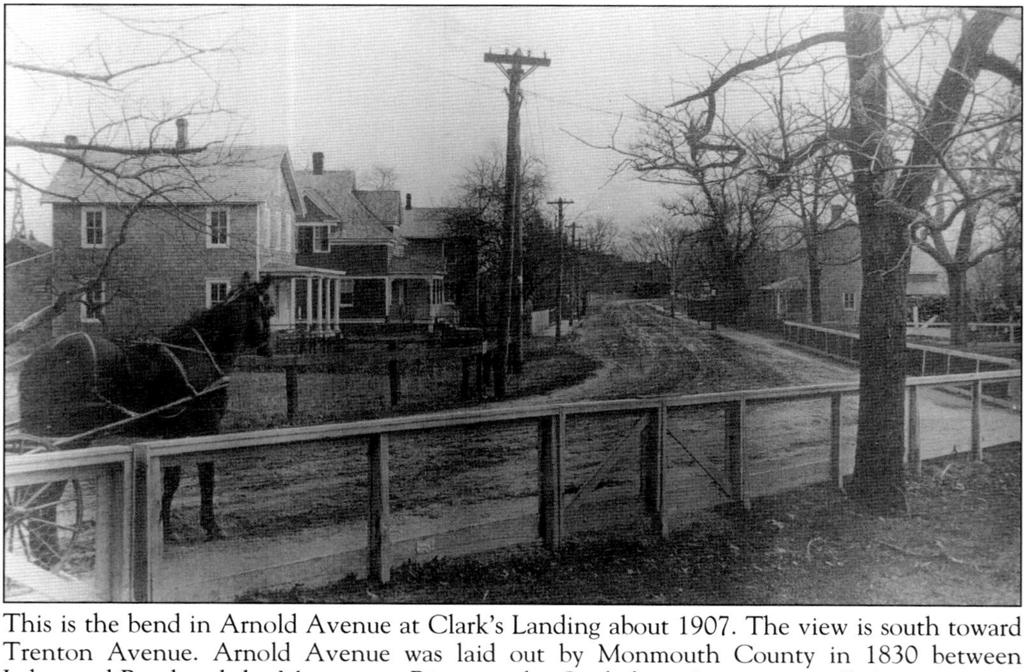

This is the bend in Arnold Avenue at Clark's Landing about 1907. The view is south toward Trenton Avenue. Arnold Avenue was laid out by Monmouth County in 1830 between Lakewood Road and the Manasquan River on the Cook farm. It was originally known as the "Road Leading to Thomas Cook's Place."

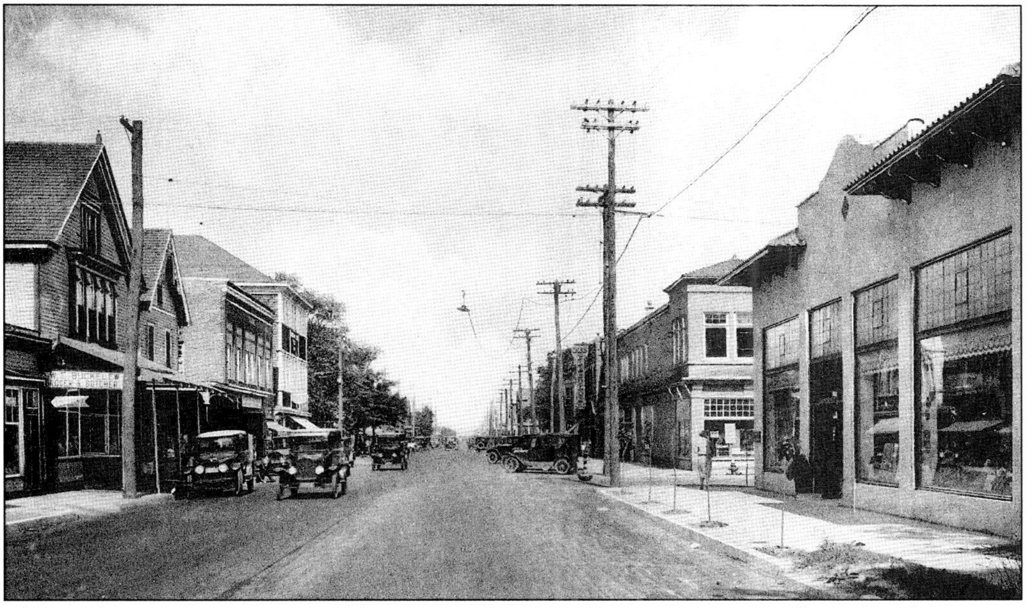

This is the view east on Arnold Avenue near Bay Avenue in 1925. The new Abromowitz Department Store is on the right, while Buckelew's Market, Point Pleasant Bakery, Gottlieb's Department Store, and Arnold Hall are on the left. This intersection was still the major center of business in Point Pleasant Beach in the 1920s.

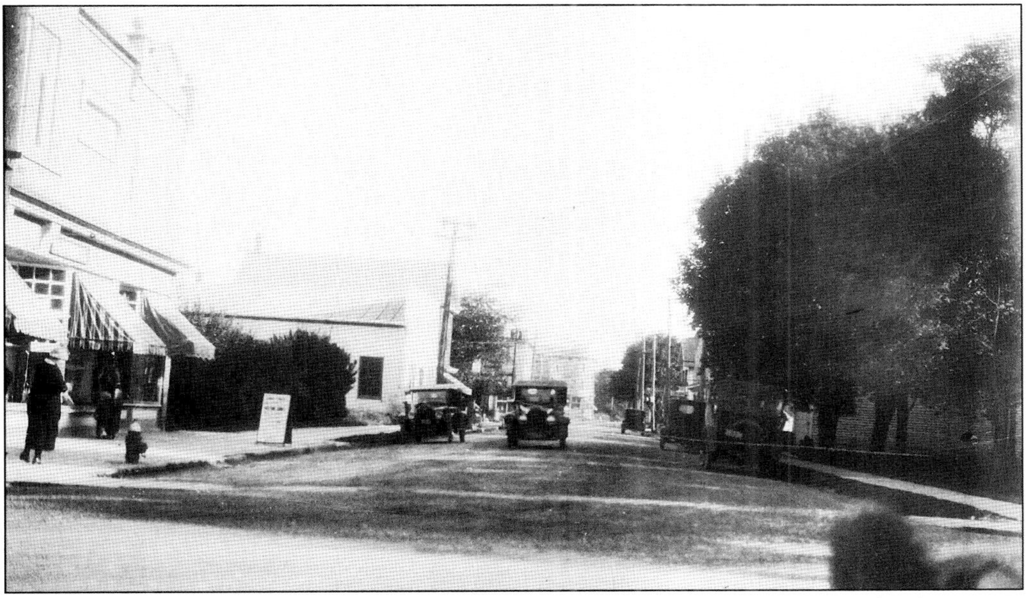

This is Bay Avenue south from Arnold Avenue c. 1918. Bay Avenue was opened by the county between Arnold Avenue and Ocean Road in 1874 and was originally known as Squan Avenue. Bay Avenue was later extended south to Barnegat Bay, accompanied by the appropriate change in name.

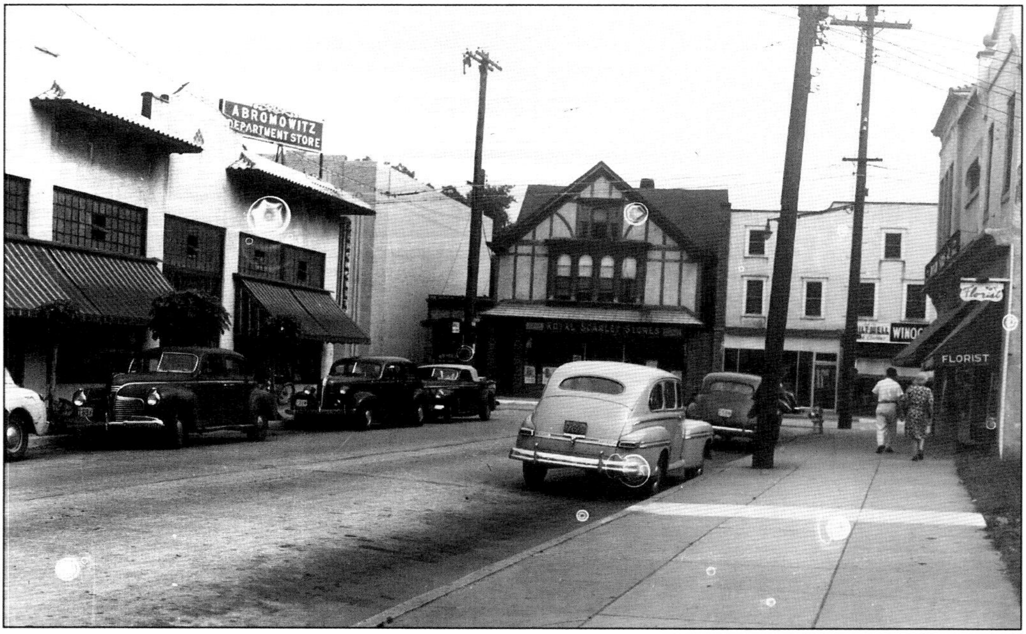

The intersection of Bay and Arnold Avenues in Point Pleasant Beach is shown here in 1947. Stores on the corner that existed at this time included, from left to right, Abromowitz Department Store, Ocean Federal Savings and Loan, Buckelew's Royal Scarlett Market, Winograd's Department Store, an American Food Store, and Dillon's Florist. Notice the spacious sidewalks that existed prior to the widening of Bay Avenue in the mid-1950s.

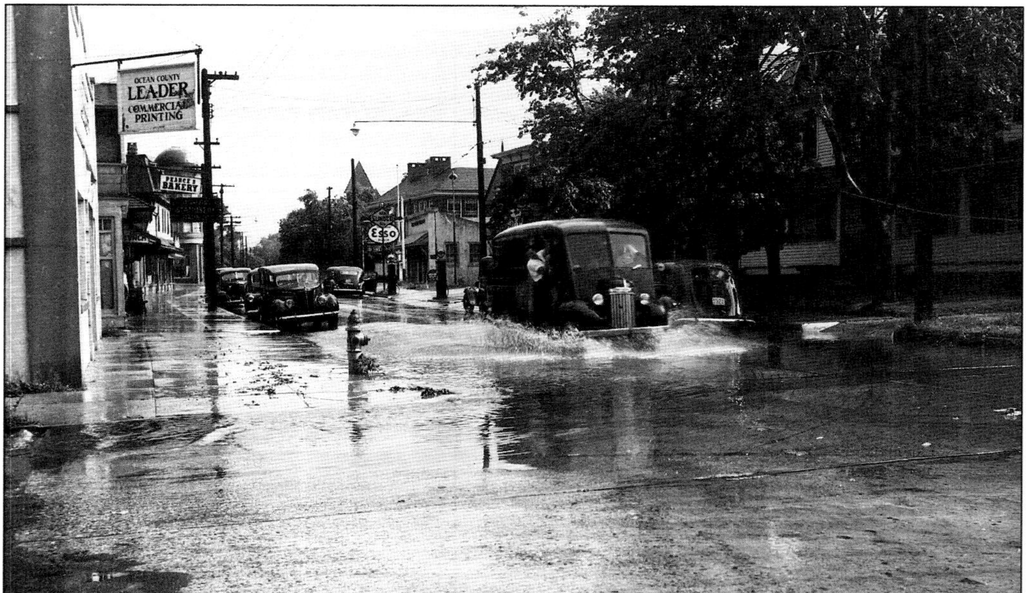

Bay Avenue had its share of problems as a busy business thoroughfare, including drainage woes and the fact that it was much too narrow. These discrepancies were corrected in 1956 when Bay Avenue was widened (at the expense of the roomy sidewalks) and electric service was moved underground between Arnold and Trenton Avenues.

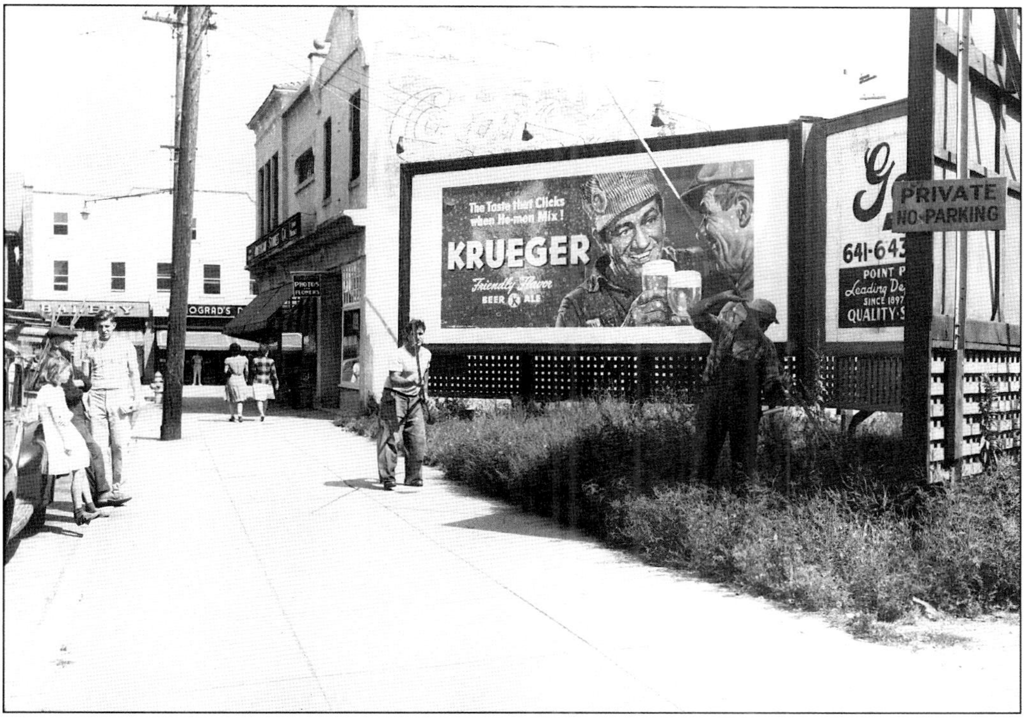

These billboards on Bay Avenue, shown in 1944, go back more than sixty years. Prior to that, the south wall of the concrete Wheeler Building on the corner was used for advertising. This was the site of the Gem Airdome open-air theater, which was operated by David Abromowitz during the summer months from 1912 to 1915.

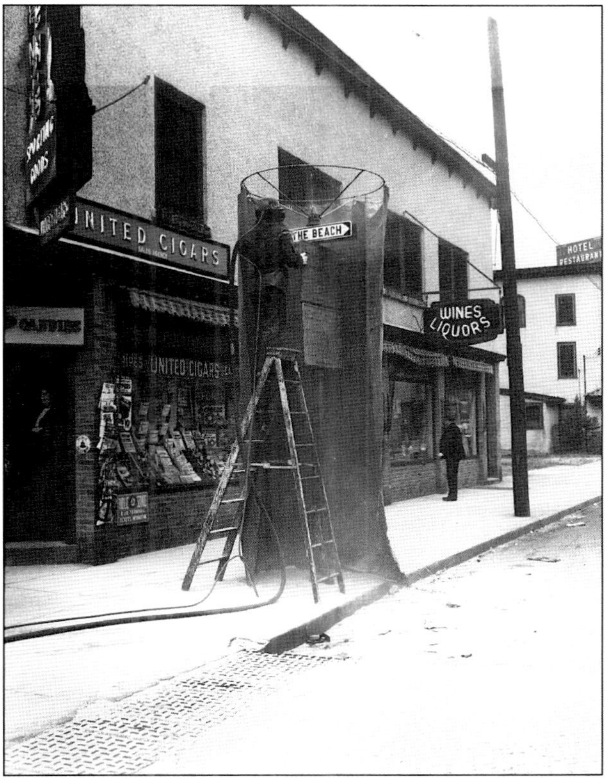

A street sign outside of Borden's at Richmond and Arnold Avenues is refurbished in 1939. These sturdy cast signs were located at every major intersection on the state highways and were routinely sandblasted prior to getting a new coat of paint.

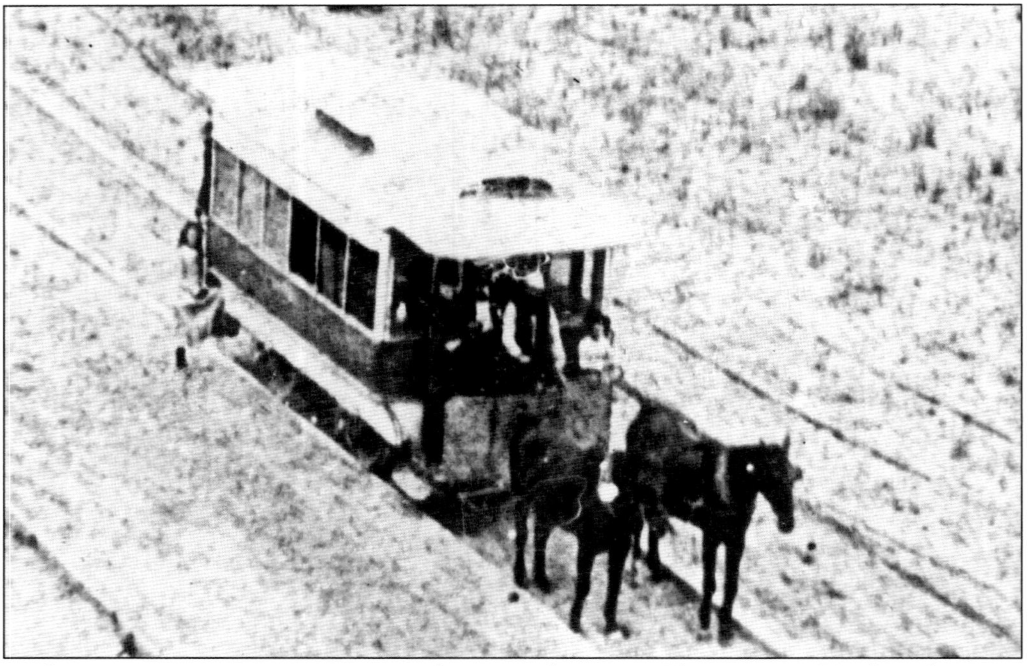

Modern mass transportation, as it was, first arrived in Point Pleasant in 1878 when the Point Pleasant Land Company began operation of a horse-drawn trolley. The tracks ran along Atlantic Avenue from the Resort House to the beach and this trolley was the first of its kind on the Jersey Shore. The horse trolley line was abandoned in 1890.

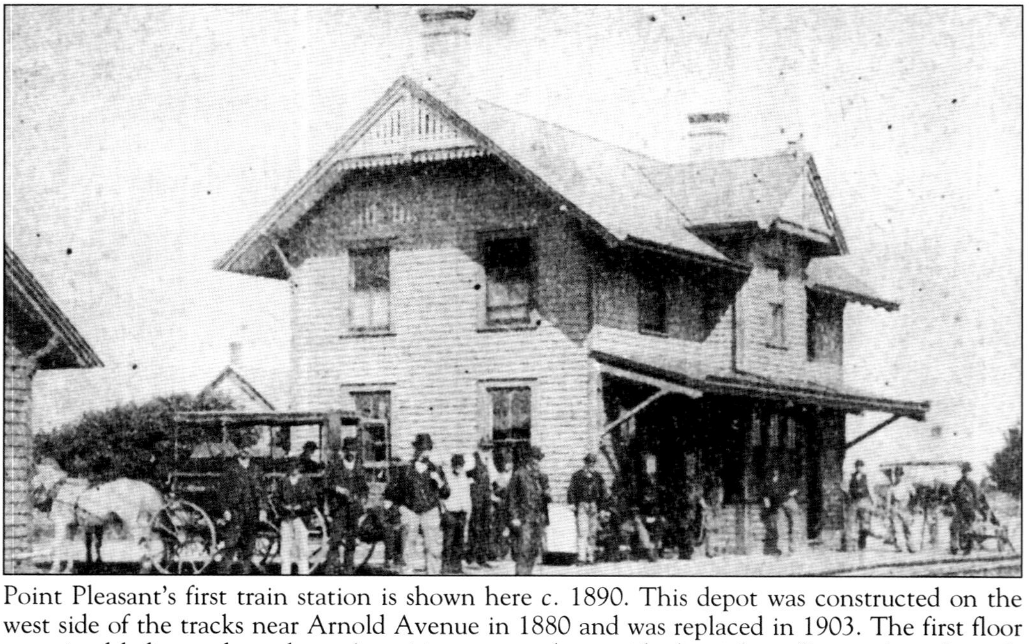

Point Pleasant's first train station is shown here c. 1890. This depot was constructed on the west side of the tracks near Arnold Avenue in 1880 and was replaced in 1903. The first floor contained ladies and gentlemen's waiting rooms along with the ticket office and a telegraph station. The second floor apartment was occupied by the ticket agent and his family. The station was moved across Railroad Square next to the bank and was torn down in 1939.

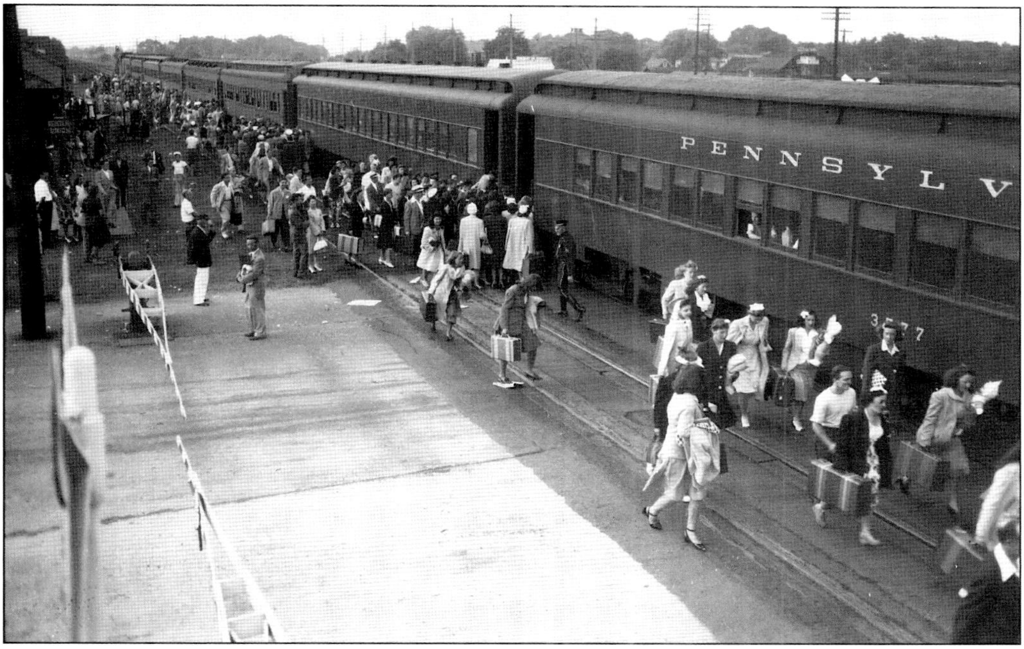

It's July 5, 1943, and a northbound Pennsylvania Railroad train rapidly fills with departing holiday vacationers. Until the completion of the Garden State Parkway in 1954, the train was still the easiest way to get to the shore from the big cities.

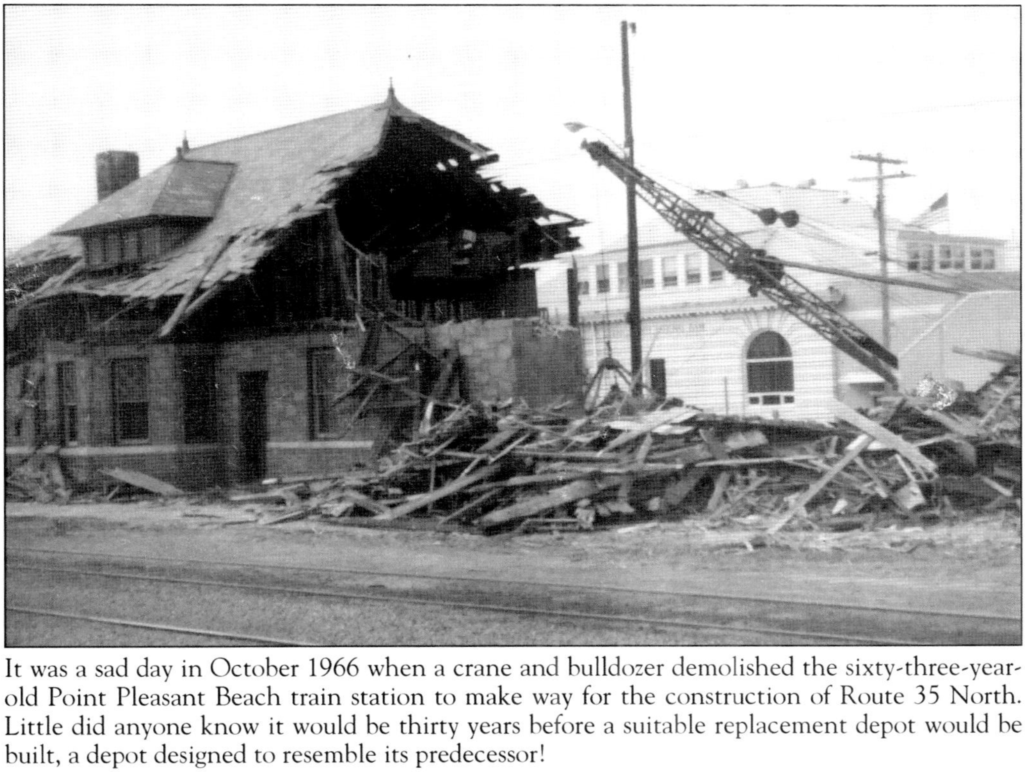

It was a sad day in October 1966 when a crane and bulldozer demolished the sixty-three-year-old Point Pleasant Beach train station to make way for the construction of Route 35 North. Little did anyone know it would be thirty years before a suitable replacement depot would be built, a depot designed to resemble its predecessor!

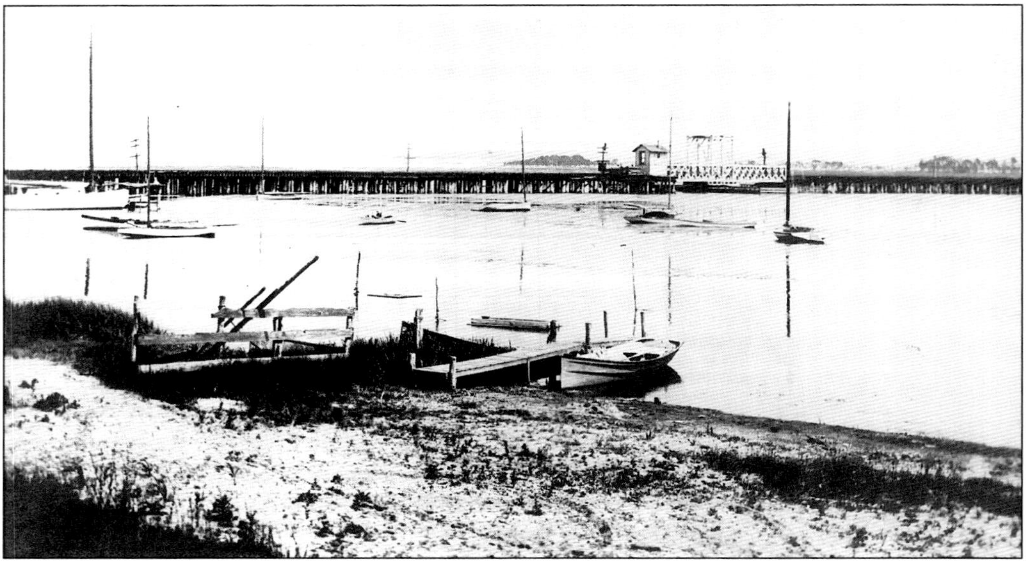

The Manasquan River railroad bridge is shown from the Brielle shore in 1906. The all-wood trestle was a source of constant headaches to railroad officials, what with worm-eaten piling, fires, and occasional storm damage. The original swing draw was replaced with another in 1895 and the southern half of the trestle was buried with fill . . . much to the protests of residents on the southern bank of the river. The railroad owners always seemed to get their way.

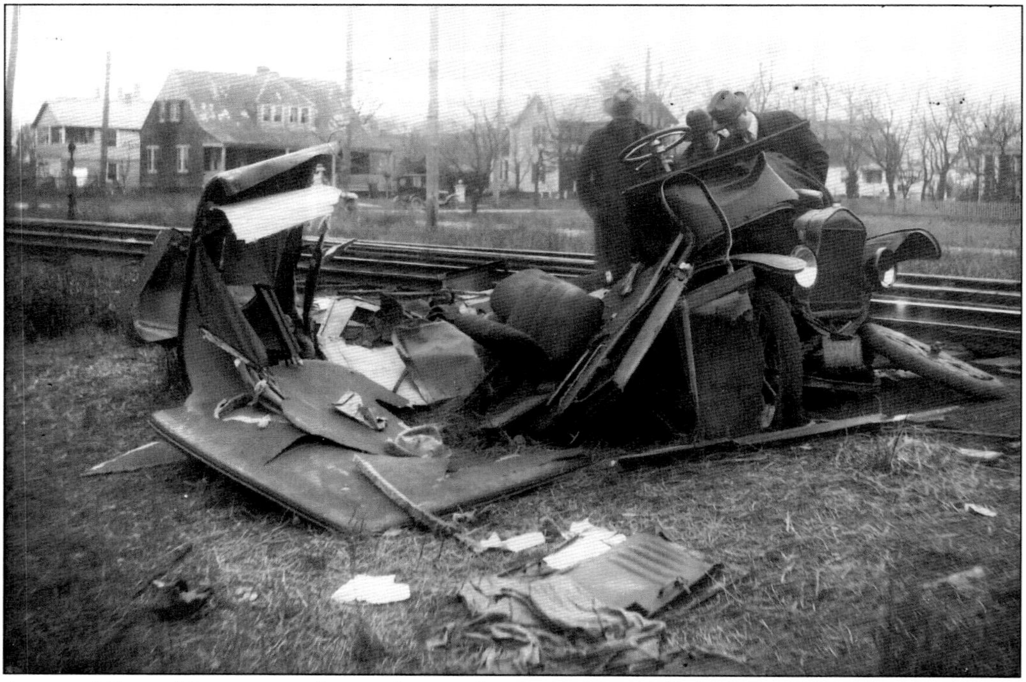

Automobile and locomotive hit at this grade crossing, as well as at many others. The lack of warning signals combined with the large volume of train activity made this grisly scene much more common than it is today. This car came to rest on the east side of the tracks between Forman and Trenton Avenues in 1926.

Six

Going Downtown

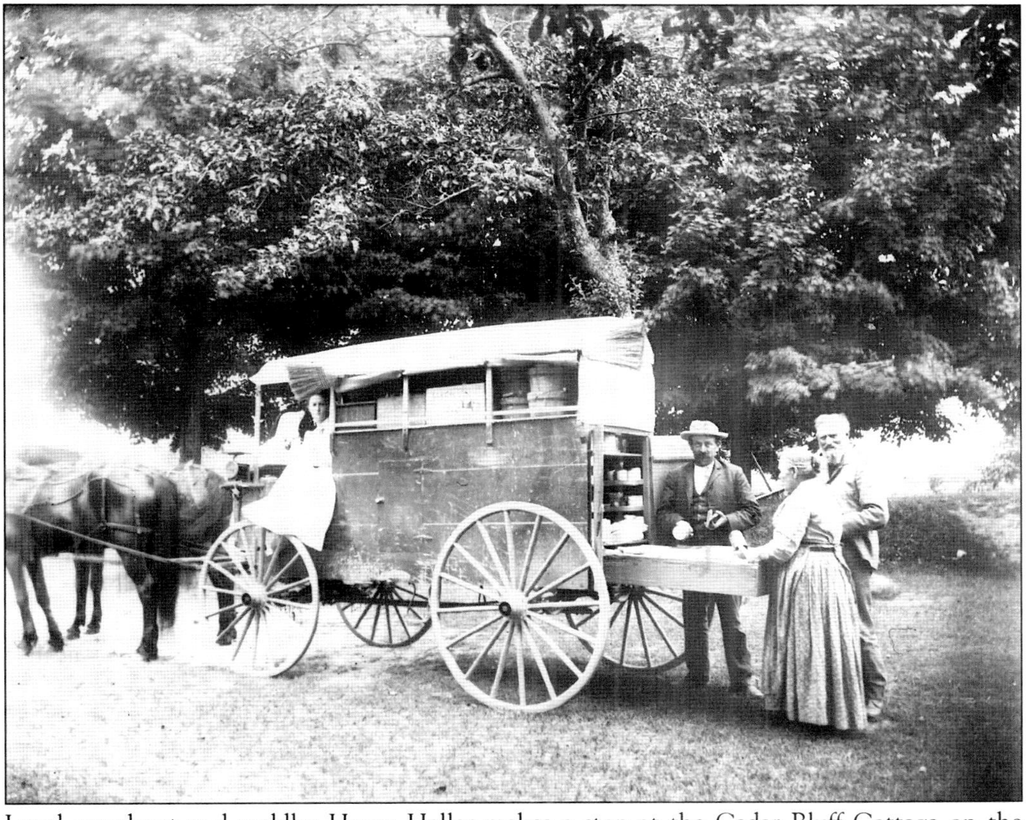

Local merchant and peddler Henry Heller makes a stop at the Cedar Bluff Cottage on the Manasquan River in 1900. Heller sold his dry goods from his wagon up and down the shore. He later purchased the Hendrickson Building on Bay Avenue in Point Pleasant Beach.

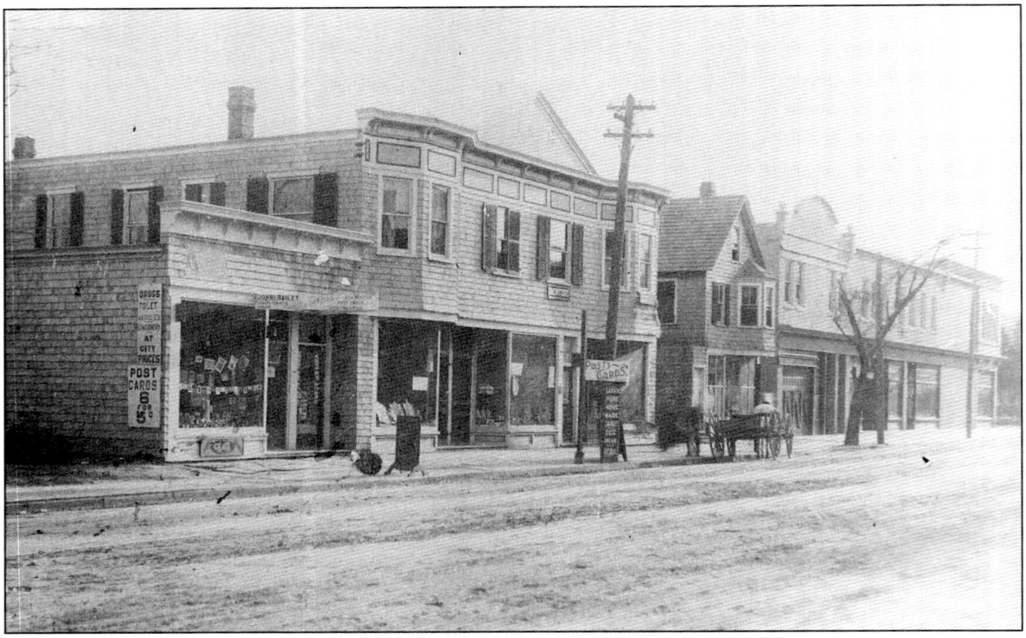

The south side of Arnold Avenue between River and Bay Avenues is shown here in 1910. The Laug Building (left), the William Todd residence, and the all-concrete Wheeler Building were all built after the devastating fire of 1906, which leveled this part of town (see Vol. I, p. 34).

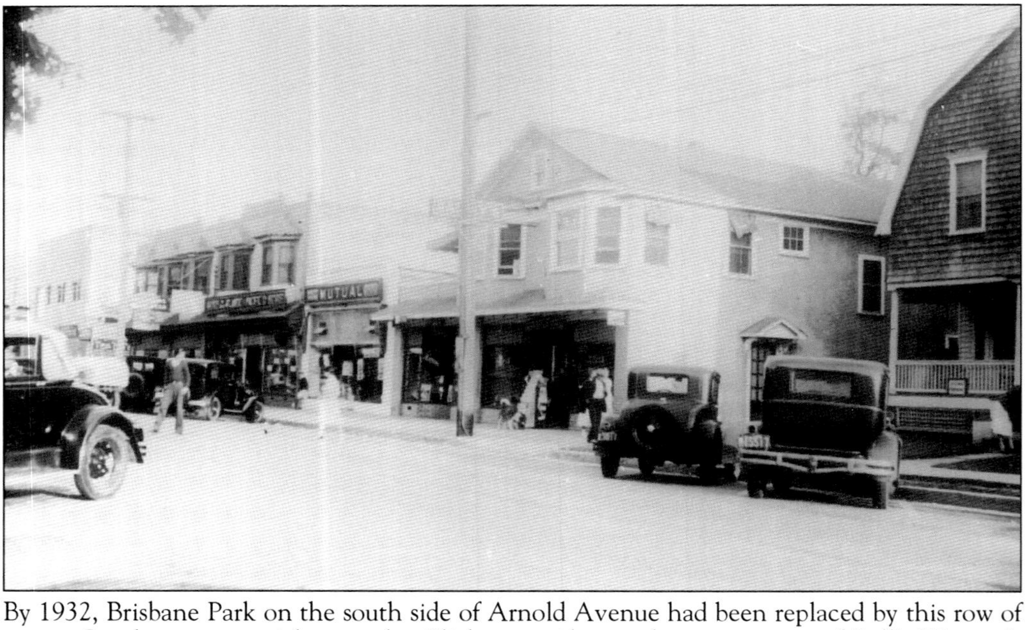

By 1932, Brisbane Park on the south side of Arnold Avenue had been replaced by this row of stores. On the extreme right was the Clickner residence, the present site of Bell's Women's Fashions, followed to the left by the John Bailey Building and the present Woolworth Building, which housed an A&P and other businesses.

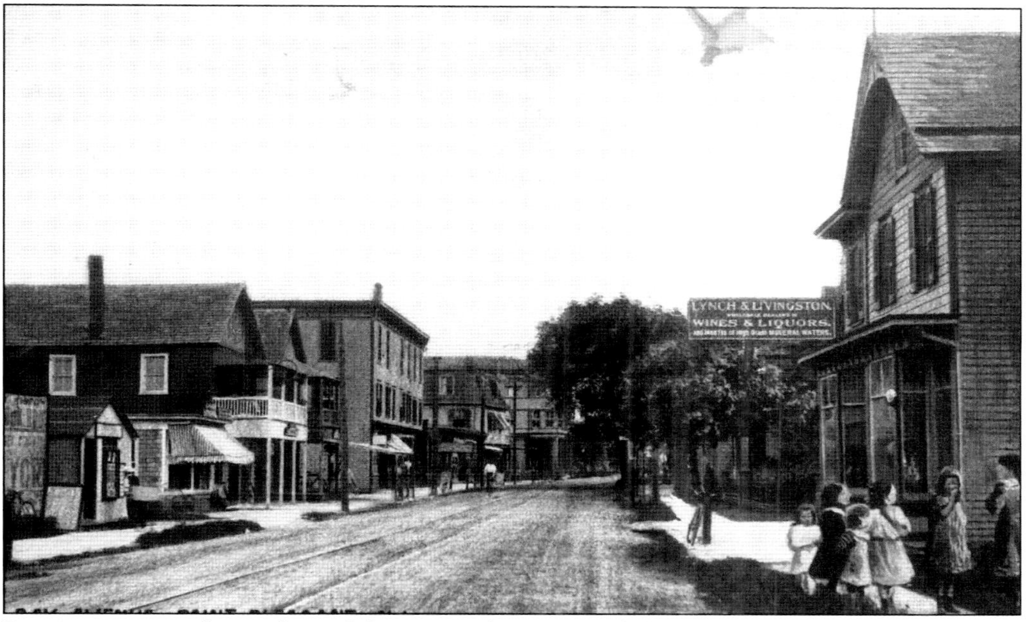

Bay Avenue was the nucleus of the Point Pleasant Beach business district at the turn of the century. The three-story structure at left center was the Hendrickson Building, the second home of the Point Pleasant Beach Borough Hall. On the right was the J.R. Lynch Bottling Company, a prominent local business that remained at this location from 1898 to 1965. Evelyn Tindell is the child outside of Lynch's on the right facing the camera.

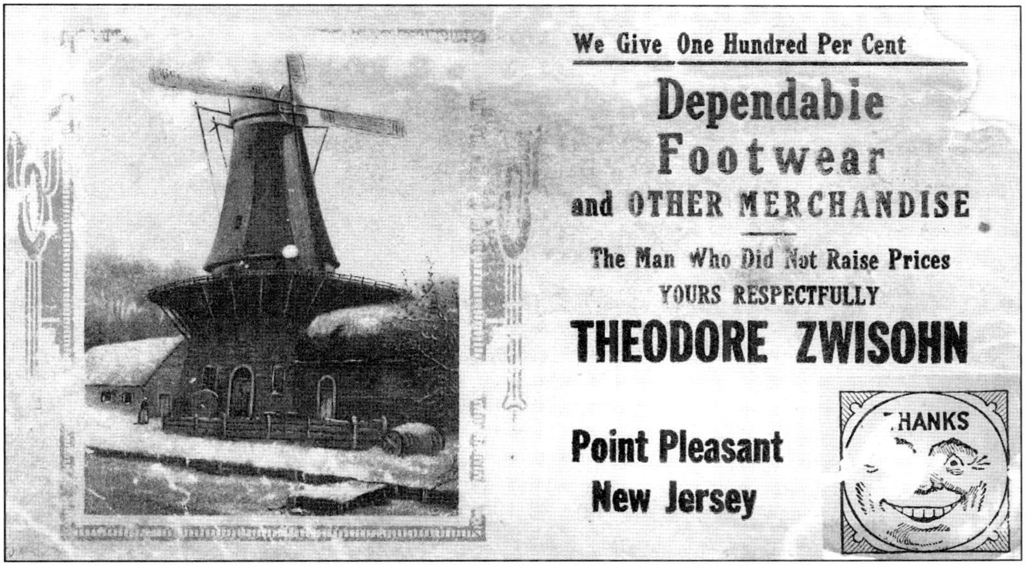

Theodore Zwisohn was one of a handful of pioneer businessmen that helped establish the business district in Point Pleasant Beach nearly one hundred years ago. Zwisohn ran his own department store on the north side of Arnold Avenue at the present site of Corona Plaza. The original Zwisohn Department Store burned in 1933 and was rebuilt minus the third floor. This second building was destroyed by fire in 1989, several years after the Zwisohn family closed the business.

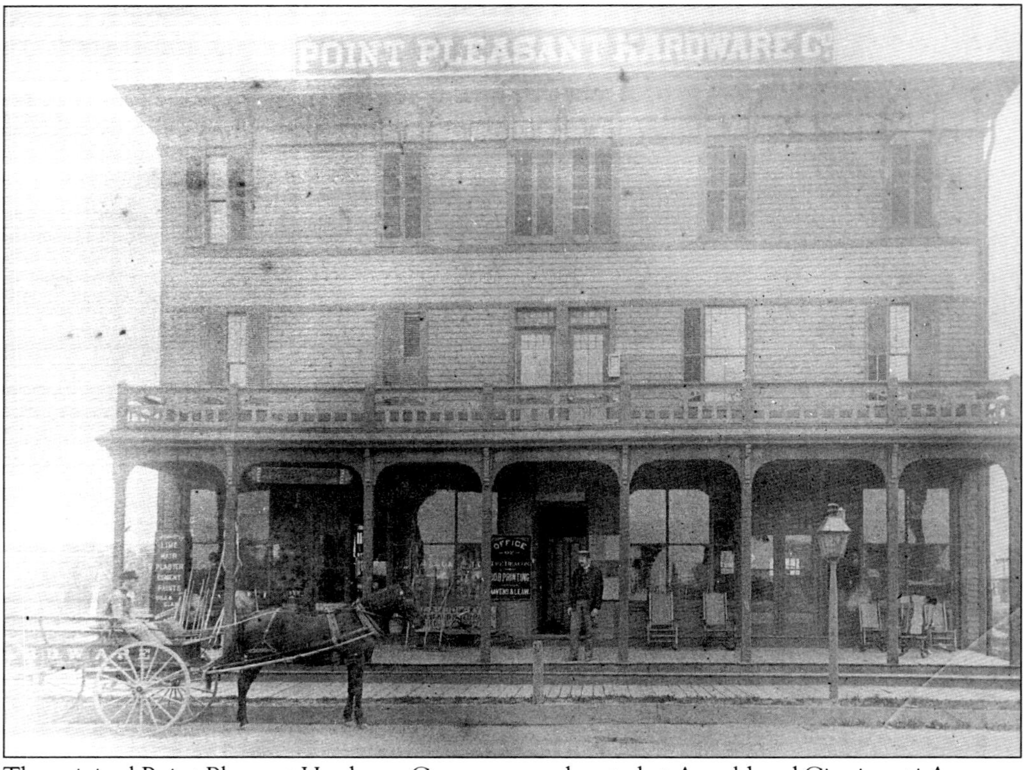

The original Point Pleasant Hardware Company was located at Arnold and Cincinnati Avenues in 1893. The hardware company remained in the Knox Building from its inception in 1885 until it moved in 1902. This building was built about 1882 by the Reverend Charles E. Knox, landowner and founder of the Point Pleasant Presbyterian Church. The Knox Building was torn down in 1943 and today is the site of Duffy's Restaurant.

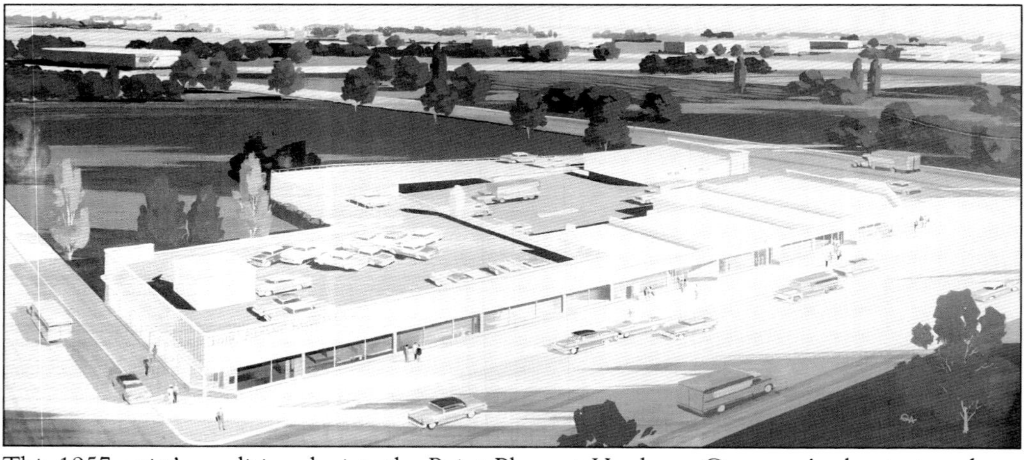
This 1957 artist's rendition depicts the Point Pleasant Hardware Company's plan to tear down the familiar Tudor building on the corner of Arnold and Richmond Avenues and replace it with a modern one-story row of stores extending the entire block between Arnold and Laurel Avenues. An interesting concept was the parking lot located on the roof. Of course, this plan never materialized.

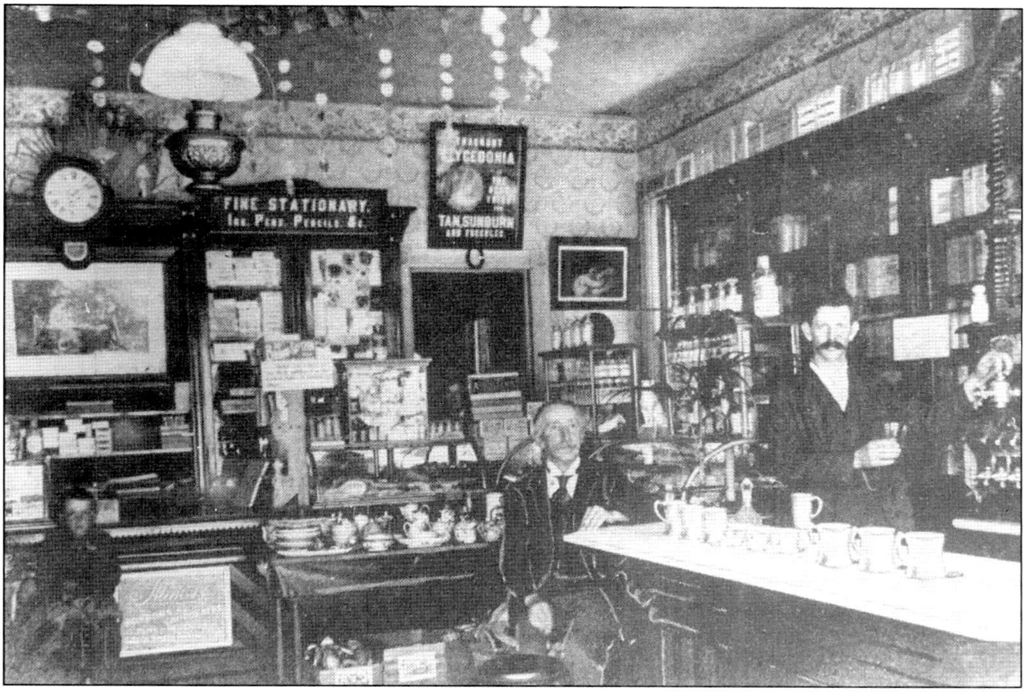

Gustavus Mangold (center) and Richard C. Marley are in Mangold's Pharmacy at Richmond and Forman Avenues in 1895. Everett Antonides of Manasquan bought the pharmacy in 1903 and ran it successfully for several years before selling it to Robert Saunderson, who continued the pharmacy into the late teens.

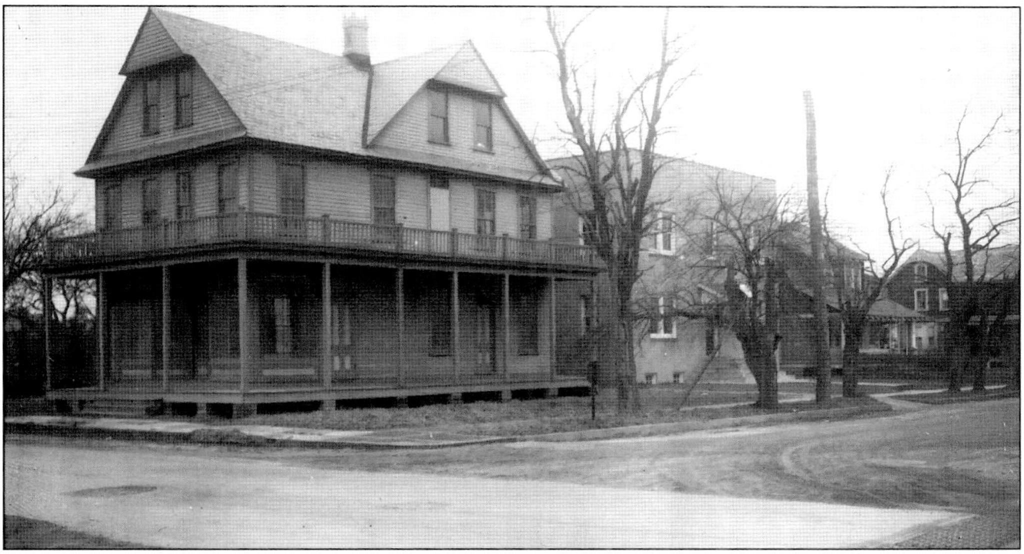

The Mangold's Pharmacy building on the northeast corner of Richmond and Forman Avenues in 1925. This building housed the local telephone exchange on the second floor between 1904 and 1925, when it was transferred to the "modern" telephone building to the rear of the drugstore on Forman Avenue, which is today the Shore Memorial Funeral Home. The old Mangold's Pharmacy was torn down in the late 1920s.

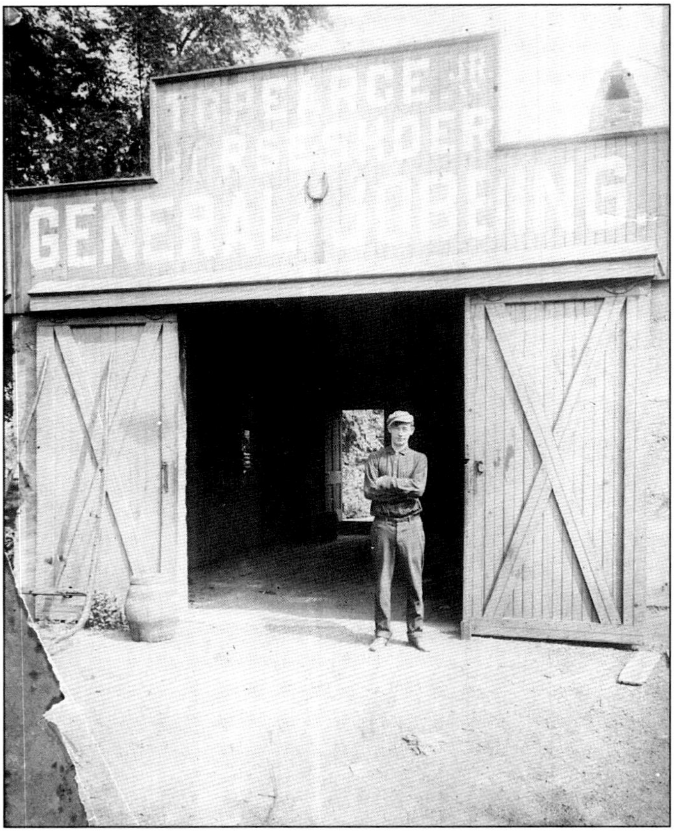

Tabor Pearce's Horseshoer and General Jobbing was located at Bay and Trenton Avenues c. 1900. Establishments of this type proliferated throughout the Point Pleasant area at this time.

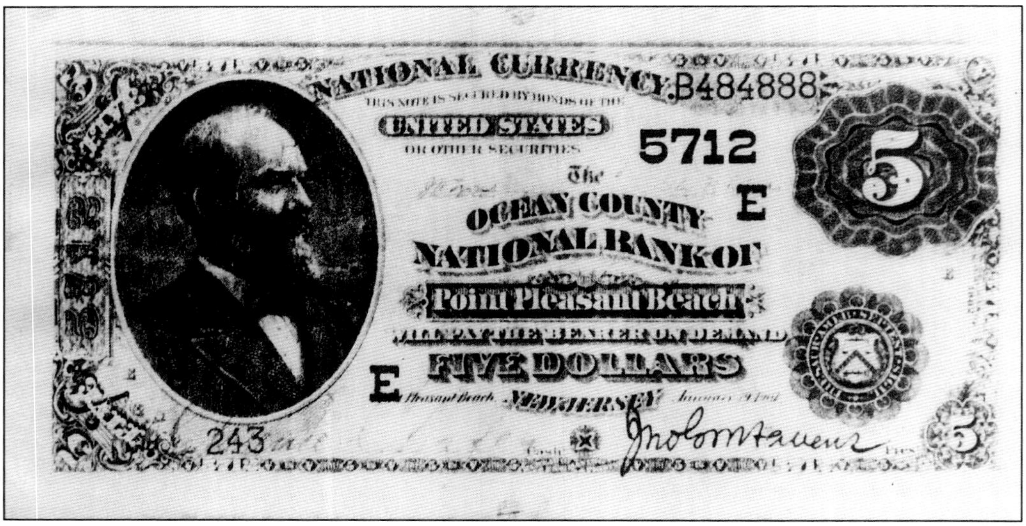

This $5 note was issued by the Ocean County National Bank in 1908 as legal tender. The practice of small community banks issuing their own paper currency would soon draw to a close. The front of the note was signed by the first bank president, John G.W. Havens, and cashier Clarence Chafey, and contained a portrait of President Garfield. The reverse side included a portrait of George Washington and the Capital building and the inscription "1882 * 1908."

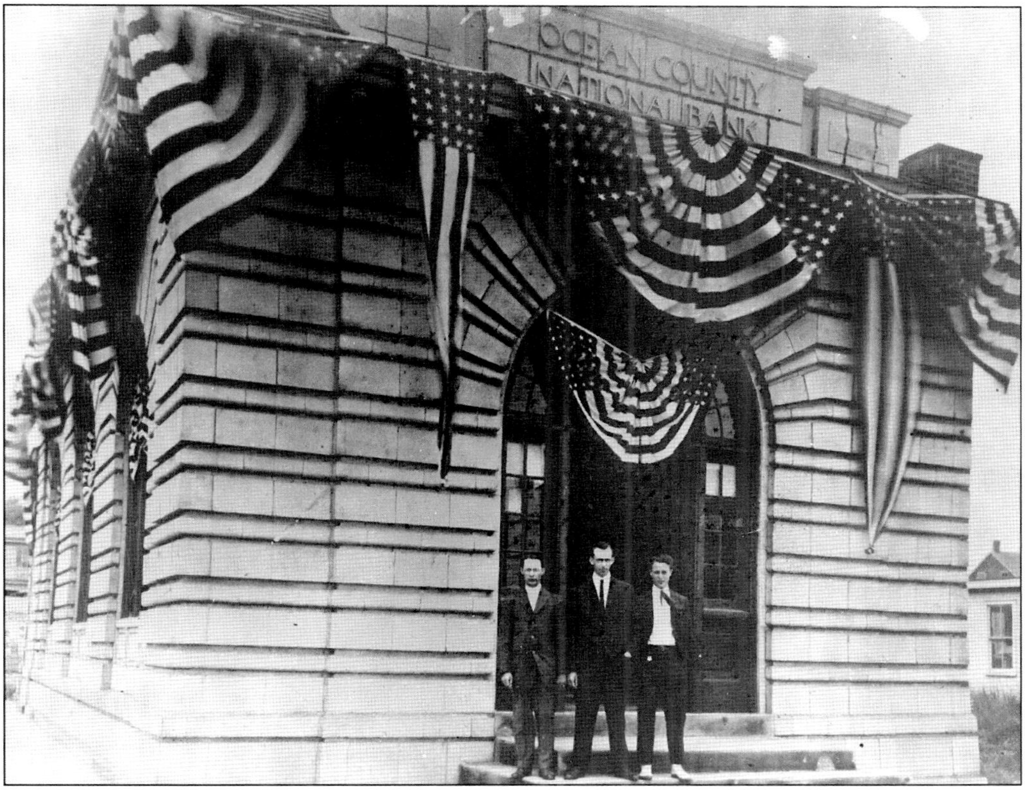

Ocean County National Bank opened for business on March 1, 1901, in a small brick structure on Railroad Square opposite the depot. After the Havens fire of 1903, the bank purchased the corner lot from Havens and erected the familiar bank building (above) with the main entrance on Railroad Square. Standing from left to right are Clarence Chafey, Joe Forsyth, and Clarence Chafey Jr.

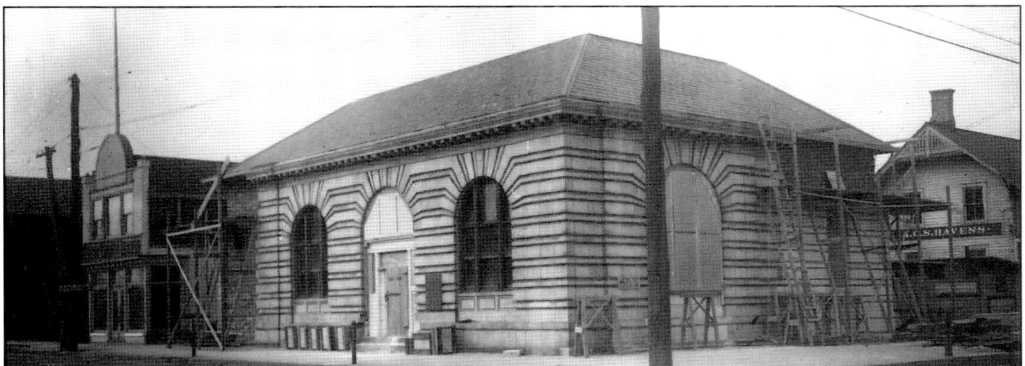

The bank's first expansion is shown near completion in 1923. Ocean County National Bank remained a solid banking institution, and became even more robust in 1983 when it became part of the Summit Bancorporation. The name was eventually changed to Summit Bank in 1993. To the left of the bank on Arnold Avenue can be seen one of the many bureaus of the *Ocean County Leader* newspaper, while on the right is the A.O.S. Havens Real Estate Office in the original railroad station building.

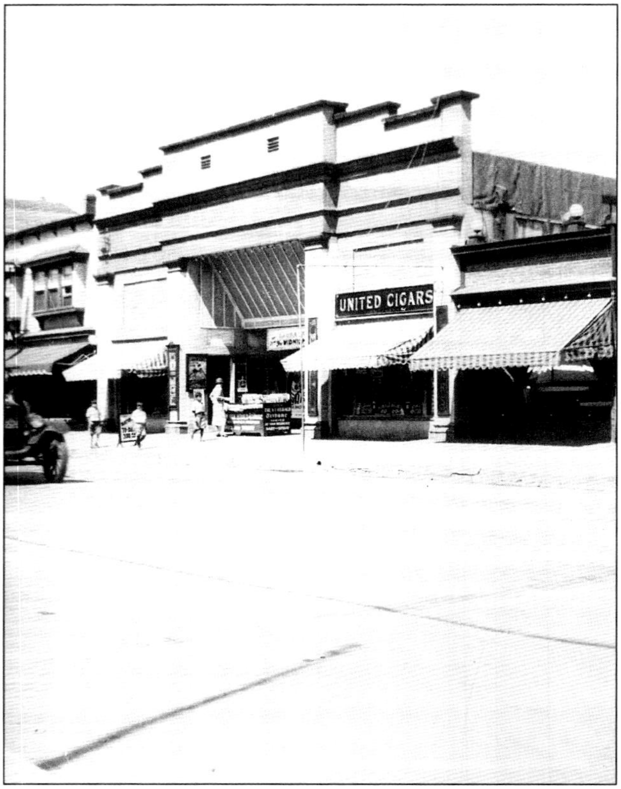

The Grove Theater and Ralph and William Borden's United Cigar Store are shown here in 1928. The mid and late 1920s saw a rapid growth of businesses in the heart of the downtown district. For example, in 1924, sixty percent of the land on Arnold Avenue between River and Richmond Avenues was vacant. By 1930, all of this prime real estate was occupied.

Ralph Borden's United Cigar Store in the Grove Theater Building *c.* 1927. At this time, Borden's offered everything from cigars and pipes to fishing tackle and ammunition for sportsmen. By the 1930s, Borden's offered a complete liquor department, which was moved across the street into the Hayes Building by Charles Mahoney in the early 1960s as Point Liquors.

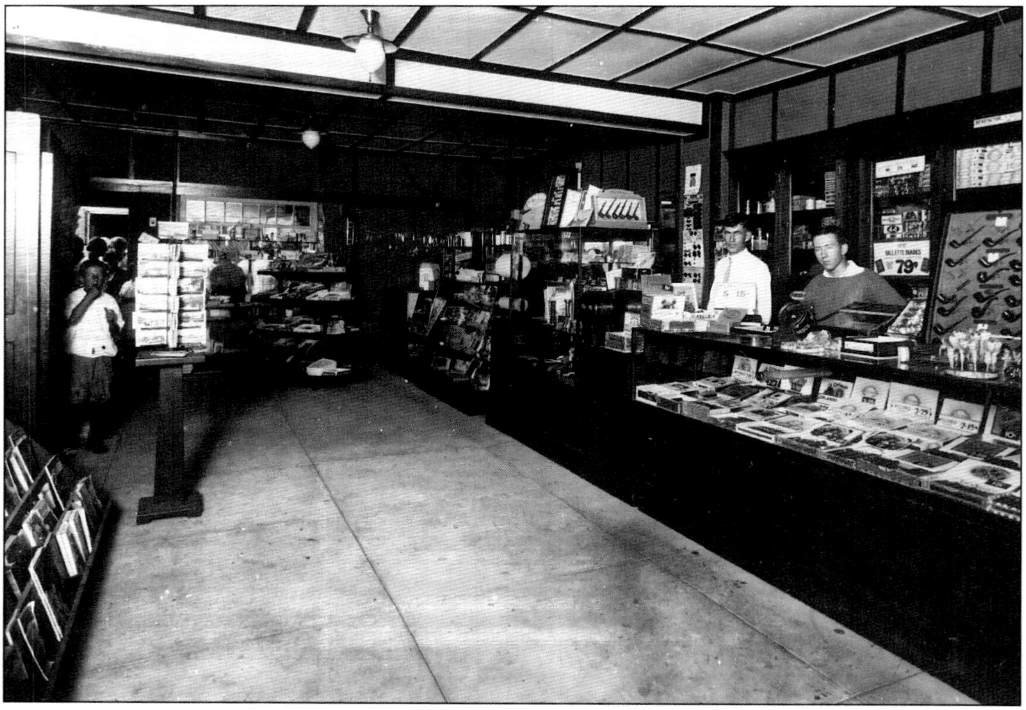

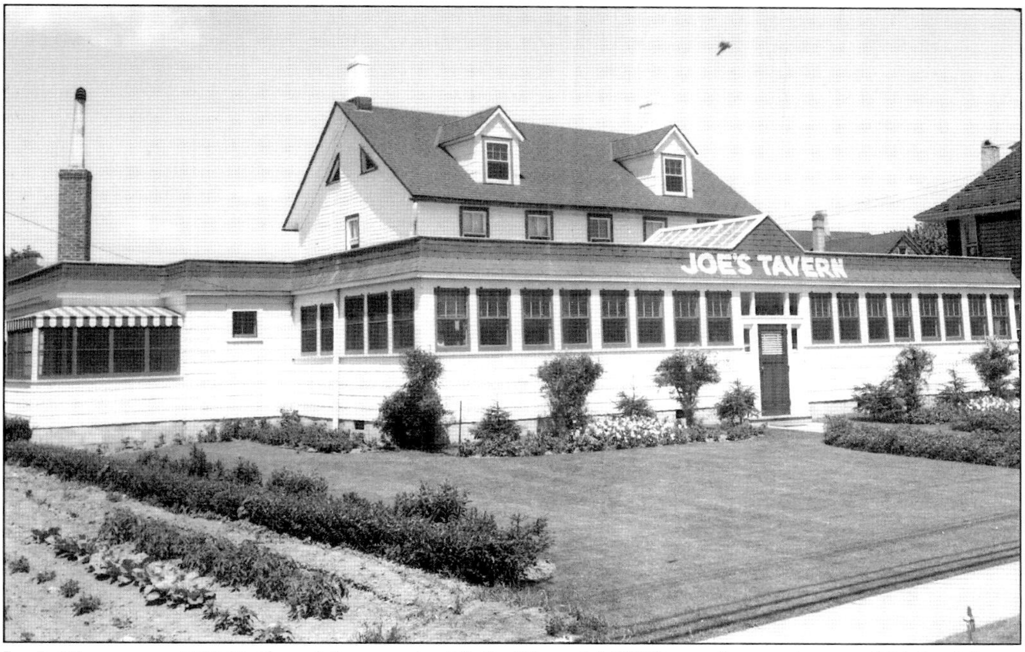

Joe's Tavern at 133 Railroad Square in 1942. The old Williams house (see p. 39) had been refurbished with the addition of dormers and an expanded porch. The Point Pleasant Community Club later occupied the building, which was torn down in 1974.

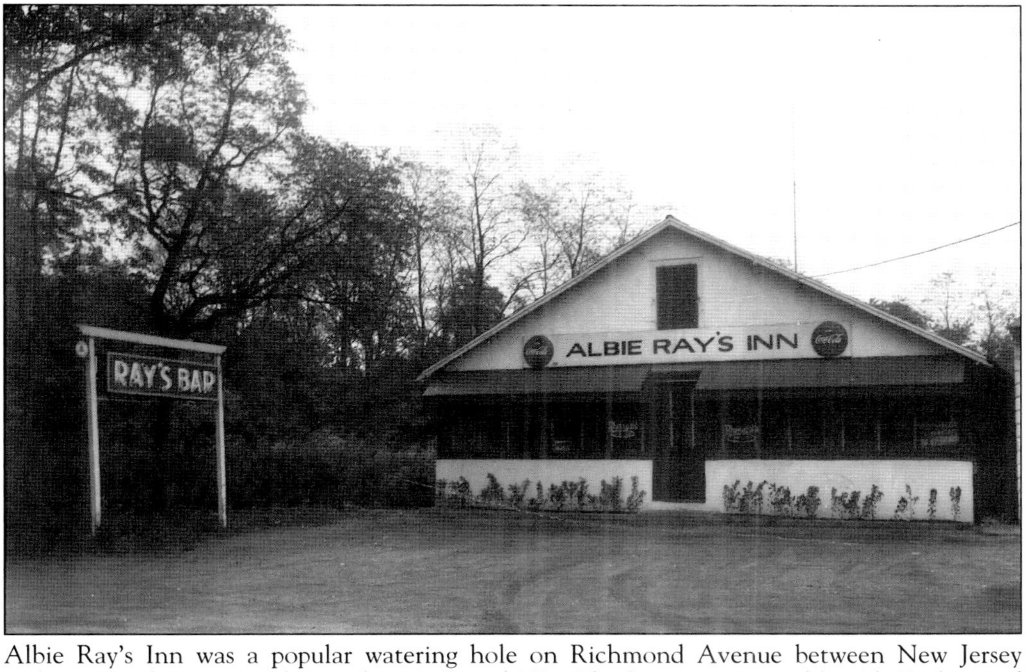

Albie Ray's Inn was a popular watering hole on Richmond Avenue between New Jersey and New York Avenues during the 1940s and '50s. The bar was operated by Al. Fischer and featured Francis Sickles and his one-man band. Ray's Bar was also the home of the original "Doghouse Club."

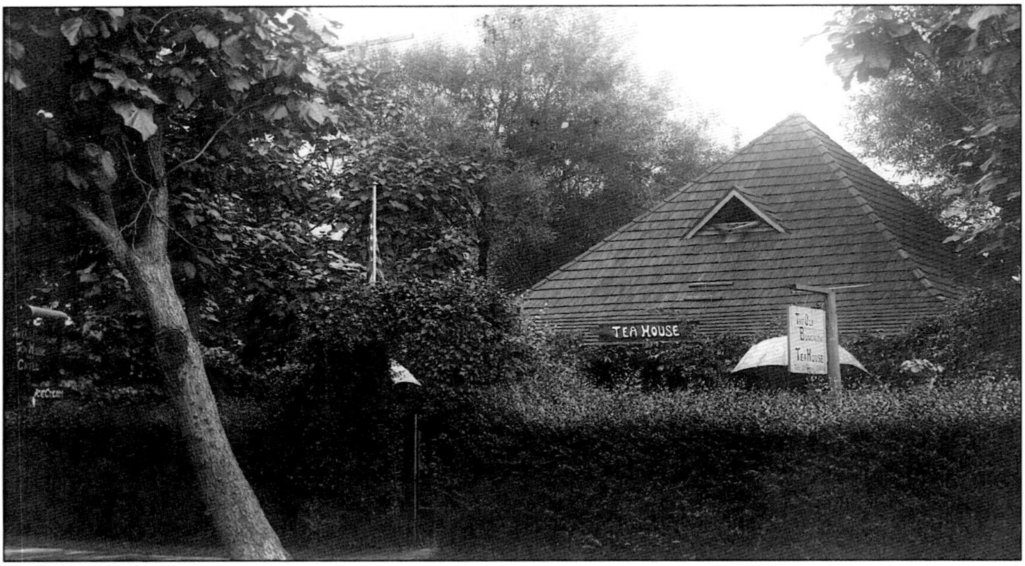

The Old Bungalow Tea House was on the northeast corner of Atlantic and Saint Louis Avenues c. 1920. Opened in 1914 by Henri Bourgeois and E.J. Forrest Greenfield, it was one of the earliest tea houses opened on the Jersey Coast and had a high reputation for serving the finest foods and tea. Miss Juanita Green was the head hostess at the Old Bungalow Tea House from its inception until it closed in the mid-1940s. The building itself existed until it was demolished around 1960.

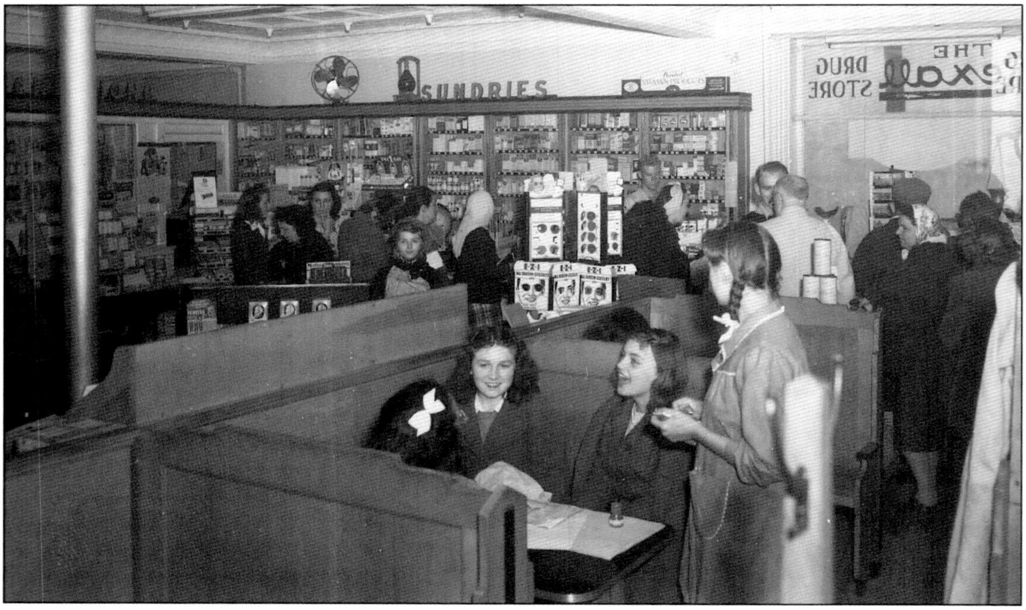

Among the several popular hangouts of the 1930s and '40s in Point Pleasant Beach was Johnson's Pharmacy at Arnold and River Avenues, shown above in 1945. Located in Arnold Hall, the business was founded in 1899 by A. Burtis Johnson and was later turned over to his son, Sykes Johnson. Johnson's Pharmacy featured a soda fountain and luncheonette. McLaughlin's Sportswear now occupies the site.

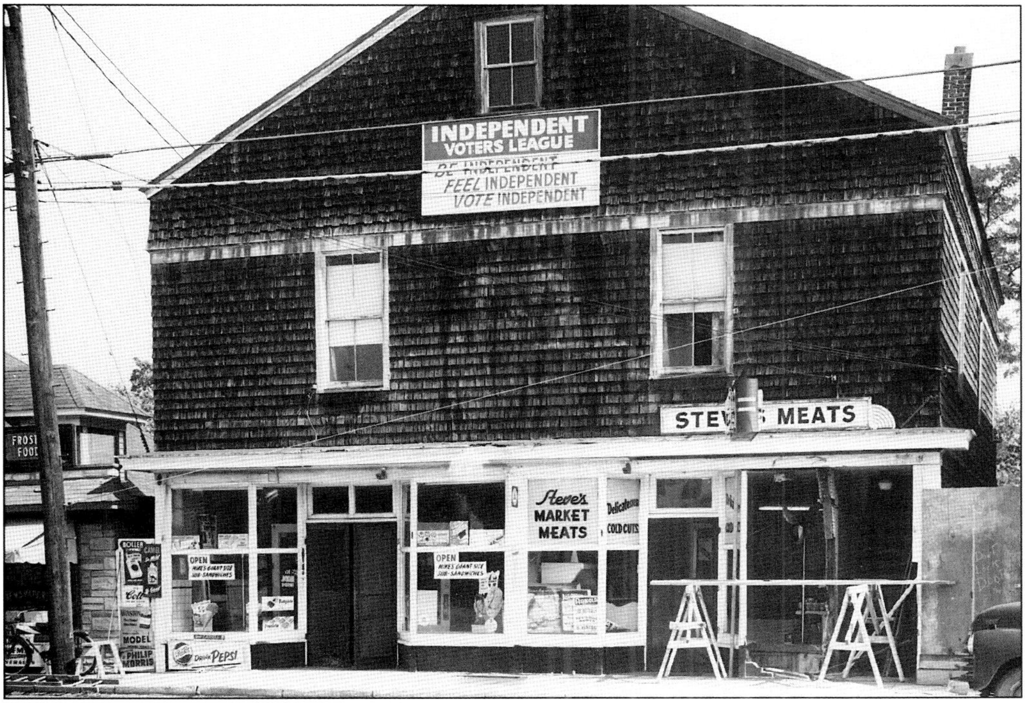

Around 1910, Point Pleasant Builder Alfred Holman built Mechanic's Hall at Arnold and Trenton Avenues. The building was named for the organization that met in the second-story lodge hall, the Atlantic Council #154 of the Junior Order of United American Mechanics, or ACJOUAM (see Vol. I, p. 79). Renovations to the deteriorating hall were made in the mid 1950s (shown above). The storefront on the left contained a fledgling Mike's Submarine Shop, the genesis of today's Jersey Mike's chain.

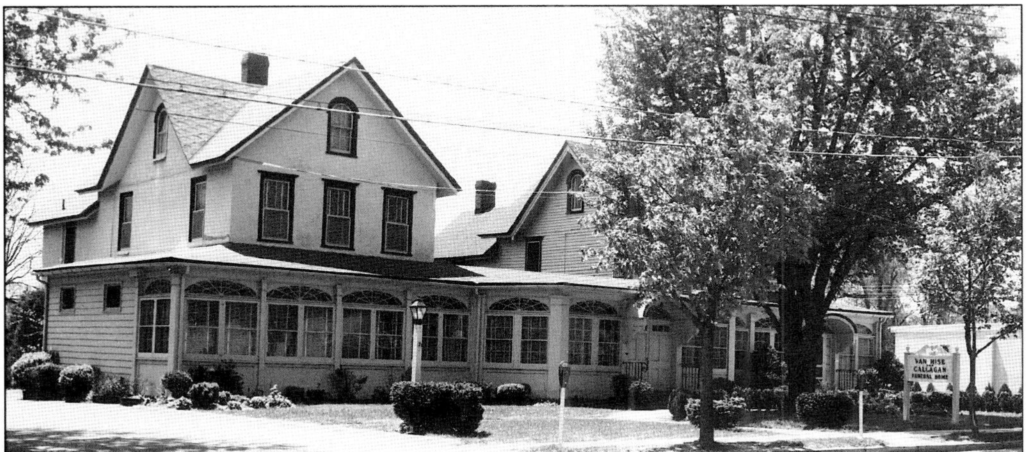

The Van Hise and Callagan Funeral Home on Arnold Avenue was established in 1876 by William Longstreet. Longstreet conducted his undertaking business out of one of two identical homes built by George Russell in 1874. Longstreet sold the business to Joseph Harvey in 1902, who in turn sold to H. Allen Van Hise in 1931. The funeral home was soon expanded to include both Russell cottages, shown here in 1960.

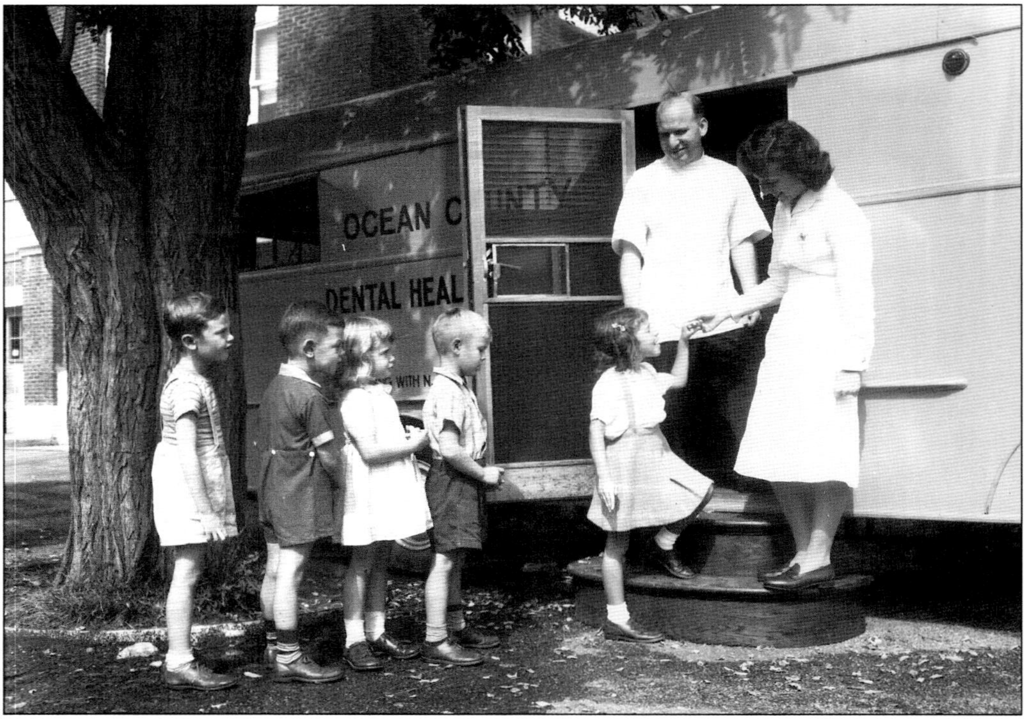

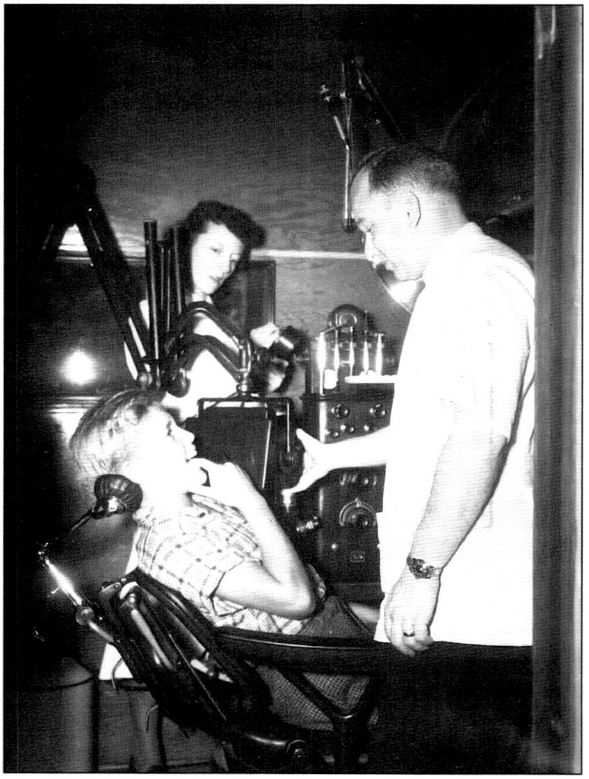

The Ocean County Dental Health Service visits the Point Pleasant Beach schools in September 1946. This fully equipped dental office in a mobile trailer made stops throughout the county in the 1940s in cooperation with the state department of health.

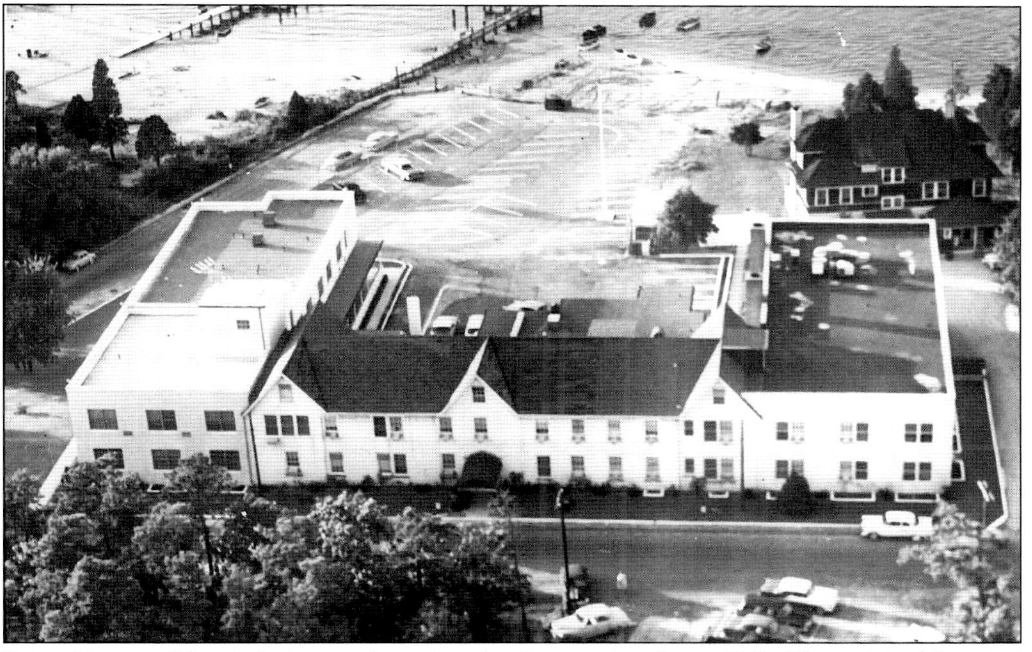

Point Pleasant Hospital is seen here in a bird's-eye view from 1960. The original hospital building is in the center, built in 1927. Hospital founder Frank Denniston's parents' house is in the upper right and was used as a nurses' home for many years. The east (Nimick) wing (on the right) was completed in 1952 and the west wing was built in 1959.

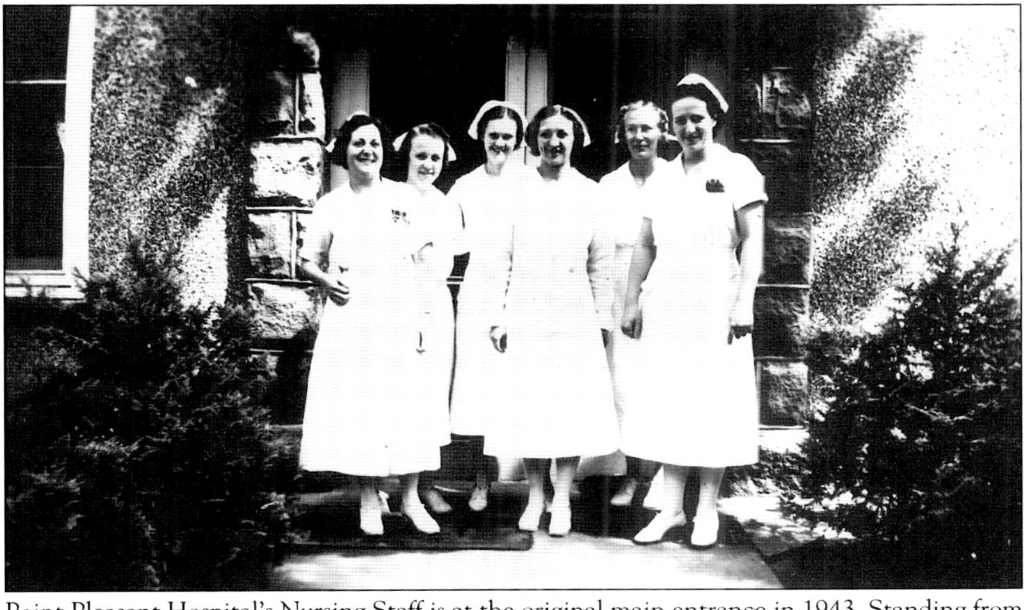

Point Pleasant Hospital's Nursing Staff is at the original main entrance in 1943. Standing from left to right are Ann Bethel, Renee Hibbs, Miss Lee (nursing supervisor), Lucille Ivory, Vonnie Kadeg, and Edith Phillips. Notice the Todd Process stone surrounding the entrance.

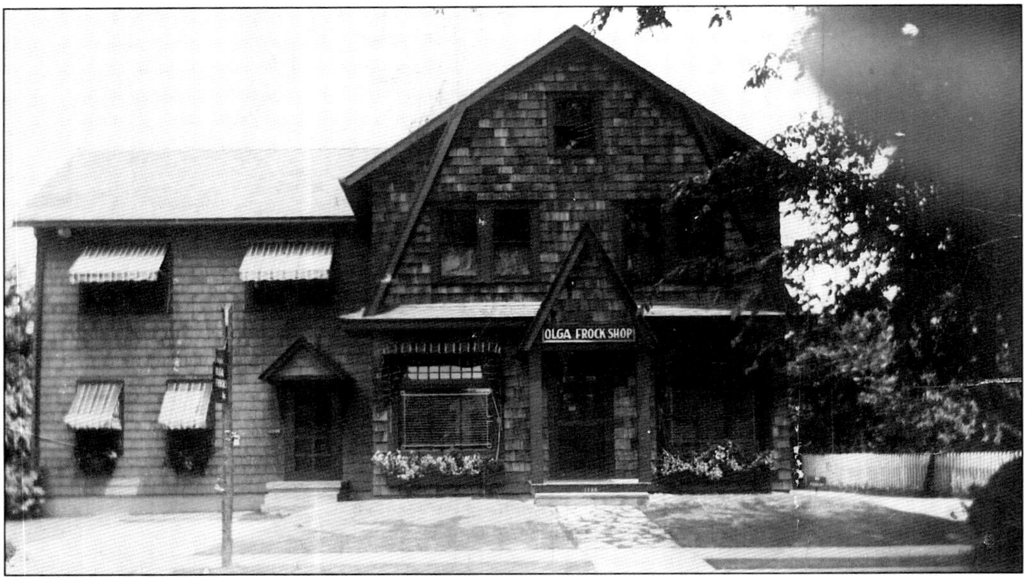

The Olga Frock Shop located at 1100 Richmond Avenue in 1936. Olive F. Gates started the nationally famous women's dressmaking business in 1927 with one sewing machine and two salespersons. The wing to the left was added in 1935 and a large modern workshop was built across the street at 1101 Richmond Avenue in 1939.

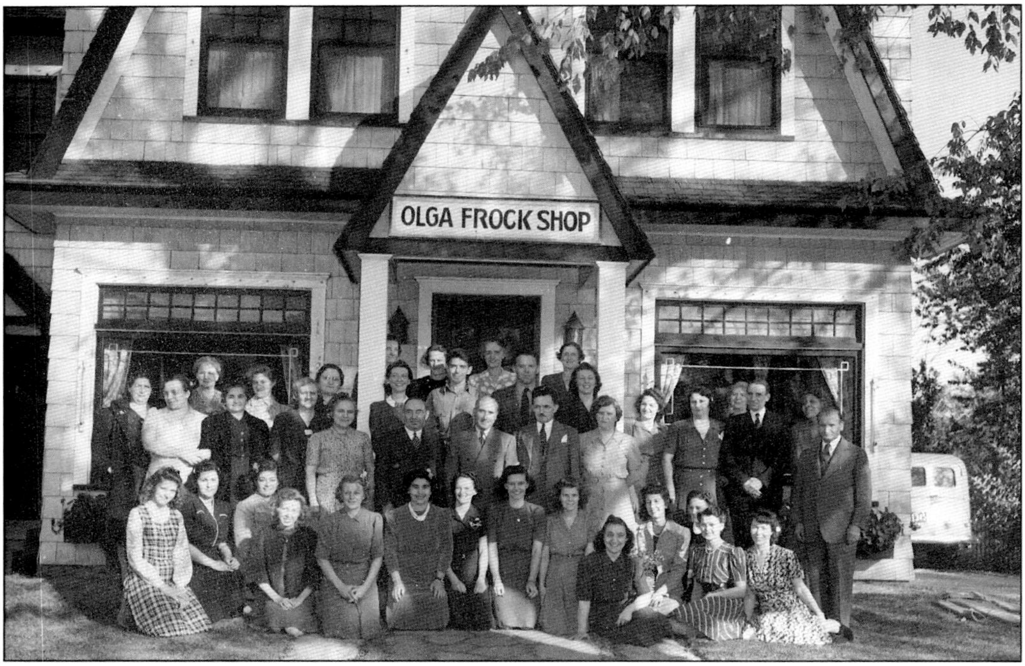

Mrs. Gates combined the first two letters of her first and last names to name her business. The Olga Frock Shop eventually employed over 70 local residents in the sewing and cutting workshop and another 150 sales representatives across the country. The original building became a retail specialty shop by the late 1940s (above). In 1960, Olga Frocks moved its headquarters to North Carolina.

In 1894, Henry Downey of Osbornville purchased a lot from Charles Knox on the southeast corner of Arnold and Richmond Avenues and built the Downey Building. This structure was moved one lot east in 1902 when Joseph Johnson built the present hardware company. The Downey Building was torn down in 1959.

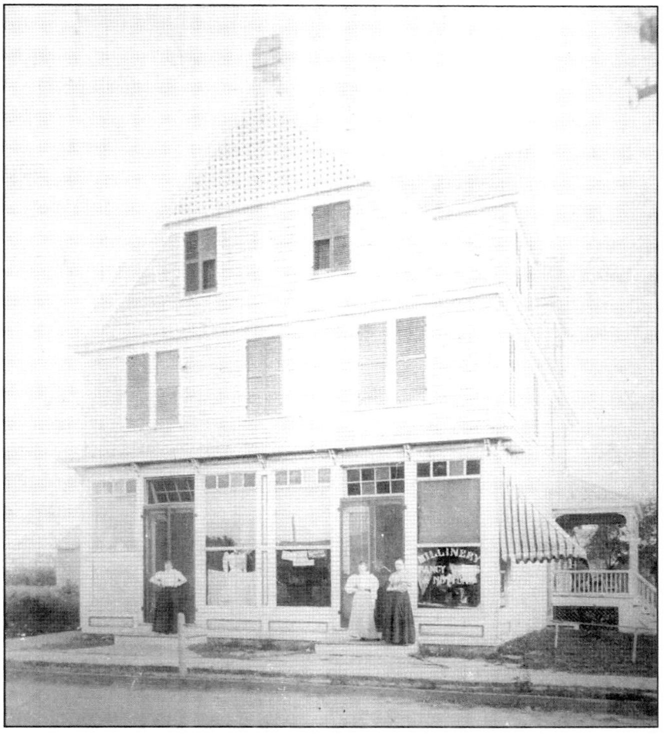

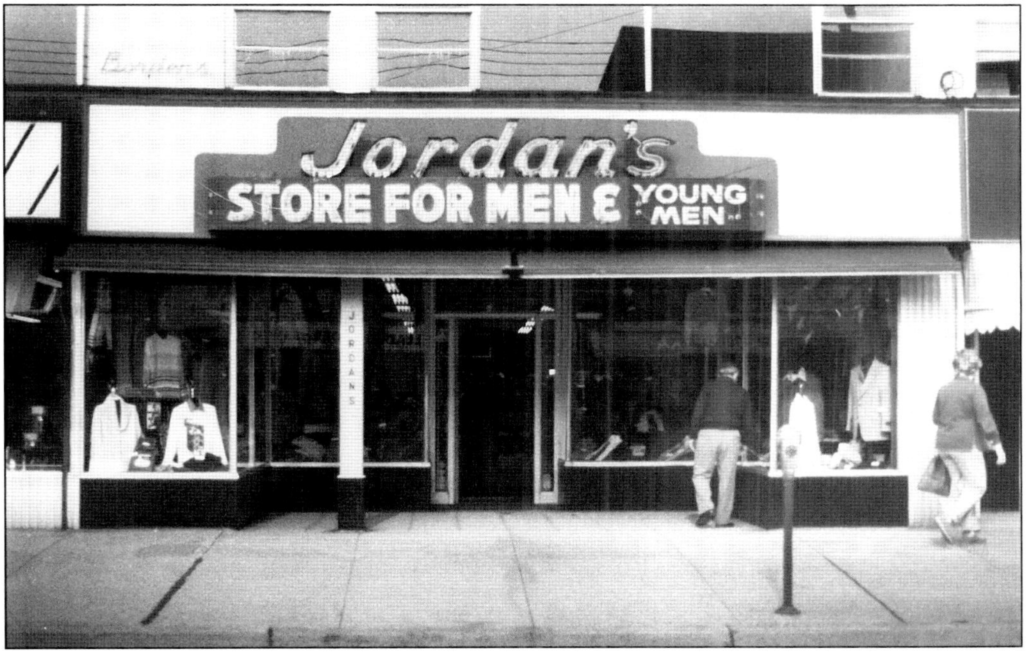

Albert Steinman and Albert Goldsweig opened Jordan's Men's Shop at 607 Arnold Avenue in 1956. Jordan's occupied the east half of the old Grove Theater Building and specialized in an exclusive line of men's clothing, sportswear, and outerwear in hard-to-find sizes. Goldsweig died in 1972 and Steinman continued to run the business until he retired in 1994.

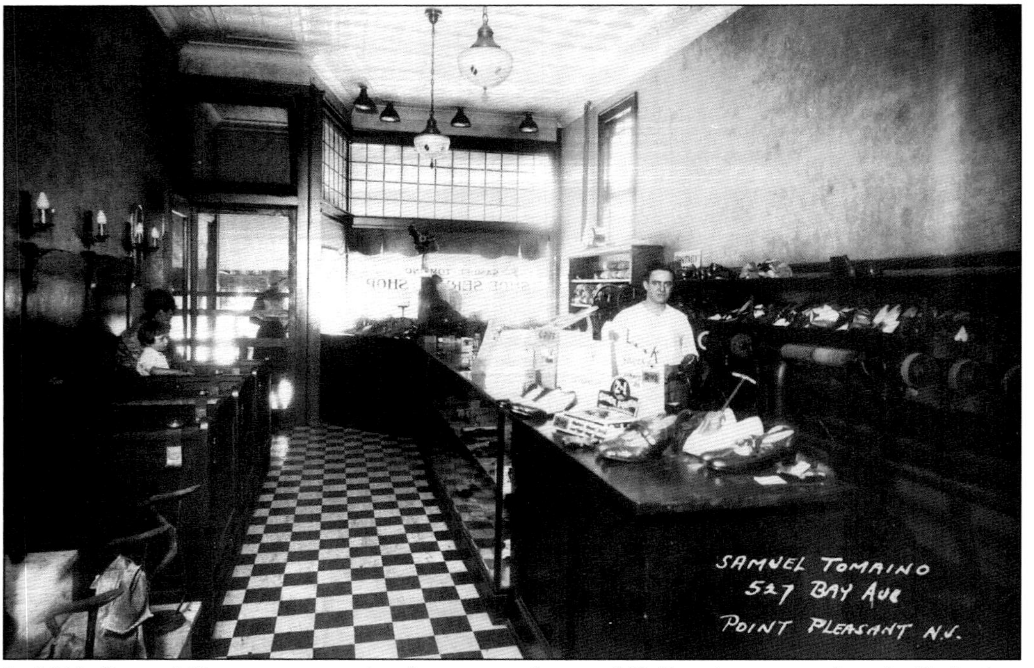

In 1915, Samuel Tomaino opened a shoe repair shop at 502 Bay Avenue and gradually built a loyal base of customers. By 1925, Tomaino purchased a house at 527 Bay Avenue, added two storefronts, and opened an enlarged shoe store and shoe repair service (shown above). In 1949, the entire building was remodeled (see below) and Samuel's son Francis took over operation of the shoe store. With Francis Tomaino's retirement, the business closed its doors in 1986.

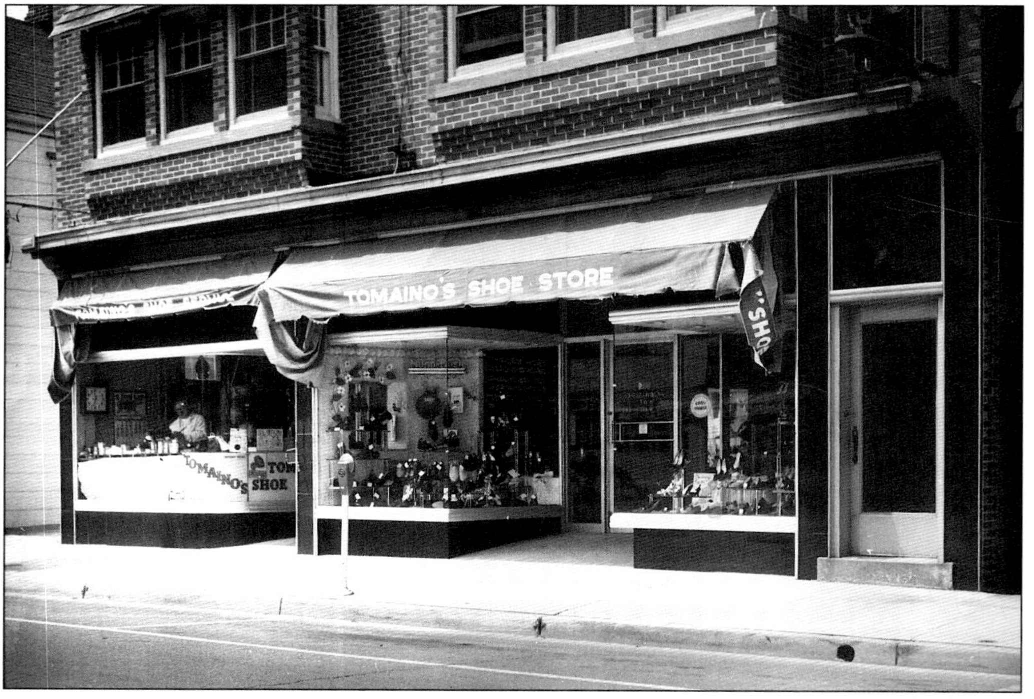

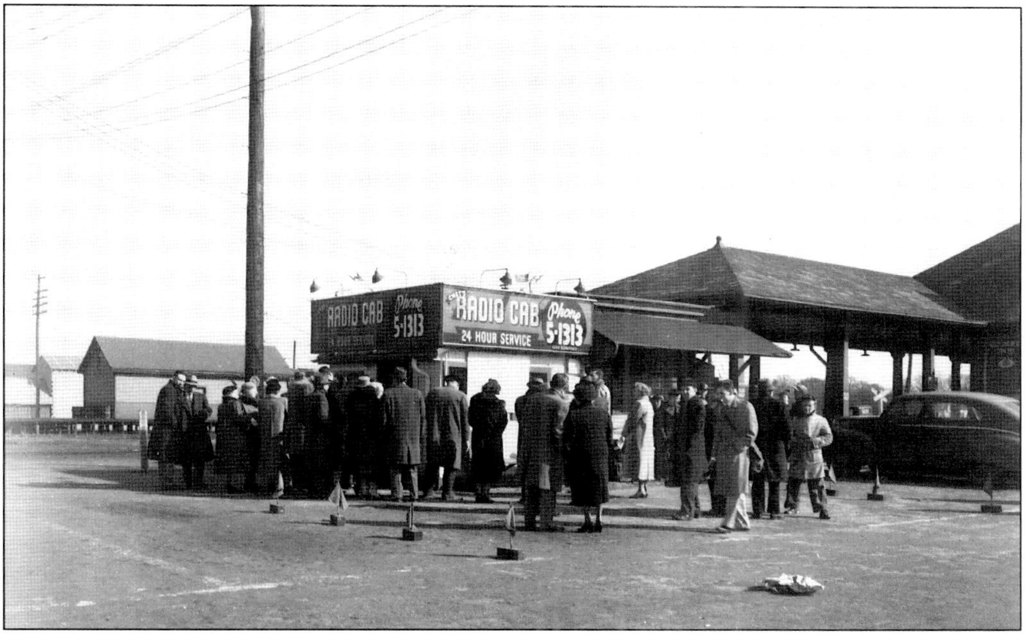

Chet's Radio Cab Service at the Point Pleasant train station draws brisk business on a cold March day in 1950. Local taxi service during the early 1900s was sporadic, but by 1920 Herb Briggs had begun Briggs Taxi and Bus service that is still in business today.

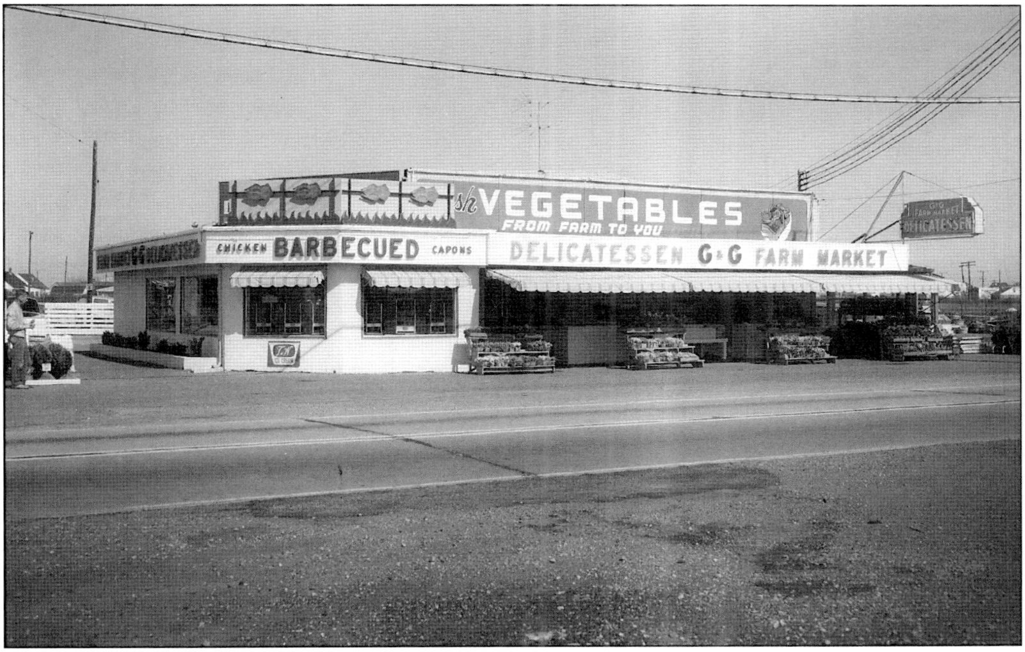

G & G Farm Market and Delicatessen was located at 1600 Richmond Avenue where Burger King is today. The farm market was started in the early 1950s and featured fresh vegetables, cold cuts, and barbecued chicken. An addition in the early 1960s included a package goods store and a branch delicatessen was begun at 115 Broadway.

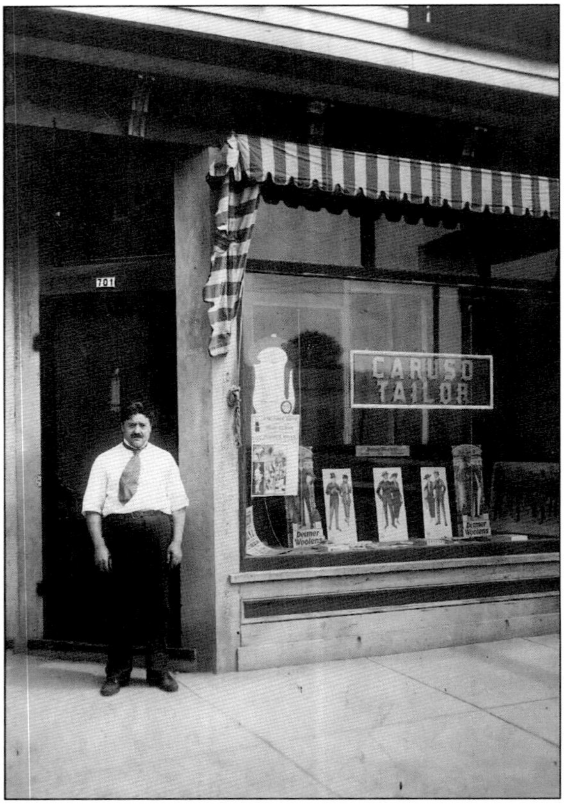

Emidio A. Caruso is outside his tailor shop in the Rogers Building on Arnold Avenue c. 1924. Caruso opened his business on Bay Avenue in 1908 and after a brief return to his native Italy, he re-opened his shop on Arnold Avenue in 1913. He later moved into the Rogers Building at Bay and Arnold Avenues and when the building was moved to make way for the new Point Pleasant Beach National Bank (now Ocean Federal), Caruso purchased it and remains at the present location at 721 Arnold Avenue.

The Joseph Backes Plumbing and Hardware Store was in the Hendrickson Building on Bay Avenue about 1899. Backes and his partner, Charles E. Cline, were the original owners of the Point Pleasant Hardware Company and sold out to Joseph Johnson and Charles Dampman in 1890 for the sum of $5,200.

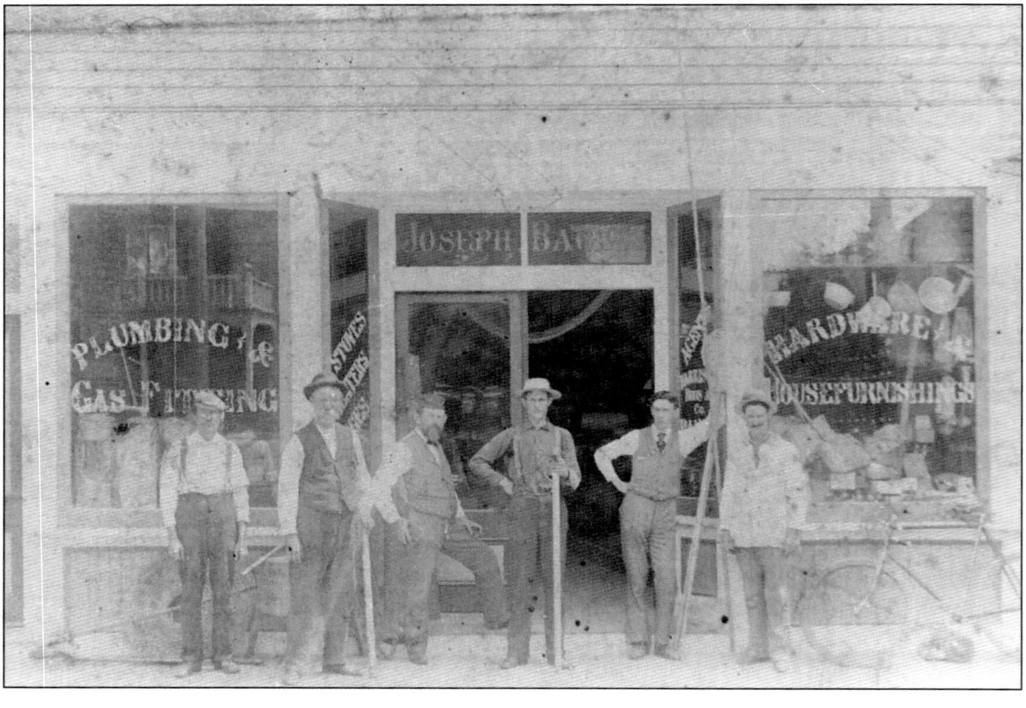

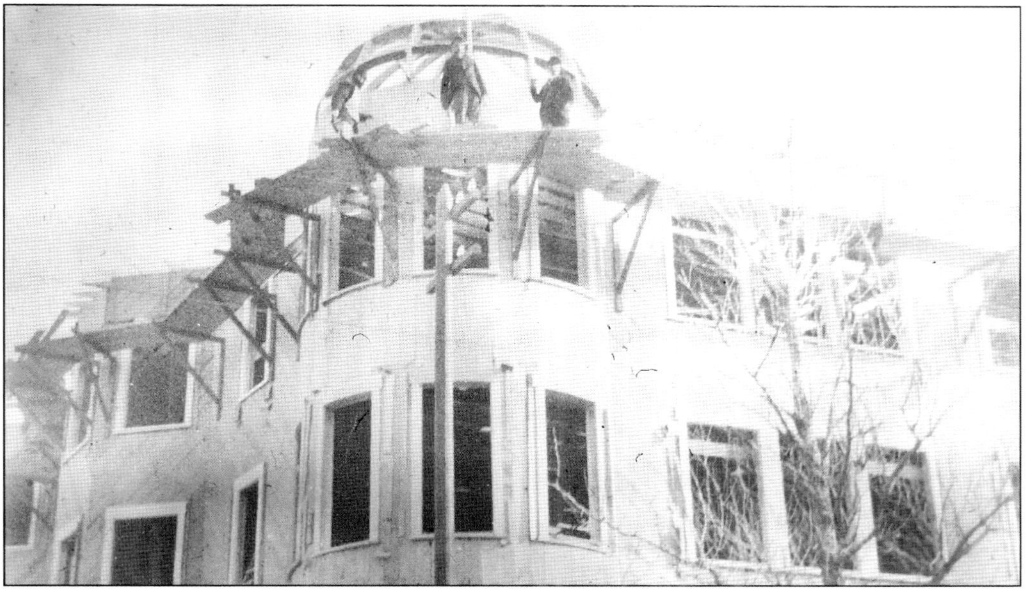

In 1902, Joseph Backes had a large three-story building built on the southeast corner of Bay and Trenton Avenues (shown above) to house his growing hardware business. However, in 1906, Backes sold his entire stock and the right to run a hardware store within the borough to Joseph Johnson for $1,000 plus the value of his inventory. Backes continued to conduct his plumbing supply business for several more years.

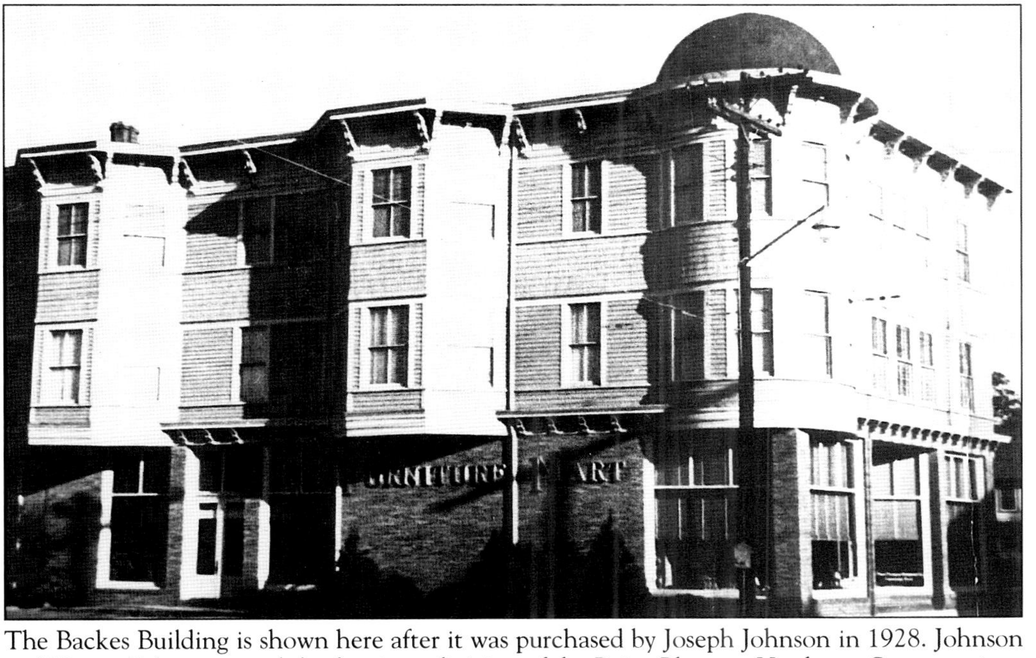

The Backes Building is shown here after it was purchased by Joseph Johnson in 1928. Johnson and Henry Osborn moved the furniture division of the Point Pleasant Hardware Company into the building, and the newly created Johnson's Furniture Mart continued to do business here until 1981, when it was transformed into the present Antique Emporium. Two additions were made to the building over the years, which doubled its original size.

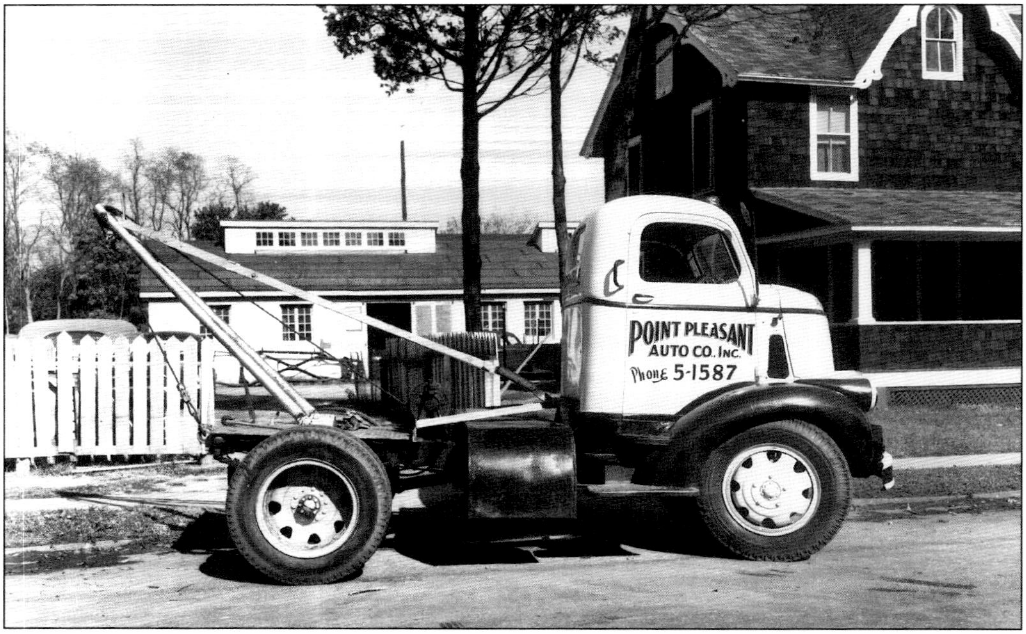

A Point Pleasant Auto Company tow truck sits on Trenton Avenue in 1948. The 7,000-square-foot auto showroom and garage at Bay and Trenton Avenues featured twenty-four-hour service on most repairs while serving as the local agency for Oldsmobile cars and International trucks.

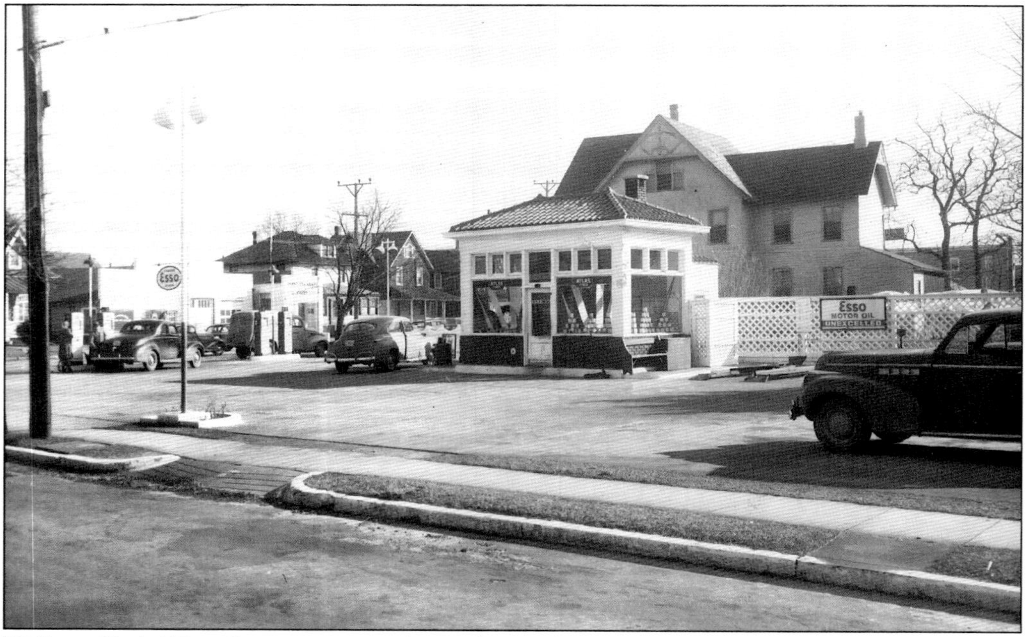

William Hicks' Esso Servicenter was located at Richmond and McLean Avenues in 1946. The house to the rear was one of the original houses built on the John Arnold Estate. It has since been torn down. Across Richmond Avenue is Feimster's Point Pleasant Dairy and Saunder's Garage, which stands on the site of Point Pleasant's first auto garage, built by Chester Clayton in 1903.

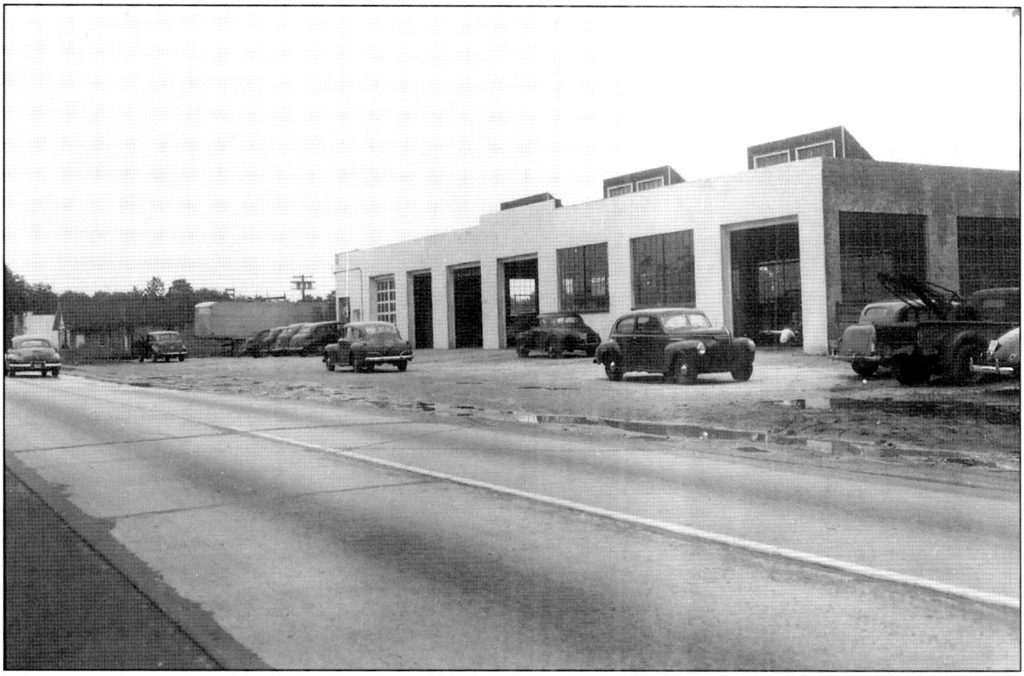

In 1946, Joseph Jacquin built this auto garage on Richmond Avenue between Washington and Newark Avenues. This building was later enlarged and remodeled into storefronts which today make up the Richmond Center strip mall on Route 35 south.

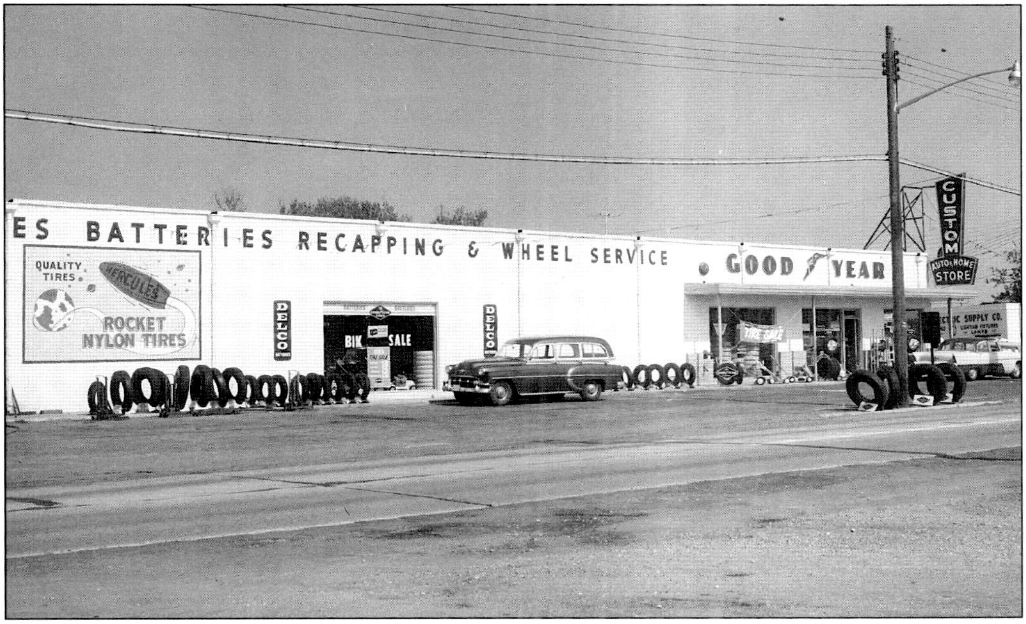

In 1955, Custom Home and Auto Store moved out of its location downtown on Arnold Avenue (see Vol. I, p. 49) and into the former Point Pleasant Moving and Storage building at Richmond and Elizabeth Avenues (shown above). Today this building houses the Tire Craft Goodyear Auto Service Center.

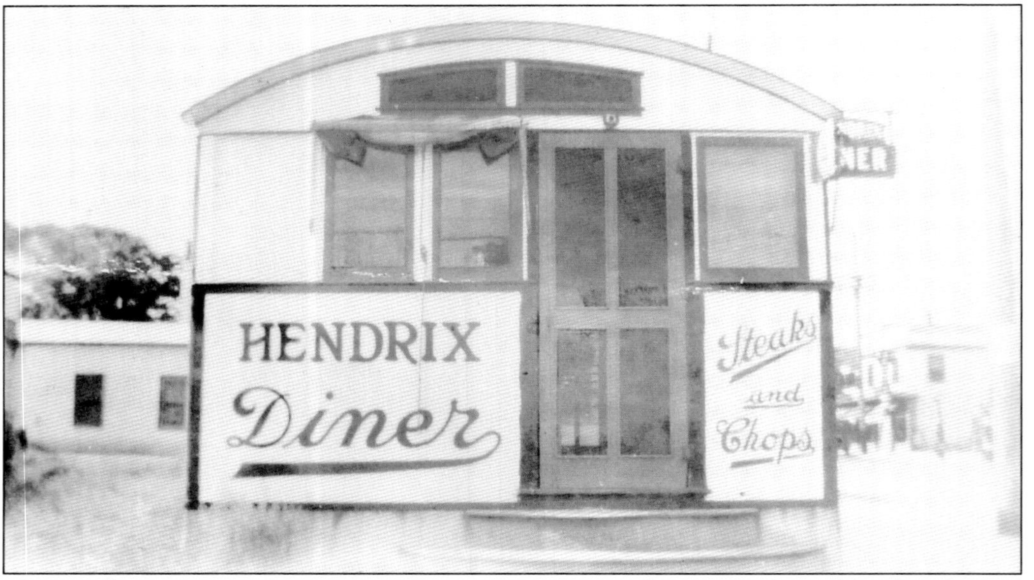

The Hendrix Diner and Restaurant was a popular eatery on the corner of Arnold and Richmond Avenues from 1927 to 1947. Olen Hendrix and his wife Stella began the business in a diner car (shown above) where Borden's stands today. The restaurant was moved across the street into the Hayes Building in 1934.

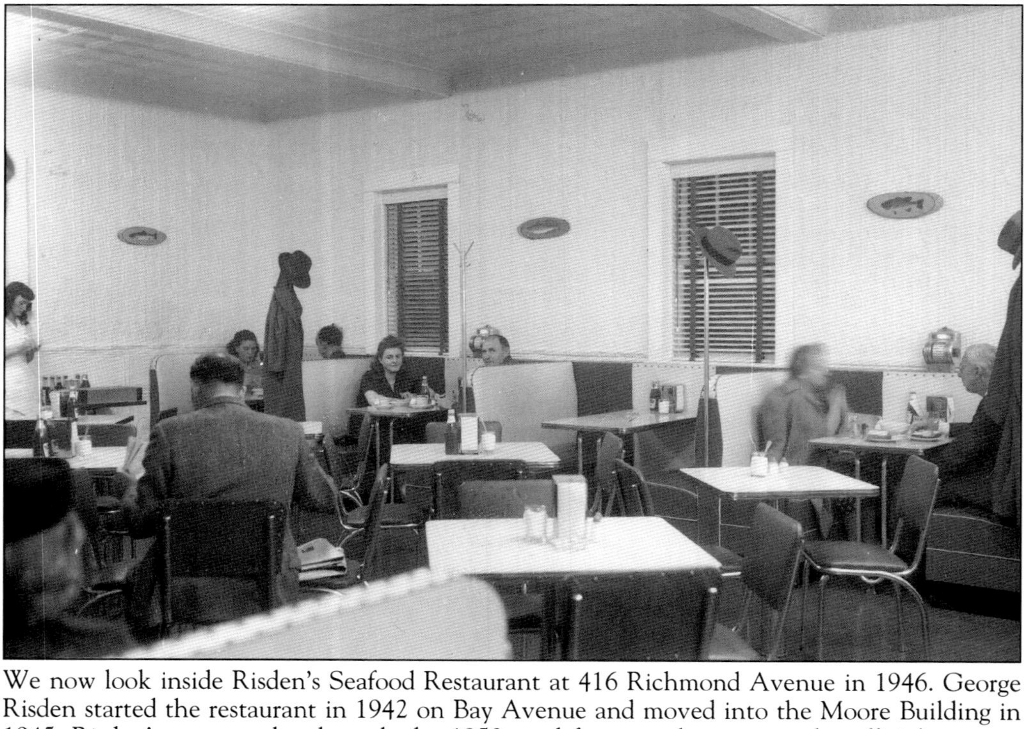

We now look inside Risden's Seafood Restaurant at 416 Richmond Avenue in 1946. George Risden started the restaurant in 1942 on Bay Avenue and moved into the Moore Building in 1945. Risden's was popular through the 1950s and for several years was the official meeting place of the Point Pleasant Rotary Club and the chamber of commerce. Pleasant Travel Service occupies the site today.

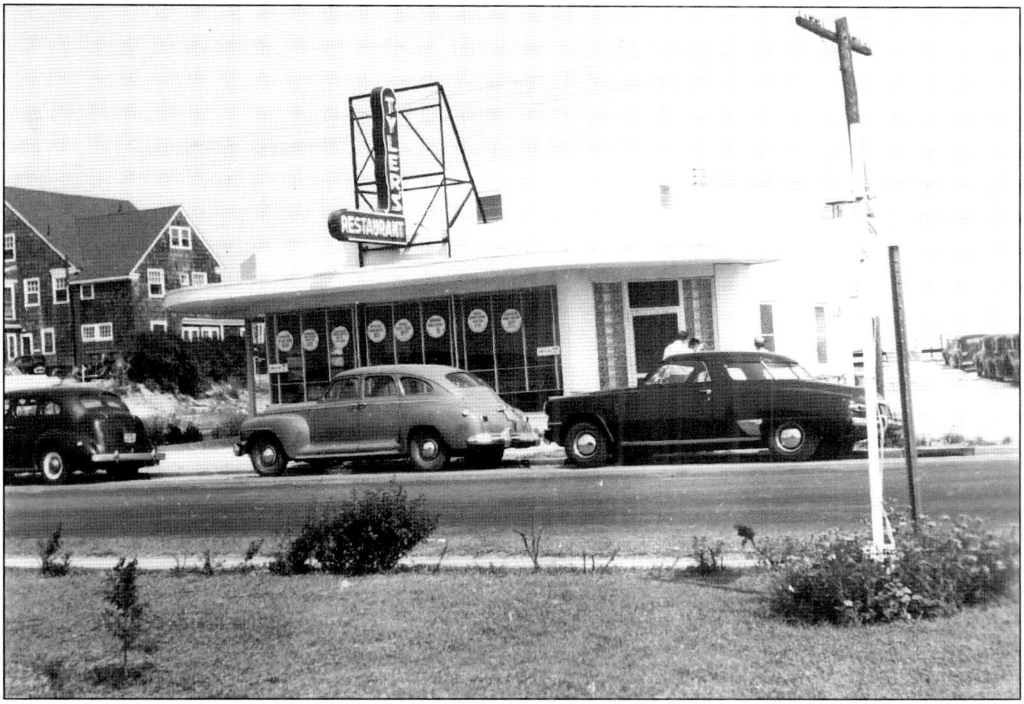

Tyler's Restaurant at Ocean and Trenton Avenues is shown here c. 1950. Today it is the home of the Natural Buffet. Other long-gone restaurants along Ocean Avenue included The Haven Restaurant, The Round House, Simpson's Seafood, Whitten Hall, and the Beacon By-the-Sea.

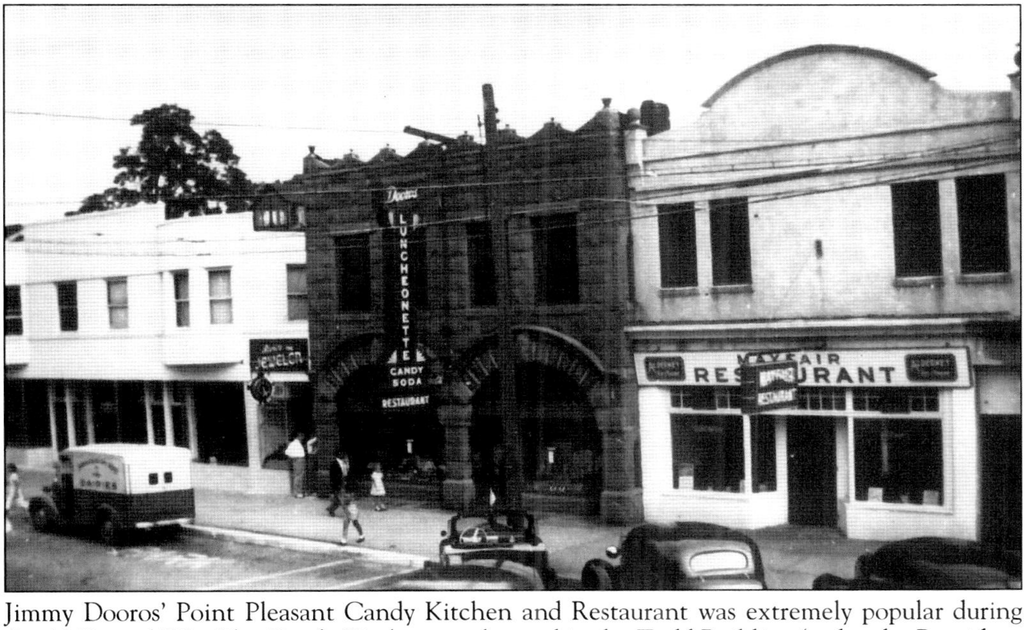

Jimmy Dooros' Point Pleasant Candy Kitchen and Restaurant was extremely popular during the 1940s and '50s. The Candy Kitchen was located in the Todd Building (today the Provident Bank) and its main attractions were the home-made ice cream and candy, the soda fountain, the dining booths, and the ever-popular jukebox.

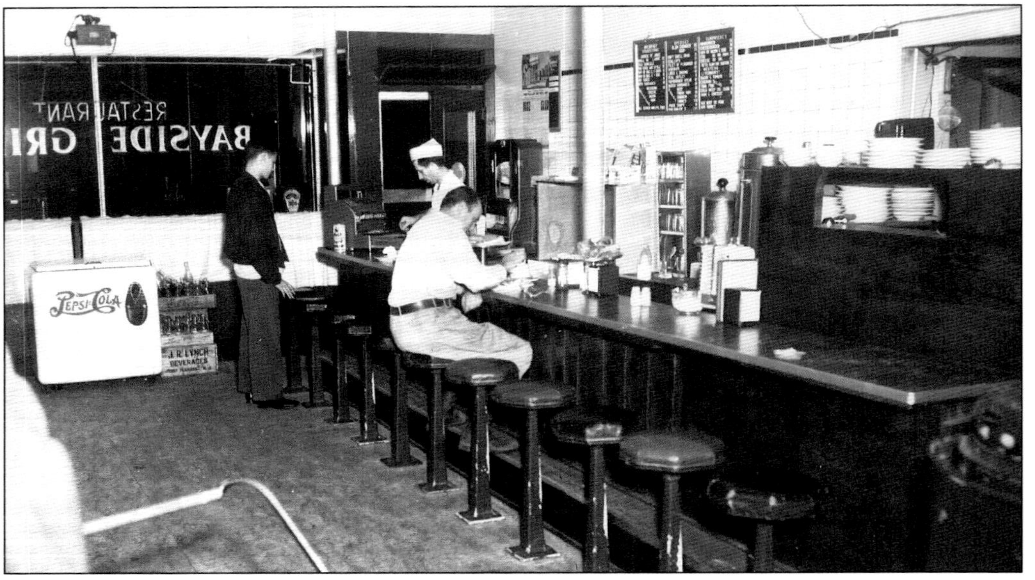

Bay Avenue also had several fine restaurants, including the Pleasant Cafeteria and the Bayside Grill, shown here in 1948. Bernadette's occupies the site today. Specials included a Hamburger Steak for 65¢, soft shell crabs for 75¢, and a Pork Chop Dinner for 90¢. Notice the J.R. Lynch bottle cases stacked next to the Pepsi cooler.

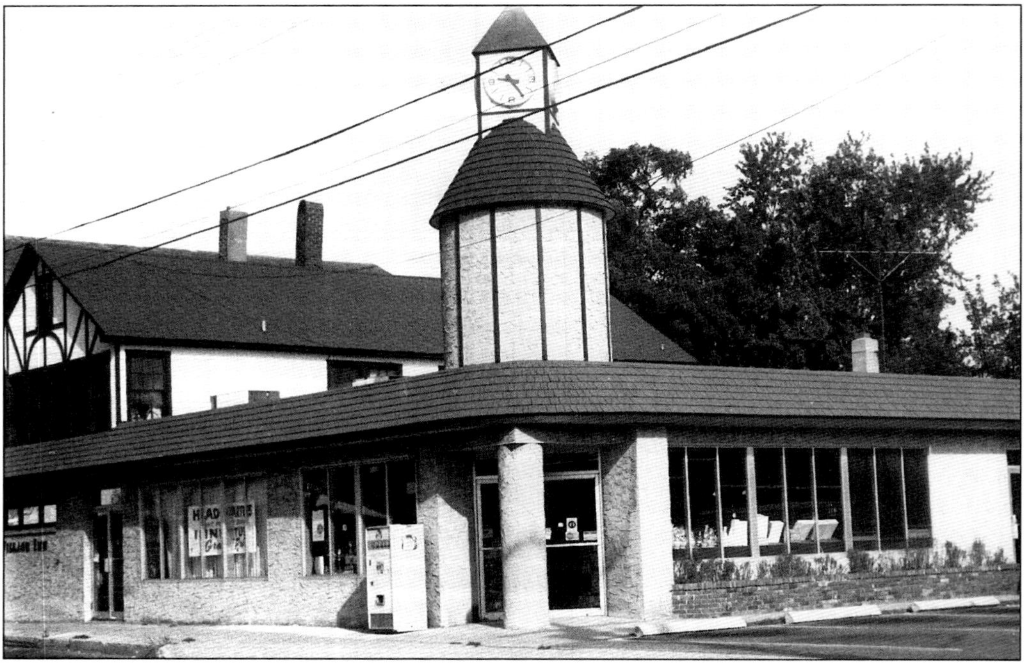

The Village Inn Restaurant was at Arnold and Trenton Avenues in 1970. The two-story portion of the restaurant (shown at left) was originally opened as a tavern in 1932 by Warren Britton. By the late 1940s the tavern was sold and renamed the Village Inn. The popular restaurant and package goods store was destroyed by fire in 1994. Originally, this was the site of Charles Maxson's Hotel (see Vol. I, p. 10).

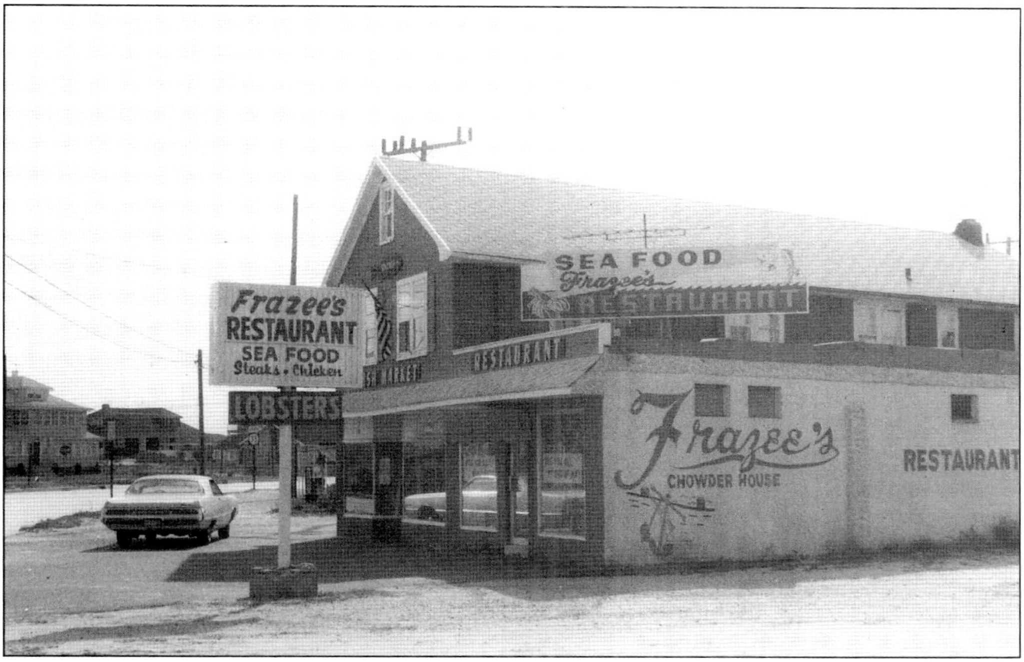

Frazee's fish market was established by James Frazee in 1926 in a small building where Burger King stands today. The market was relocated to the familiar two-story building on Sea Avenue in 1929 (shown above in 1972) and remains in business today.

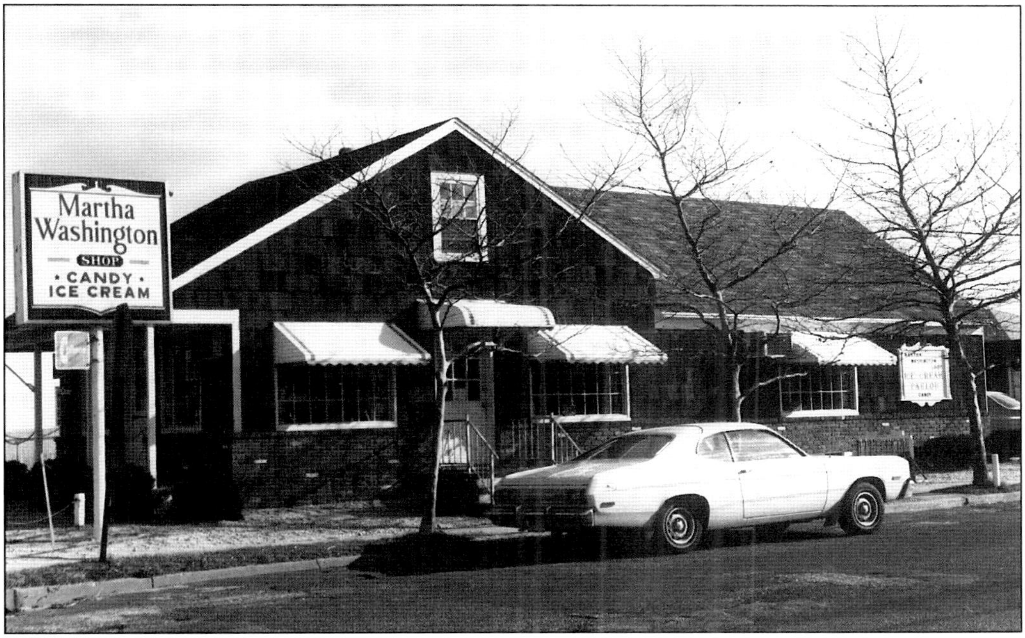

The Martha Washington Ice Cream and Candy Shop was located at the corner of Broadway and Saint Louis Avenue during the 1960s and '70s. The shop featured an old-fashioned parlor with thirty flavors of ice cream, fudge, salt water taffy, sodas and sundaes, and hand-dipped chocolates.

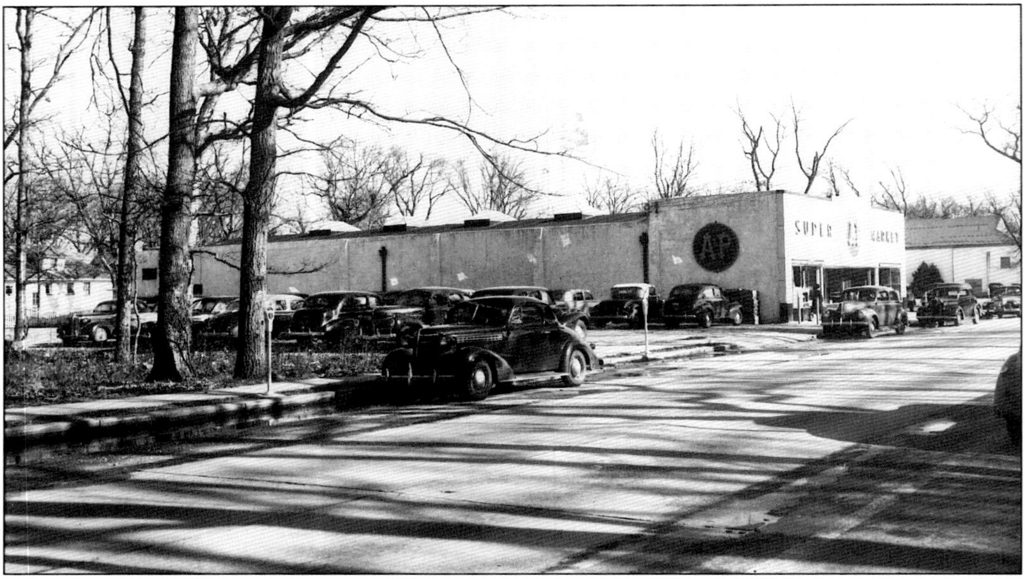

The A&P supermarket is shown here in its third and largest location on Arnold Avenue in 1949. Today this building houses the Summit Bank Corporate Center. The A&P was earlier located in the west half of the Woolworth Building and on Bay Avenue in the Height and Lawrence Building. Other supermarkets in the area included an American Stores at Bay and Arnold Avenues and an Acme on Richmond Avenue at the present site of Foodtown.

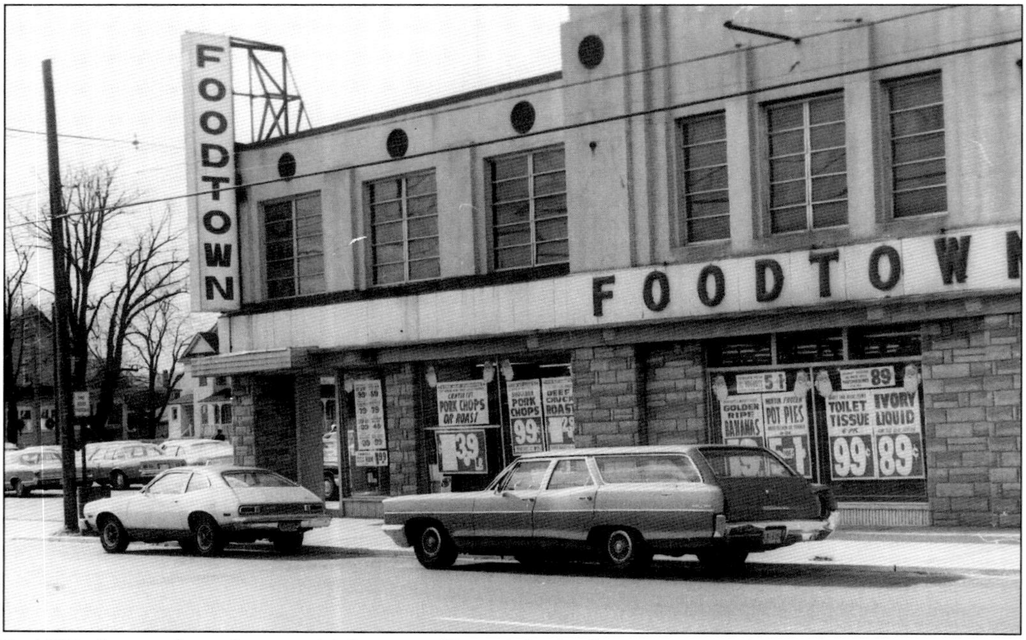

In 1930, former Seaside pound fisherman Harry May had a new movie theater built on Richmond Avenue, but he quickly ran into money problems and the building stood unfinished for several years. In 1939, an Acme supermarket moved into the completed building with offices and meeting rooms on the second floor. The original facade of the proposed movie house, minus the marquee, can be seen in this 1975 photograph.

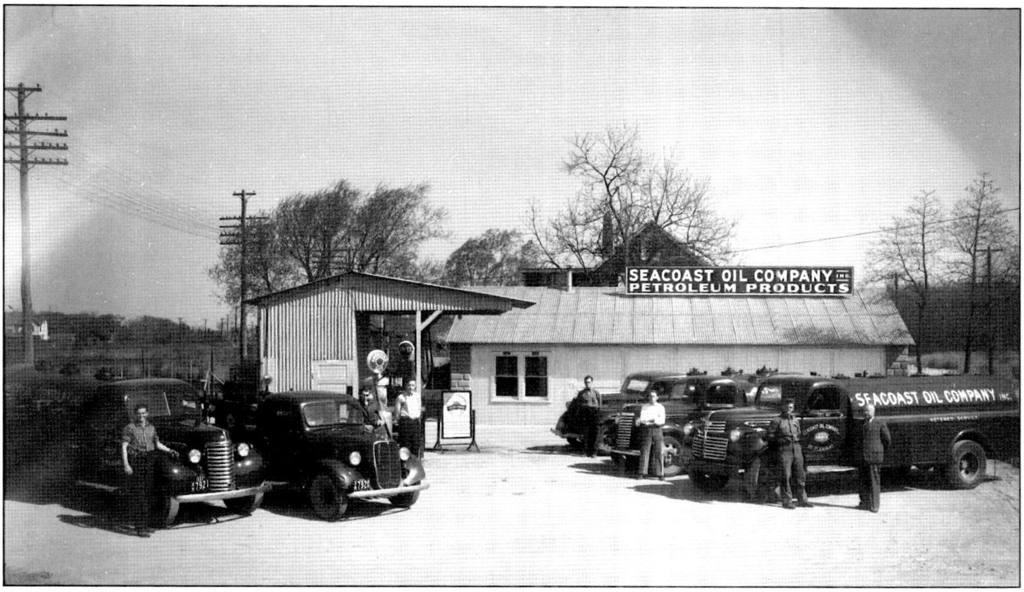

The Seacoast Oil Company was located at the intersection of Cook's Land and Cook's Road in 1941. Seacoast started doing business in the Point Pleasant area in 1930 and was one of the first local distributors of home heating oil, fuel oil, and gasoline.

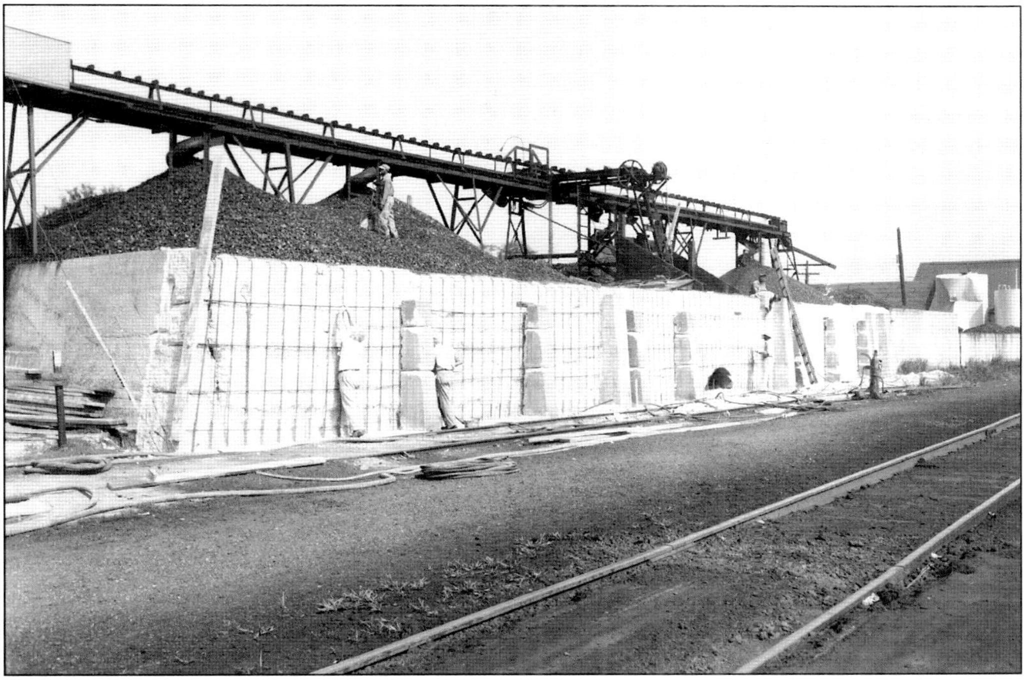

The chief method of heating homes until the mid-1940s was with coal, and the major supplier in Point Pleasant was the Point Pleasant-Bay Head Ice and Coal Company, now Point-Bay Fuel. Coal was delivered by railroad hopper cars and dumped into a conveyor and distributed into the coal pockets, as shown here in 1948. The coal pockets and retaining walls still remain today at the Hawthorne Avenue facility.

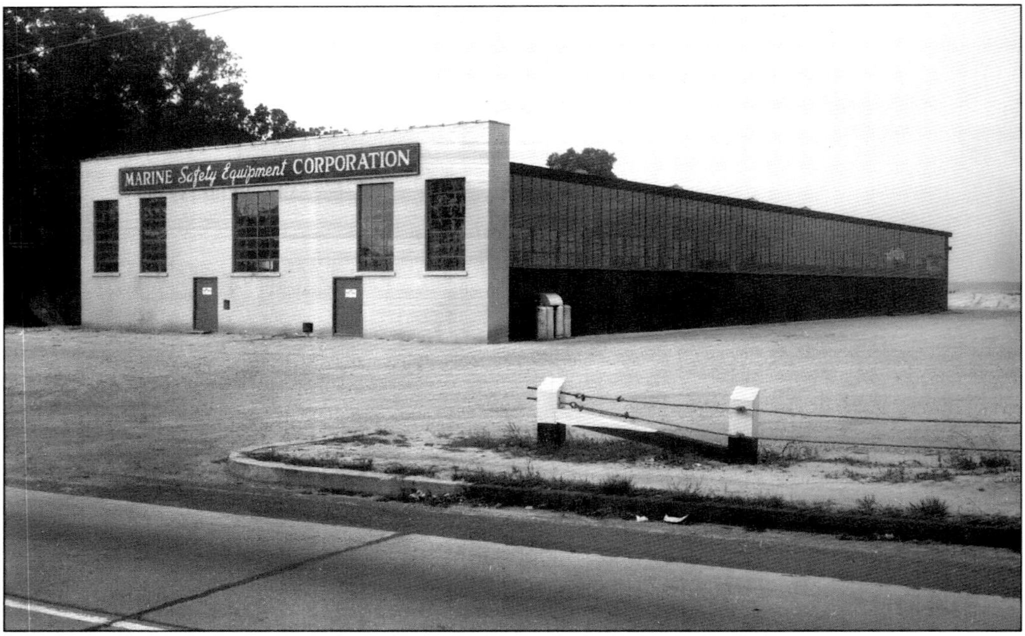

In December 1945 John Harkrader and his wife Evelyn established the Marine Safety Equipment Corporation at the base of the Route 35 Manasquan River bridge. MASECO, as it was known, manufactured lifesaving equipment such as rafts, davits, and lifeboats, which were loaded onto rail cars and shipped throughout North America.

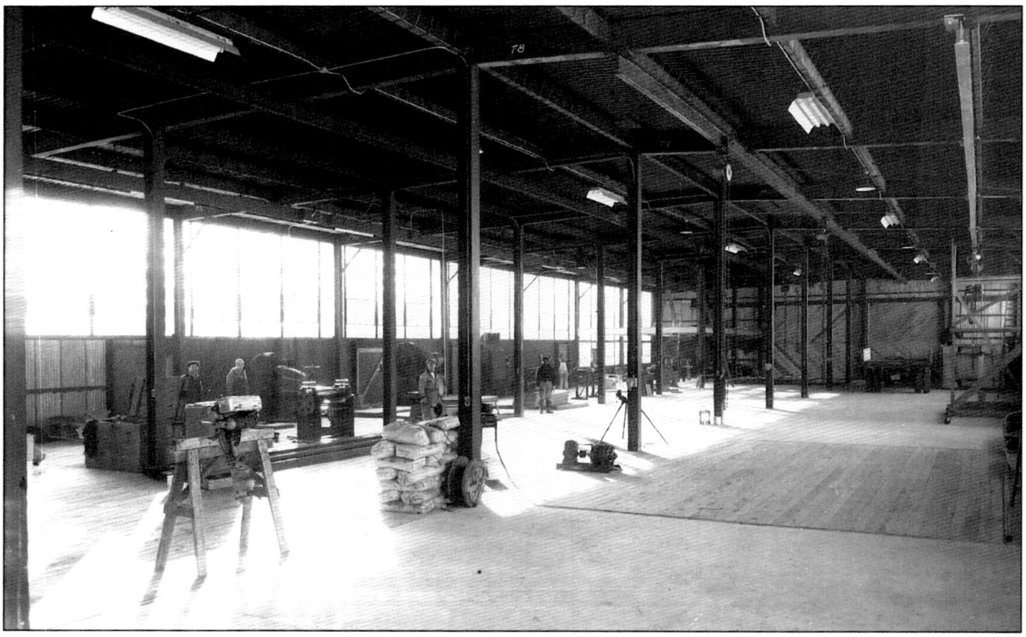

The MASECO factory, shown here in 1947, was one of the largest industries in the area. Equipment for numerous tankers and cruise ships was manufactured here, including 36-foot lifeboats for the cruise ships *Constitution* and *Independence*. At that time, these were the largest lifeboats ever manufactured in the world.

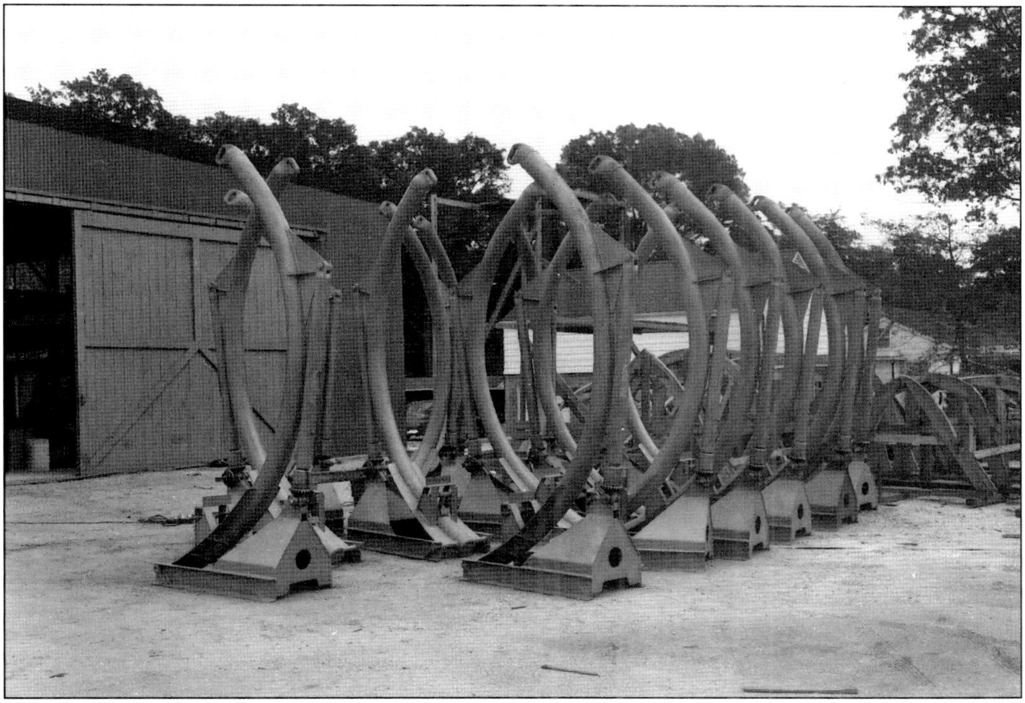

Ship davits are lined up outside the MASECO plant in 1948. These davits were used to hold the lifeboats and lower them over the side of the ship in an emergency.

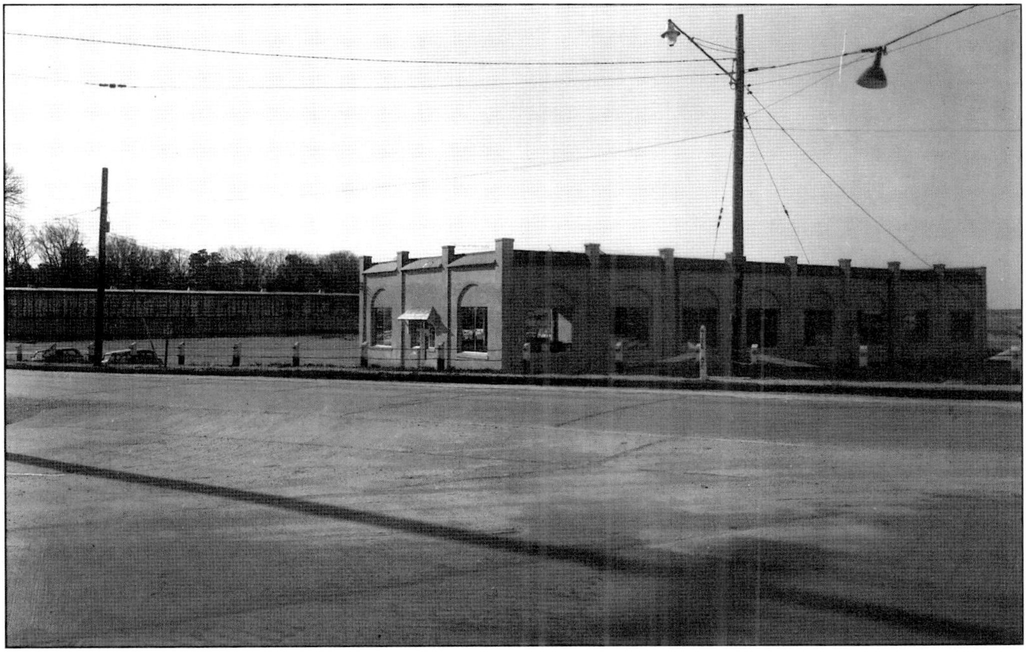

The intersection of River Avenue and Broadway in 1947 shows the just-completed Seasports boat showroom, later to be expanded and become New Jersey Yacht Sales. In the background is the Marine Safety Equipment Corporation.

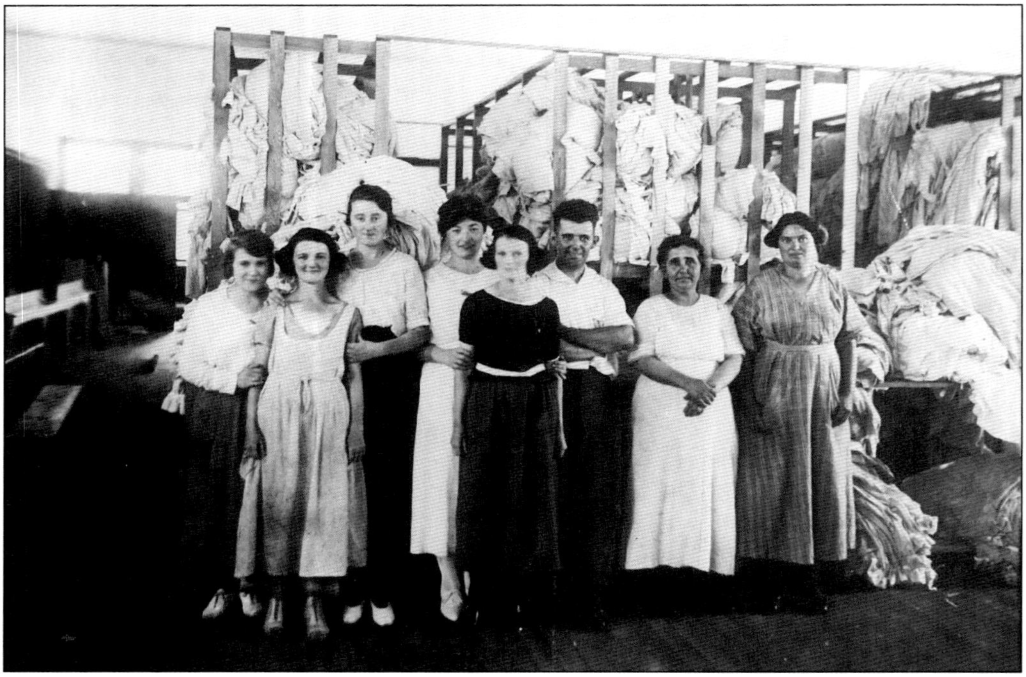

Linens and bed sheets from Point Pleasant Hospital tower above the staff at the Point Pleasant Steam Laundry in 1933. The laundry building was located at the rear of 707 Grove Street and was later known as the Point Pleasant Laundry Service. A fire in 1990 demolished the building and ended the business.

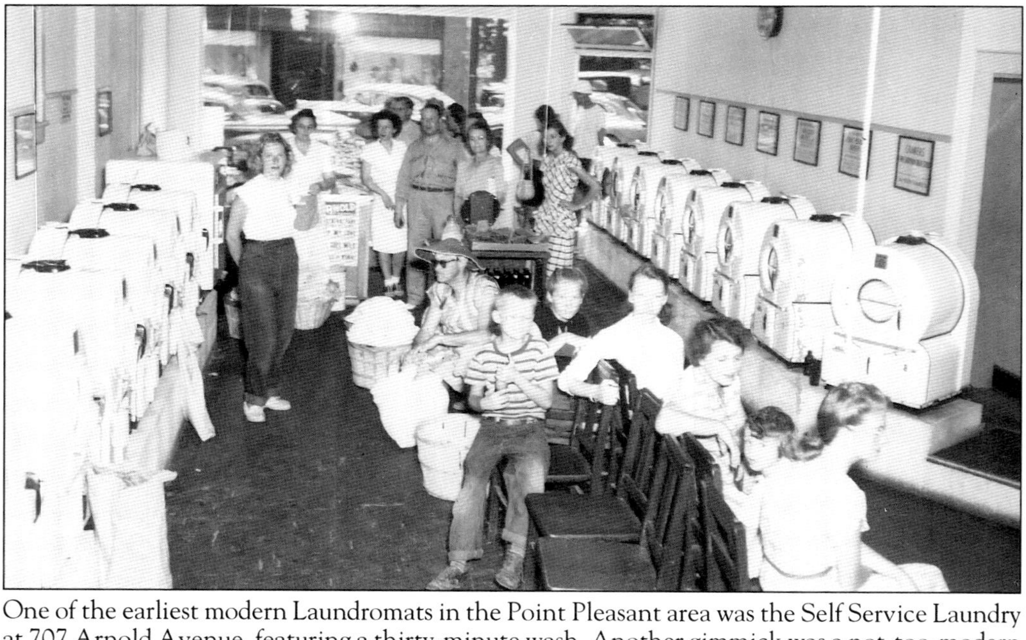

One of the earliest modern Laundromats in the Point Pleasant area was the Self Service Laundry at 707 Arnold Avenue, featuring a thirty-minute wash. Another gimmick was a not-too-modern pick-up and delivery service; this involved an employee on a bicycle pulling a wagon-full of laundry bags. The above photograph was taken in 1948.